Comments From Readers

"The Valeo Method is a soulful guide that will lead you on a path of self-discovery that will touch every area of your life. It will expand your vision, free your spirit and help you to achieve your life's purpose."

– Jim Britt,
Best-Selling Author of Rings of Truth & Unleashing Your Authentic Power

"Benny Morris demonstrates how to meet the challenges of life and overcome them in a positive way. He takes the hand that is dealt and makes it a winning hand. Benny takes the lessons of his life and refines them through the Valeo Method into powerful principles for living a life of passion and accomplishment."

– Dr. Herbert Harris,
Author of The Twelve Universal Laws of Success

"Many will encounter struggles and challenges in their lives. However, few will endure such defeat as Benny has faced, and overcome. I am forever grateful for the strategies I have learned from Benny that has allowed me to persevere in times of struggle. Within this book, you will learn how to tap into the power of your natural spirit and overcome the limitations of life's temporary challenges."

– Jake Kevorkian,
Founding Partner, Numis Network

"Benny Morris cuts to the core of life's most difficult question: What is your purpose or calling in life? His breakthrough Valeo Method can lead you to the life you were meant to live. Inside these pages are a treasure trove of transformational concepts that provide a step-by-step system to finding your passion and your Divine purpose. Have the courage and make the commitment to read and implement the system today. It changed the course of my life."

– George Veronis,
Entrepreneur / Sales-Training Coach

As I write this, I'm on a mission trip in Haiti to help rebuild an orphanage. Everyday I read The Valeo Method, and I'm in awe of how much it's in alignment with the path I need to be on.

– Burke Hedges Jr,
23 year old college student

The Valeo Method™

Live Victoriously

Dr. Benny Morris

The Valeo Method™

FIVE STEPS TO LIVING THE DREAM OF YOUR SOUL

By Benny Morris

~

Copyright © 2010 by Backbone Worldwide, Inc.
First Printing July 2010

Printed in the United States of America

ISBN-13: 978-0-615-37129-0
Cataloging-in-Publication Data is on file with the Library of Congress

~

Book and Layout design by Sadie Johnson-Mellowatts
Editing by Catherine Van Herrin

Published by Backbone Worldwide, Inc.

Website: www.ValeoMethod.com
Email: info@thevaleomethod.com
Phone: 800-943-0013

Dedication

I dedicate this book to the Lord my God

Thank you for giving me the dream in my heart to write this book and the courage to see it through.

TABLE OF CONTENTS

Acknowledgments 13

Introduction 15

Forward 17

Part I: THE FOUNDATION 25

Chapter 1:   The Underdog Champion 35

Chapter 2:   The Comeback Kid 39

Chapter 3:   The Quest for Wholeness 41

Chapter 4:   Shoot for the Moon 43

Chapter 5:   The Need for Healing 49

PART II: THE VALEO METHOD

Chapter 6:   What is the Valeo Method? 55

Chapter 7:   Which Dream Are You Living? 57

Chapter 8:   Memoralize Your Experience 65

PART III: DISCOVERY

Chapter 9:   Know Thyself 73

Chapter 10:   The Awakening 75

Chapter 11:   The Power of Awareness and Clarity 79

Chapter 12:   You Can't Stop the Clock 83

Chapter 13:   Healing the Mind 87

Chapter 14:   The Emotional Body 93

Chapter 15:   The Rule Book and the Play Book 99

Chapter 16:   Documentation Beats Conversation 113

Chapter 17:   Belief and Perception 123

Chapter 18:   All Excuses Are Equal 133

Chapter 19:   Love and Fear 137

Chapter 20:   How Much Pain Before Change? 143

PART IV: RELEASE 153

Chapter 21:   The Sacred Wish 159

Chapter 22:   Is Your Faith Trapped? 165

Chapter 23:   The Thinking Process 171

Chapter 24:   The Real You Loves You 177

Chapter 25:   Catch and Release 181

Chapter 26:   Ego and Emotion 185

Chapter 27:   Transitional Language 193

Chapter 28:   The Power of Words 195

Chapter 29:   Acting on Purpose and With the Flow 209

PART V: EMBRACE 227

Chapter 30:   The Sources of Wounding 229

Chapter 31:   The Sensitive Self 233

Chapter 32:   Role Models 239

Chapter 33:   Fear, Anger, and Grief 241

Chapter 34:   Forgiving Your Parents 247

Chapter 35:   Tired of Self-Sabotage? 253

Chapter 36:   Understanding Suppressed Feelings 257

Chapter 37:   The Fragmented Personalities Dilemma 263

Chapter 38:   Child Abuse and Adult Consequences 267

Chapter 39:   Co-dependence Kills the Dream of the Soul 273

Chapter 40:   Reaching the Innermost Self 277

Chapter 41:   The AFIG Process 287

Chapter 42:   Controlling Anger 299

Chapter 43:   Recognizing Intuitive Experience 309

Chapter 44:   The Four E's "For Ease" 313

PART VI: ACTIVATE AND ATTRACT 327

Chapter 45:   Do I Really Have a Purpose? 331

Chapter 46:   Dreams Ignite Purpose 339

Chapter 47:   Creative Visualization 345

Chapter 48:   Future Framing Your Dreams 349

Chapter 49:   WOWIE "I Am" 355

Chapter 50:   How To Get Anything You Want 371

PART VII : MANIFEST AND MAINTAIN 389

Chapter 51:   Living in God's Economy 401

Chapter 52:   Pride VS. Authentic Power 407

Chapter 53:   Why Trust God? 411

Chapter 54:   A New Level of Thinking 421

Chapter 55:   Meditate and Open Up the Flow 429

Chapter 56:   Prayer Role In Manifestation 441

Chapter 57:   At Last...Faith! 447

Chapter 58:   Launching the DREAM 453

PART VIII : TEAM

Chapter 59:   TEAM (Together Everyone Achieves More) 457

Chapter 60:   People Will Do Anything to Be on a Team 463

Chapter 61:   Share the Love – Don't Dump on Your Team! 467

Chapter 62:   Team Spirit 471

Chapter 63:   You Are the Movie Director 473

Acknowledgments

Although the writing of this book has been a wonderful and transforming experience for me, it has also been difficult. I could never have completed it without some very important people around me. First, I have to thank my precious wife Kim for her support and belief in me. She is my encourager, my earth angel, and my gift from God. Thank you Honey for believing in me and this message, even in the toughest times when it seemed like it was only a dream, you never gave up.

I am grateful to my Mom and Dad, Roy and Betty Morris, for giving me the example of how to raise a family, live with honor, and for showing me the power of kindness and humility.

Thanks to my son Kyle for believing in me so much. Thanks for being such a great kid, wonderful son, and now an amazing father yourself. You are my best friend. I am so proud of you.

Thanks to the most awesome brothers on the planet, Steve, Kevin, and Chris your love and support has gotten me through some rough spots, I love you.

Special thanks to my incredible father-in-law and mother-in-law, Sammy and Judy Hodges, for your loving kindness and support.

Thank you so much to Burke and Christina Hedges for your belief in this project and your unwavering determination to get the message out no matter what it took. I am so grateful to you both; you are a blessing and an inspiration to me. Special thanks, Burke for your editorial contribution and the awesome work on the conceptual development of the cover!

Thank you to my sister-in-law Carrie Hodges who was so helpful in the early stages of getting the manuscript developed.

Thank you to Catherine Van Herrin for your tireless dedication and brilliant editing to pull the manuscript together in such a great way. You are the best.

Thanks to Karen Lacey for the beautiful job of proofreading and finishing touches. You did a stellar job.

Thanks to Sadie Johnson ~ Mellowatts for the beautiful cover design and layout and your total commitment to excellence and perfection.

Special thanks to my early career mentor and coach J. Tom Murphy who helped me take my thinking to a higher level and for encouraging me to always be a leader and a champion. Your teaching still affects me today.

Thanks to Derrick Wiley for your foresight and belief in The Valeo Method and for your determination to get this program to over 400 people that desperately needed encouragement.

God Bless all of you!

FOREWORD

The moment I met Benny I knew he was a winner. His passion for life and compassion for helping people inspired me more than 20 years ago before he became Dr. Benny. He and his lovely wife Kim are amazing souls with hearts bigger than all the universes put together. His vision is crystal clear, but it is his uncompromising devotion to encouraging people to live the dream of their soul that's truly inspiring.

As you will soon realize in the pages ahead, *The Valeo Method* is not just another me too self help book with the same old rehashed information. It's a "Divinely" inspired masterpiece, a real original, and written as though he was speaking directly to you.

The key to *The Valeo Method* is that Dr. Benny fully understands what it takes to be an authentic success, what it takes to overcome the most horrific of circumstances and to come out on top and live victoriously in every vital area of life. Those areas I'm referring to are: your health (physical, mental, and spiritual), the quality of your relationships, your financial prosperity, your true happiness and purpose. When you figure out how to love what you do and do what you love you will be living the dream of your soul.

What *The Valeo Method* did for me... is it gave me a blueprint to equip myself with the tools to lose twenty pounds and keep it off; to be happy, joyous and free; to appreciate the source of true bliss, how to worry less and be more and in turn discover the dream of my soul. If it did it for me it can do it for you too.

Do you want to live your dream? Then put *The Valeo Method* to the test. Discover what is now possible for you. Release the ball and chain of self sabotage. Embrace the real you. Activate the unlimited power inside of you and manifest the potentiality of your dream.

The amazing transformation you are about to experience is a gift. It found me and now it has found you. There are no coincidences. A gift is not a gift until you give it away. Pay it forward and be the change you want to see in your life and in the world.

You are the master of your fate and the captain of your soul; therefore, if you can dream it... then you can live it.

Burke Hedges,
Tampa Florida

Author of "Who Stole the American Dream?"
& six other books with over four million in print.

INTRODUCTION

Live Victoriously!

Getting this message to you has been my most singular passion for the past four years. I have spent countless hours writing this book with a sense of relentless determination like no other I have ever felt before. All this time, I have lived with a deep, burning desire to share the words in this book with you because I know they will begin to make an immediate difference in your life. The principles covered in The Valeo Method have been tested, re-tested, and involved trial and error in both personal and group situations. And now that these principles have been refined, it is with my deepest sincerity that I share them now with you.

I pray that you will recognize that there are no "accidents" or "coincidences" in life and that you are reading this right this moment because you were meant to. I wholeheartedly believe that God takes us where we need to go and places what we need to learn within our sight. I also pray that you will use this book as a stepping stone to take your life to a new level and remove any obstacles that have been holding you back. I believe in this book because it works. I have seen the power it has unleashed within people who have traveled through these steps — breakthroughs that most people never experience in a lifetime. I have watched hundreds of seriously depressed and down-and-out people prevail over their limitations and demons.

The steps outlined in this book will awaken you to your unique purpose — that seemingly elusive treasure with which each of us are born and which God wants us to play out on His magnificent stage. And when you find your purpose, you will clearly see the path to the dream of your soul — that place where only you can claim a new future and relish in new possibilities. The state of true, whole happiness is within your reach — it is right here on earth, and it is often much closer to you than you may realize.

We all have the same questions about our existence, and they play out in an endless loop in our minds. "Who am I?" "What is my purpose?" "What am I supposed to be doing with my life now?" "Where am I along this journey called 'my life?'" These questions will either cause a cancer of the mind until we do something about them, or, too often, they will lead us to lose hope altogether and become a source of endless pain. Then, to "avoid the void" in our lives, we will begin to anesthetize ourselves with many harmful distractions (drugs, alcohol, sex, gambling, overeating — anything to distract and dull our senses) and miss the message our spirit is trying to send us instead of discovering our true purpose — our calling. This book and the processes within will gently lift you out of your self-imposed prison, along with the thoughts, beliefs, and emotions that keep you shackled to a life of limitation.

The Valeo Method is based on five simple steps that are built around practical techniques to create change through absolute self-awareness. Within these pages, you will begin to change for the better in one of two ways: either you will gradually begin to notice and feel the subtle effects of positive change, or you will experience a jolting breakthrough that will shock and astonish you into your soul's deepest needs and desires. I have witnessed this transformation many times, in every seminar and workshop I have led; I have seen depression, addiction, and desolation vanish in the faces and spirits of those with whom I have worked, and I know without a shadow of a doubt that this book will do the same for you. After all, the genesis of this book began with me — when I realized that my life had become an uncontrollable series of highs and lows, I knew I needed change, and I needed it fast. I was failing myself. I was disappointed in me.

The Valeo Method will show you how to get back in the driver's seat of your life — to regain that control that brings happiness and an overall sense of well being that you have known before but have talked yourself into thinking that you can never reclaim it. This book will remind you who you were born to be all the time and help you reconnect with the strength and holiness of your soul. Then you will be free – free to express victory in your life, to seize opportunities to prosper and grow, and to naturally seek things and people that are in perfect alignment with your purpose. You don't have to work as hard at living as you think! The steps within the Valeo Method will allow you to visualize, recall, and recapture the dream of your soul. Being and living in connection with your soul never feels like work!

Can you imagine what it feels like to experience and recognize, within a single moment, that the child inside you has never died at all, but that you have simply forgotten it was there? Do you realize the kind of impact this discovery can have on your life? Do you have the uneasy sense that you are blindly accepting who you are based on your past experiences, future projections, and the opinions of those closest to you? And do you realize that in reality, this is the opposite of what is true about you?

This inauthentic mindset, this skewed way of thinking, keeps us from uncovering our true identity and the joy and happiness that God intended us to have. Throughout this book, you will read many stories that will remind you of yourself – people who, just like you, were living a false, unhappy life that they were able to change forever simply because they followed the Valeo Method. This book is chock-full of detailed, intense, even shocking stories of people's lives before they put the Valeo Method to the test. You are no different; if you are reading this now because you are seriously seeking relief, change, and control of your life, you will not be disappointed.

"What do I have to do to make this happen?" you may ask. All that is required of you, the reader, is a conscious, disciplined commitment of attention and intention. The rewards and benefits far outweigh the input – the discovery of your genuine soul, life purpose, mental and emotional cleansing, and a new awareness of the most sensitive, cherished part of yourself.

Are you ready to stop clinging to a fading past and an uncertain future with a lack of hope and promise? Are you ready to let go of the buried, unprocessed pain and memories that no longer serve you? Are you ready to open yourself to a wiser and more powerful you, filled with renewed confidence and courage?

I really believe that if you apply the principles in this book to your life, you will add ten to twenty years to your life — starting right now. You don't have to wait until the end of your life for the changes to occur! I know, because it happened to me. This process allowed me to hit fifty in the best shape in my life mentally, emotionally and physically. It enabled me to lose eighty pounds (and keep it off) and stop taking three types of blood pressure medication. In the gym, I out-train, outrun, and outwork most guys half my age. My wife and I feel like college students again. Life is vibrant and passionate, and we continually look forward to this renewed phase of life that is the most exciting we've ever experienced — with no fears or worries. We seize every moment and live "in the now" because we know we are living out God's plan for us.

When I finally realized that I had to write this book, God became my editor-in-chief — my constant source of information. I just held the pen; God worked through me for the nearly four years it took to write this book. With every page I wrote, I humbly thanked God for allowing me to be His servant — the conduit through which I could carry out my own dream of the soul — to help and encourage those who were struggling with life and in need of a "lift."

Sure, many times I wanted to give up — sometimes it seemed like too much work, too much responsibility for just one person, but then I always remembered -- I wasn't alone; God was working with me. I pray that this book touches that specific area of your life where you need the most nurturing and help. The part of the Valeo Method that still fascinates me is how effectively it seeks out pain, like a heat-seeking missile, and ministers to and heals the parts of a person that need the most relief and attention.

I know this book will help you. I say that with complete confidence and straight from my heart and soul. As I continued to "take dictation from God," I began to realize that this book took on a kind of life of its own that really had nothing to do with me — it was always, even from its inception, simply about helping people find their way and overcome the obstacles that were keeping them from enjoying a fulfilling, happy life. Now, you, too, can help others by paying it forward by introducing the methods used in this book with those you love, as well. There's no feeling like it, I promise you!

I hope to meet you in person, talk to you, or get to know you through email very soon! Please contact me at the address on the back of the book to tell me about your results and breakthroughs, and please don't forget to tell everyone you love about the Valeo Method.

God bless you, have fun on your journey, and be encouraged!

Benny Morris

PART I

THE FOUNDATION

Everyone in this world is born with a "calling;" a sense of themselves that is uniquely their own and comes from the truest, deepest instinct they know—the instinct that tells them, "*This* is what I am meant to do."

Anyone who is *not* doing what they are meant to do knows the feeling—it's a dull ache in their soul because they are not living their lives' purpose—and this ache means that their calling is suffering.

Everyone's life is meant to be happy, joyful, abundant, and filled with peace. So how do we get to that point? How can we get the most from our experiences in life? That is what this book is about. I wrote this book because I used the principles and techniques that I have described here, and they resulted in a profound and lasting change in my own life.

In addition, after sharing these discoveries with many others over several years and seeing a consistent success rate in creating lasting, long-term changes in their lives, I knew I had to write this book and share my discoveries with the world.

Many of the things you read here will be familiar to you in one way or another. Nonetheless, pay careful attention because what makes the Valeo Method™ special is the power of the principles' *order and synergy*. As a person goes through them they create momentum. The big payoff? Lifelong, lasting results!

The foundation of this book began during my own personal quest to understand how the mind works. In particular, why are some people happy no matter what they have, while others can't find happiness at all. I kept asking myself, "What is the difference between success and failure? Does it have to do with our background or education, or is it in our genes? Could it be timing or luck? What is it?" These questions arose during a twenty-year, non-stop quest for my own happiness in which I experienced ups and downs in all areas of my life. I went from the highest of highs to the lowest of lows and more than once. Many times I felt perplexed, sometimes I felt jinxed, and other times I felt invincible and that the world was my oyster. Along with this roller coaster ride came a challenging plethora of emotions. In retrospect, I understand it was all part of my journey. It was my intended path to have these experiences so I could discover answers to help myself and then share these answers with others.

After searching through hundreds of books every year, attending seminars and listening to every audio self-help program I could find, I realized something profound. Though many awesome writers, teachers, doctors, philosophers, and spiritual leaders helped me along the way, I identified five areas in my life that needed to be addressed. These areas were keeping me from discovering my calling and my bliss, and not one book or program addressed all five. I needed to work on these five particular areas in order to lift my own obstacles and be able to enjoy long-term success. Since then, these steps have worked for many others facing a broad range of challenging situations.

I realized that the average person didn't have the time to search relentlessly for the truth like I did for all those years. It is overwhelming to try to determine which program works best for you. What if you choose the wrong one? The program might be good but it may not adequately address your personal challenges and needs. This is why I have devoted my life to teaching the Valeo Method, my proprietary five-step system for lasting change.

I will show you how to find your personal power—that deep, essential "you" that has been locked away and dormant for so long; how to influence people with your renewed sense of confidence; and how to prevail over any obstacle that shows up in your path. I will challenge you but I will also entertain you with some remarkable stories of accomplishment and how to overcome setbacks; and I will teach you skills you will be able to use for the rest of your life.

First, however, it is important we understand what comprises our individual personalities. I call this the ABC's of our personal reality. It is created by three things: our appearance, our behavior, and the circumstances of our lives that we identify with at any particular point. These three components create who we think we are as an individual. The complexity of this False Self covers up the Real Self and, along with it, the key to a life that is on target with your individual destiny. The Valeo Method reveals powerful truths about how to take control of thoughts, beliefs, emotions, and issues from the past that block your way. This opens up the pathway and the flow into a life of purpose and total fulfillment in all areas of your life. You will also learn why many traditional techniques and solutions to overcoming setbacks and disappointments have temporary success or none at all.

Psychology is the study of the mind and its mental processes, especially as it is related to behavior. Just as medicine serves to heal our bodies without any recognition of the soul, psychology seeks to heal the personality without recognition of the soul.

I certainly do not mean to belittle the field of psychology or the professionals who work on its behalf. The whole purpose of the Valeo Method is to teach awareness of why things are the way are, and what works and what doesn't work toward making our lives the way they were meant to be. Some people stay in therapy for years and are never "healed" because they are treating their symptoms, and not the *cause* of their symptoms. The real problem is not at the personality level—it is at the soul level. Simply put, we heal the soul by bringing it from the dark into the light.

Discovering and understanding your intuition is a big step toward healing your soul and releasing the Real You and the God-given dream of your soul, your purpose. The word "purpose" is defined as "original intent." In other words, your purpose is not what you decide you are supposed to do, but what you were *created* to do, be, and have in your life. Within this understanding is your pathway to bliss.

Intuition is the voice of the non-physical world speaking to you. It is through this communication system that you are released from the trap of a limited, five-sensory being, and awakened to a multi-sensory, unlimited being. Becoming whole means allowing the spirit/soul personality to blend seamlessly and in harmony. People who are unhappy have a fragmented and splintered combination of these three energy dynamics, the spirit, the soul, and the personality. The key to taking control of your life is to understand what the spirit is, what the soul is, and that there is a difference—and only then can we understand what each wants and needs.

With the Valeo Method, you will recognize the energies that operate in harmony with the soul and those that operate in opposition to it. A personality connected to a soul dominated by the ego and fear-based emotions is unaware of this harmony because there is always interaction between the soul and the personality.

For example, when the person (personality) is not attached or aware of the spirit (the original source or intent) he or she is easily lured into physical matters and the material things of life that seem to matter a great deal. Yet these physical/material desires are far from the source of the authentic power of an unencumbered spirit/soul. If you are aware of and receptive to your spiritual energy you will be guided by it. However, when the personality part of the soul is dominated by the ego, it can interfere with and cut off the guidance of the spirit and want no part of it.

All spirits are meant to evolve into wholeness and to return to their original source. When and how that happens boils down to the effects of egoic interference and choice, or free will. This means we have a choice: we can take charge of our will and direct our own lives, or we can float down the river of life in a boat with no oars, letting the egoic mind (False Self) control us while we wait to see what happens.

Similarly, we experience doubt when we are being pulled in two directions at the same time. When we are doubtful, the ego is in control. There are two forces at war inside us. This internal war can cause us to become stuck in a place of unrest or dis-ease in our mind and body. Doubt, however, is also there for a good reason—to teach us. When we *choose*, we get to *learn*. If we choose as an ego-dominated five-sensory being, we are guaranteed to learn through pain and suffering. The more we choose as aware, intuitively guided, and multi-sensory beings, the more we will experience the love-based emotions of joy, peace, and happiness.

Sadly, for most of us it takes a crisis, trauma, or some other cause of suffering to make us seek answers and to evolve. The ego and spirit compete for dominance of the soul through the personality. The personality is driven by the emotions we experience; the good emotions from the spirit and the negative emotions from the ego determine our personality—how we view the world and ourselves. The strongest emotions dominate, and they usually win.

The Valeo Method will teach you how to release your negative energies and fear-based emotions that create a reality in your life you do not want. This will allow you to choose authentic power and embrace the good of your spirit. Remember, you learn through awareness, which affords you access to wisdom instead of uncertainty. You will learn to recognize the difference between the spirit/soul and personality and to take control of your destiny.

When we experience pain or negative emotions it is the soul's way of bringing attention to those areas of itself that need help and healing. Negative emotions are not necessarily bad; they simply act as messengers, passing energy from the aware self to the unaware self. The nervous system is the body's way of letting us know it is experiencing pain and, in a similar way, emotions are the soul's way of letting us know it is experiencing pain.

The Bubonic plague killed millions of people until it was discovered that it was caused by unsanitary living conditions and rodents. When people learned to sanitize and clean up their personal environment, the threat of the disease lessened greatly and finally disappeared. It is the same way with a hurting, unfulfilled soul—awareness of the "plague" of the soul is the first key to healing. This is the power of awareness in your life. If you are unaware of the part of you that causes your negative emotions like fear, anger, worry, and jealousy, you can't gain control of it. Compassionate understanding of this concept is the only way we will ultimately heal the world on a global level—there is simply no other way.

What are your genuine needs? What needs have you created to get what you want, control others, and receive attention? You must learn to know yourself deeply and clearly to find joy and purpose in your life. This means learning the difference between your authentic needs and artificial needs. In other words, what needs sustain the ego and what needs sustain your spirit/soul.

For example, the needs of the spirit/soul are to give and receive love, to release creativity, to manifest good will toward others and to release our God-given gifts and talents that are waiting to become apparent to us. We need to know how to nourish and cultivate our spirit/soul instead of giving our energy to the non-authentic needs of the ego that constantly drain the life out of us.

Real, authentic power is created by tapping into and releasing the intention of a spirit-dominated, not ego-controlled soul. Power is constantly flowing out from the soul through fear-based emotions. This places a drain on the energy that you need to be in control of your life. The loss of this energy creates physical weariness, loss of motivation, depression, and discouragement. Then, your natural defenses are weakened and unable to protect you from other negative energies in and around your environment that are constantly trying to get in.

Success is always tied to the satisfaction of the soul.

Let's look at it this way: emotions like anxiety and fear are simply energies leaving the soul, and that translates into loss of power. These energies only take away and bring nothing back. In contrast, love-based emotions are spirit-based energies which leave the soul to connect with and reflect the same, thus charging up and not draining the soul. In other words, authentic power only attracts love energy! So think about it: when your soul is love-dominated you have chosen to release the Real You and live your purpose! You have a humble, love-attracting soul that is attracting and extending an aura of good around you every day, everywhere you go.

An unempowered soul, or a person who is suffering emotionally or who has confidence and self-esteem issues, is the stronghold of an ego-dominated soul. This person has little chance of completing their calling and living the dream of their soul unless they regain their sense of self. A person will never be continuously happy or fulfilled until they walk and experience the path their individual soul was meant to walk. There will always be something missing; a sense of emptiness that will never be satisfied as long as they yield to the ego and live by artificial power instead of the spirit.

The ego rarely aligns with the dream of the soul. This is the very reason there is so much suffering in the world—so much internal conflict, strain, and pain in so many people. Most people's lives are consumed and sometimes destroyed when they try to heal, mask, or eliminate this pain. In reality, the only way to stop going without, is to go within. The dream of the soul sits dormant, awaiting the energies and attention that activate it. Unfortunately, these energies are not likely what the ego or our personality would choose. The ego seeks to keep our attention with fear-based emotions which strengthen the identity of the ego.

Yet, when you no longer allow fear, you allow your authentic power to reside within you, and fear has no choice; it has to leave. Fear cannot compete with the Real You when you tap into the authentic power of your spirit. The more you become aware of the ego and the energy dynamics that go on inside of your mind, the more you will be able to use the techniques of the Valeo Method. The undesirable feelings and emotions and the causes behind them will begin to float to the surface to be exorcised, one at a time. The process strengthens your faith which is, in essence, your belief in your authentic self—and this is how you are able to exorcise your own demons.

Sometimes we can't see our calling because we have convinced ourselves we are on the right track, yet in reality we are opening doors that take us nowhere. Are you tired of missing the mark? There comes a time when you have to let go and be who you are. Just trust; trust God and your role in His universe. If we can just learn to say and believe, "Thy will be done," and let it happen, we can gain so much peace.

I am not talking about letting go of life's responsibilities but about releasing your ego's hold on you and allowing your life to manifest. This is the final piece of the puzzle. Are you ready to get in alignment with God's universe and live your role in His cosmic play, which is your original intent (purpose) and the dream of your soul? By the way, your intended purpose may not be what you think and that may be why you feel like something is missing! But don't worry; whatever it is, you will love it, you will connect with it, and nothing will ever make you happier.

Okay, is it time? Are you ready? Hasn't it been long enough? Is it time to pay attention to the intentions of your heart? Is it time to listen to your heart and not your mind? If you are truly ready to live, love, and be happy, please pay particular attention to this: God is not in your mind; God is in your heart. Unless you remember your missing part, your authentic self, you cannot experience your true, authentic power until you become conscious of what you feel in your heart.

What path have you chosen to learn? The path of pain and suffering, or the path of growth and empowerment? Isn't it time to set your intentions based on what your heart is telling you and stop being led by your ego and the negative energies it draws from society's collective consciousness?

Many people miss the mark when it comes to manifesting what they want in their lives because they confuse two things—they don't understand belief and they don't understand hope. Let us be clear: Faith and belief are the same thing, just as hope and expectation are the same thing. Think of it this way: Faith is belief when it is rooted in authentic power, and expectation is hope in action.

If you create something with your expectation and you believe in it, something magical happens. When you have awareness of your authentic power and your ability to manifest, then what you believe in changes from just a belief about something into faith about something. It is then you experience that feeling of certainty, a knowing that what you intend is absolutely going to happen. You just know, and you know that you know!

This is what you are about to learn and experience as you read, understand, and apply the precepts and principles of this book. You will learn that what you have faith in and hope for with great expectation will manifest. That's not my own or any particular person's prophecy or prediction as much as it is just fact—the science of cause and effect—and mostly because that is just the way God set it up. You can either go along with nature, science, and God's Divine Plan, or you can fight your way upstream with your ego pushing you all the way.

Most people in our lives are not happy; they aren't fulfilled or leading exciting, purposeful lives. Most of them don't do a great job of coping with the problems of everyday living. Most people settle for mediocrity; they have resigned themselves to "just getting by" as a way of life. The feelings of inadequacy that arise from this mindset cause them to blame society, circumstances, and other people for their lack, disappointments, and failures. We have become so conditioned to accepting that people and situations control us that normally we don't even respond to other suggestions or ideas. In fact, we get so caught up in following the parade that one day we look up and discover the people we thought we were following were actually following us! The opposite of courage is not cowardice; it is conformity. The Valeo Method will challenge you to step out of the box and boldly take back control of your self-confidence, self-esteem, and your life.

Be encouraged! The Valeo Method will teach you how to develop the skills to live by the beliefs that are fueled by faith and hope. This is the best part and you will hear it all the way through this book. You will begin to want to use your skills to help others do the same and that, my friends, attracts more and more good energy and blessings into your life, your environment, and your personal economy.

Let's get busy! The ego and its false beliefs can seem real and intimidating but in reality they are no match for your authentic power that will emerge when you learn and apply the five simple and duplicatable steps of the Valeo Method.

Be encouraged! So, are you ready? Let's get started!

Chapter 1
The Underdog Champion

Courage is going from failure to failure without losing enthusiasm.

Winston Churchill

Why does everyone love the underdog? The movie Rocky and its many sequels were huge box office successes. It's the story of an unlikely guy from a meager background and with little experience as a heavyweight fighter who nonetheless goes on to become a world champion. He had something special going for him; he had a big heart, and he wouldn't give up.

I cried at the end of the first movie. I'll never forget leaving the theater as a kid, feeling something touching my heart. It was a feeling that made me want to take on the world. I thought, "Just give me a chance." It made me start asking myself those "What if?" questions. Dreams of many possibilities raced through my mind. I loved the way I felt. Can you remember the last time you had that feeling?

There is an underdog in every one of us. When we see movies like Rocky, hear stories of accomplishment or of someone overcoming big challenges, it stirs up the underdog inside each of us. But what is that part? Why does it motivate some to action and others just let it slip away?

If you are going to have heart surgery do you want a doctor who has completed many challenging and successful operations? Or would you consider a doctor fresh out of medical school with little experience, including close calls and even failures?

This book was written by an underdog who wants to help you discover and inspire the underdog in you. The information is not only based on real-life situations and experiences, but theory and application within large groups in some of the most difficult and challenging situations life can dish out. It comes from hard work and relentless trial and error. It comes from studying devastating disappointments contrasted against astounding successes and comebacks against the odds.

Would you like to find out why you make mistakes in life? Would you like to learn how to avoid making them again? I used to beat myself up and wonder why I kept repeating my mistakes and sabotaging myself. When things seemed to be going great I would then somehow mess it up. Yet I was always able to climb back up Success Mountain one more time and plant a "Conquered!" sign at the top.

Then another area of my life would start to unravel. Why is it so hard to get it together in all the areas of life such as career, relationships, finances, and our physical, emotional, and spiritual health? Why do so few seem to reach an ongoing level of joy and fulfillment in their lives?

What is your life situation now? Are you broke, lonely, sick, in prison, depressed, discouraged, confused, or battling an addiction? Do you have some great things going on in your life but other parts are miserable? Do you have secrets that eat at you or do you listen to an internal dialogue that keeps you distracted? If these questions stimulate your curiosity, keep reading, because many answers and discoveries lie ahead.

This book is about going from losing it to finding it. It is based on a process that teaches you how to see beneath the surface of life to the deeper level of the authentic self; the source of your life. It is about learning what is causing your problems, disappointments, and shortcomings. Most of us complain about the effects and never address the causes. It is much easier to address what causes the undesired results.

For example, when my thoughts kept causing me to sabotage myself, I didn't want to admit that any of it was my fault. I thought I had all the answers. I thought I could fix or outrun any challenges that came my way, and I did for a while. Then I realized I was doing it the hard way.

Even though I overcame my challenges and many times achieved grand results, the success never lasted. I felt like a juggler trying to keep more and more balls in the air. My world was constantly building up to great heights and then collapsing. My battle cry used to be, "I'll bite off more than I can chew and chew it anyway." I also said, "I'm going to the top of Success Mountain, and one of two things will happen: I'll be waving from the top or I'll be dead on the side. I will succeed!" It almost killed me! In reality, I had discovered how to create an outward appearance of success. It took me years but I read book after book, listened to thousands of hours of audio recordings, and attended every seminar I could find. I even tried to model myself after successful people I met.

The success *was* there in many ways. The information and skills I learned were valuable and empowering, and for a while it seemed I had everything it took to be successful. In reality, I had only about 80 percent; the information and skills. The remaining 20 percent I lacked was momentum which, if I had pursued my level of success further, would have led to purpose, wholeness, and peace. Does it really matter what is happening in your life if you have these three things?

In the pages ahead I will share with you what I did to get that 80 percent. More importantly, I will show you how I got that illusive yet all-important 20 percent that so many of us never find. Not only that, but I will also reveal an even more important secret: how to keep success and how to enjoy it once you get it.

It doesn't impress me when someone is rich and successful through inheritance or luck and writes a book about how to be successful. Don't get me wrong, God blessed them and I am happy for their good fortune. But give me a story about an underdog, a guy or gal who prevailed against the odds, and then you have my attention, because I'm one of those guys!

I was born in a small Southern town. My parents got married, dropped out of high school, got blue-collar jobs, and had me at a very young age. There was an abundance of love in our home, but not an abundance of money or what it could provide. As I grew up I saw what it took to survive and realized it would take a lot more than what my parents had to give to thrive.

After I finished high school I decided to go to college and my parents were able to support me though the first year. With three younger brothers, however, I felt guilty; I was taking away from them due to my parents bearing the burden of my college expenses. So, I quit college and went on my quest for the American Dream. I didn't come from wealthy circumstances by any means, but I did have an above-average desire to learn and a willingness to work.

What follows are the ideas, concepts, and strategies that influenced the development of what became the Valeo Method. This system involves a process that rescues underdogs and people who aren't ready to give up. My hope is that while reading this book you will realize, "If this guy can get it together, so can I."

I screwed up in many different ways over the years. I had failed marriages, failed businesses, health problems, and poor self-esteem. I lost everything twice and I even went to prison. I've been emotionally and spiritually bankrupt.

I've also had a successful career as an insurance salesman and manager. I've been a successful real estate investor, restaurant owner, and I even owned a thriving health club. I worked as a top associate distributor and lecturer with Anthony Robbins, I wrote a successful book, and I am a personal empowerment coach to thousands of people. I'm the father of an amazing, well-balanced, and successful son. I found and married the girl of my dreams. I earned a doctorate degree in religious studies. I've even lost 80 pounds and kept it off for years and at the same time gotten off three kinds of blood pressure medication and haven't needed them for years (even though my doctor told me it would never happen).

I am not telling you these things to brag or to get you to feel sorry for me. I am sharing this with you because I want you to know I have been through a lot of challenges and prevailed in many areas. I can relate to your struggles whether they are with finances, relationships, weight and appearance, or self-esteem.

I am an Underdog Champion. I came back in all areas of my life. I do have it all now and I am passionate about sharing how I did it so I can help you, and then you can help yourself. But even more importantly, the concepts you will learn here will allow you to help others to find their way, as well, and that is what my life is about now. I want to give hope and encouragement to as many people as possible as quickly as I can, and that begins with helping you, my friend.

Chapter 2
The Comeback Kid

Go ahead and make mistakes.
Make all you can, that is where you will find success.

Tom Watson, Founder IBM

Anyone who looks at all my successes and failures will get a good idea why I qualify as an underdog. I got discouraged and wanted to give up many times, but I didn't give up on myself and actually learned something every time I failed. As a result, I was always able to make a comeback. Something inside me would never let me give up, and that something was that God didn't give up on me, either.

The Valeo Method is designed to help you find the strength of the underdog and give you the courage to get through difficult decisions and make difficult choices. It will give new hope to you, whether you feel pain and suffering or just seem to live a life that has no purpose.

You have something special hidden deep within your spirit. To smell the beautiful fragrance of a flower the petals have to open. Consider the many times you have never allowed yourself to open up to the beauty and purpose within you. This process will give you the opportunity to open up in all areas of your life so you can enjoy and pursue a life with true purpose and intention.

Loss often precedes gain. Unfortunately, it often takes a major tragedy like the loss of a loved one, a life-threatening illness, or the loss of career or financial distress to create the motivation to change. But it doesn't have to be that way. What if you could tap into the advantage of creating change *without* enduring loss, trauma, or any other upsetting circumstance to jolt you into action? What if you had the ability to just turn on your authentic power and get the results you wanted? This is about to happen if you are ready to take your life to a new level, and you are open-minded and willing.

Suffering is a natural part of life. It is vitally important you understand this and that suffering affects everyone, not just you. Some people don't get it and therefore get stuck—so much so that suffering actually becomes a habit to them. Do you see how this can happen? Life acts like the ocean, kicking up waves of turmoil only then to settle back down to low tide—ever-changing, yet always the same. How you interpret the waves determines how well you enjoy your life. The idea is not to skip over life's challenges and disappointments, but to transcend them. You really *need* failure because within *every* failure lies success, just like *every* success holds failure. The challenge here is that most people just don't know how to get from low to high tide, or from failure to success and so forth.

There are going to be mountains and valleys in life. Sometimes the valleys, the low spots, seem to go on forever. Yet you can illuminate the valleys and make them shorter and fewer if you choose. However, there are certain things that just can't be taught. You have to discover them for yourselves. The Underdog Champions of the world learn to grow from their challenges and adversities in order to build their future mountains on top of them.

Chapter 3
The Quest for Wholeness

Your vision will come clear only when you can look into your own heart. Who looks outside, dreams; who looks inside, awakens.

Carl Jung

As a human being you are on a journey; you are here for one primary purpose and that is to become whole. As you search for healing you must learn to accept everything and then choose the best. Deep inside you long to embrace your destiny, your place in eternity. You are restless to satisfy the mystery of your existence. You have a strong sense that all is possible in your life and you long for it. The more you accept and say yes to your innate goodness, the sooner you will find and live your true purpose. That process is about embracing the opportunity to grow in your true spirit, your authentic self.

A mountain climber slipped while on a high, steep mountainside. He tumbled downward but was able to grasp a branch with one hand. He held on for life. Never much one for praying before, he decided to try. He looked up at the heavens and prayed, "God, please help me, please save me." The sound of a deep, powerful voice powered out from the sky, "Let go and I will save you." After a few moments of thinking his situation over the mountain climber replied, "Is there anyone else in today that I could talk to?"

Are you holding on to limiting beliefs, doubt, and fear because you are afraid to let go? Are you afraid to try out yourself or God? I have certainly been there many times. I finally learned that for things to change, I had to change. For things to get better, I had to get better. Just like the mountain climber, I had to release my grip and stop holding on to the things that were limiting me.

Are you a mountain climber ready to let go of your fierce grip? Are you an underdog ready to make a comeback? Are you ready to make your mark, stake your claim? Are you ready to write your own Underdog Champion story? Are you satisfied to let your life play out on the same old track? Does that thought scare you, make you depressed, or motivate you? Are you ready to become a better steward at this time in your life and make it count?

Through my many experiences of trial and error I discovered something that changed my thinking forever. There are two ways to learn in life: the school of hard knocks, and the school of modeling successful people. They both work, but one is the hard way, so I decided, why do it the hard way? If someone else has already had a similar experience and discovered an effective and easier method, why not at least give it a try?

Sometimes the most successful people have also been the biggest failures. It often takes many failures to achieve success. There is an old saying that the key to success is to keep going from failure to failure until you find success.

A recurring message you will notice in this book is that everything happens for a reason and a purpose, and that it serves you. Pain and suffering serve you in many ways if you pay attention. Saint Paul reminds us, *"You also rejoice in your sufferings, because you know suffering produces perseverance; perseverance, character; and character hope, and hope does not disappoint you."*

So I pray, my friend, that my own suffering, struggles, and mistakes will serve you. I hope you allow this process to help you avoid unnecessary pain and suffering while finding your way to wholeness.

Chapter 4
Shoot for the Moon

Go for it now. The future is promised to no one.

Dr. Wayne Dyer

I Will never forget the summer before I went to high school. I was a shy and introverted kid. I wanted to be popular in high school but I was scared and nervous. I told my dad and he gave me a book titled, *How to Win Friends and Influence People,* by Dale Carnegie.

Reading that one book changed my entire life. It gave me the confidence to make many new friends. I became vice-president of my class, was elected to the student counsel, and was voted "best personality." I am not telling you this to impress you, but to impress upon you that sometimes it doesn't take much to make a huge difference. There I was, an impressionable, shy, 13-year-old kid whose outlook changed forever because of one book.

In fact, that one book changed my perspective so much that it launched me on a lifelong search for purpose and potential. I started wondering where I could find other books that were full of those kinds of golden nugget ideas. I was just a kid but I started reading anything inspirational I could find. Mostly I read autobiographies of successful people in history. Then, I graduated to self-improvement and personal growth.

The books were filled with ideas that motivated and inspired me and made me want to succeed. One book I read said you should "shoot for the moon; if you miss, you still land in the stars." I decided to go for it. Another book said that success is simply buried past frustration, so I learned to accept and even expect frustration as a precursor to success. I was moving along!

My commitment to learn fueled my success. Yet as the years went by great success was followed by sometimes even greater failures, followed by another success, and the cycle went on. After years of this scenario I decided to figure out what was happening to me. I was sick and tired of sabotaging my own success and I was getting tired of running up and down Success Mountain. I decided there had to be better way and I was determined to find it.

Finally, I found the answer—the missing piece of the puzzle—and it wasn't what I was expecting. It was there all along; I just didn't see it so I couldn't understand it.

By applying what I discovered, I was able to bring everything together in all areas of my life at the same time. I was on a roll. Everything was perfect, and the best part was I knew how to keep it that way, once and for all.

Then it happened. The worst nightmare I could possibly imagine—a life-wrecking experience. I had to go to prison.

A few years earlier, a man I had known and trusted for more than twenty-five years hired my company to create marketing materials and a national recruiting plan to help his company increase sales, as they were planning a public offering in about a year. Because I trusted this man I violated a policy I normally strictly adhered to when my friend told me it was not necessary. I did not run a background check on his partner.

The arrangement appeared quite successful until I encountered a delay in the documentation of insurance renewal and the company stopped providing its monthly bank statements. I was concerned but my desire to keep the arrangement going clouded my judgment. I made a big mistake. Although my intentions were good, and the owners convinced me to be patient, in my gut something didn't seem right. The company turned out to be operating illegally, and the owners were indicted for fraud. This was the third similar fraud charge for the majority partner—the one I didn't check out.

Toward the end of my relationship with the company, whenever things appeared to be in disarray, the owners were always quick to offer excuses and financial incentives to keep me going. Since I wanted to believe them, against my better judgment I wound up staying involved too long. As a result, I paid a big price.

I fought and defended my position for two years and gave my life savings to seven lawyers. In the end I took a plea bargain for aiding and abetting mail fraud. The government took everything else I had left. I prepared to begin what would be a three-year prison sentence at a federal prison camp in Miami.

Little did I know at the time that this experience would serve as a springboard to take my life to a whole new level. Many times things happen to you to get you ready for something special you are meant to do, be, or have. I believe this event occurred to transform my life and give me the tools, knowledge, and experience to help others even more—which was what I had always dreamed of doing, anyway.

As my wife and I pulled away from the camp on my last day we stopped and prayed. We shared tears of joy and relief. I knew I still had a big hole to dig out of, but the worst part was over. It was difficult and challenging but finally I could use this experience to help others. It was time for a comeback.
But three years earlier, it was a different story. I walked into the camp in a state of shock. This was a big adjustment and would become my biggest challenge yet.

There was a diverse assortment of personalities at the camp, and they came from a wide variety of backgrounds. The non-violent charges ranged from drug-dealing to white-collar crimes committed by accountants, lawyers, investment advisors, doctors, and politicians. Some people came from troubled childhoods, and some from broken homes and families. There were people who had been wealthy and in positions of power. There were people who spent their lives just trying to survive. But the one thing they all had in common was the challenge of putting a life back together.

This environment would provide the perfect opportunity to put the Valeo Method to the test. I could use the opportunity to help people who were at a low point in their lives—people who had lost their spouses to divorce and people whose family and friends had deserted them. Most people had either lost everything or were financially challenged. They dealt with emotions ranging from discouragement, depression, poor self-esteem, hate, anger, and the residues of addiction.

I needed to get permission and support from the administrators at the camp to create a teaching environment. I needed participants, a classroom, and a schedule. That proved to be one of my biggest challenges and it almost didn't happen. Right when I was about out of ideas and had tried everything I could think of, the director of education stopped me in the hallway. I will never forget it because I was so happy. He said, "You'll try your course one time; if you get good feedback, you will continue. If not, you are finished with it." I think the only reason he gave in was that I was so persistent, he figured I was either a nut or I really had something good up my sleeve.

I put the course together as a ten-week personal encouragement program based on the five steps of the Valeo Method. Since there were no types of rehabilitation programs at the camp which housed more than four hundred inmates, my proposal made sense and many inmates were anxious to enroll. The program consisted of a one-hour class once a week for twelve weeks with about an hour of homework. There was a constant inmate turnover rate at the camp, but during my three years there more than four hundred inmates completed the course. It was a resounding success—so much so that the classes always filled up in advance, leaving a waiting list for the next class.

The director of the resident drug abuse program at the camp even requested that the information be taught to participants in that program, as well. I received more than two hundred handwritten testimonials with touching and heartwarming stories of new hope, confidence, and courage from the graduates of the class, like this one:

*After understanding the concepts of the Valeo Method,
I feel strongly that I can have what I really want. I can
realize the dreams I gave up on before. This news really
helped me as I am leaving prison after nine years to face
a new world on one hand and a new me on the other.
Yes I can, yes I will; I will follow these steps, stay focused,
and I will succeed.   William*

Seeing the positive results in those individuals who had
so much to overcome, and after what I had personally been
through and been able to change with the Valeo Method, convinced me without a doubt I had something unique and special.
If those guys in that environment of incarceration and in such
dire life situations could make the major changes I witnessed,
there was no limit to what could happen for people in normal
life situations.

The Valeo Method stresses a "me too" thinking process. It
teaches a person that they can transform their underdog status
and become a champion. How? By learning a duplicatable
process modeled after the proven success of others. Your natural instinct is to think negatively about your problems, limiting
beliefs, bad habits, or excuses. Through your thinking errors,
you make choices that influence the direction of your life. If
you don't find a way to change, your life is just the same song,
second verse.

So why do some people overcome life's challenges yet
others struggle and fail? Why do so many get sucked into the
drama, trauma, and suffering of life? How do you get in the
flow of a positive, fulfilling life and stay there? Life is like a
river; when you are in the flow things go smoothly, almost
without effort. When you are not in the flow, you hit the rocks
in the dark.

Chapter 5

The Need for Healing

*In the depth of winter, I finally realized
that deep within me there lay an invincible summer.*

Albert Camus

You can heal your mind. It simply requires that you let go of old, limiting beliefs about who you are. It is about releasing the thoughts and memories that keep you chained to what you don't want. When you heal your mind you not only affect your mental health, you also change your emotional, physical, and spiritual health. Healing the mind is the key to overall wellness. There is no other way. True happiness doesn't come along and just happen; it rests within you as the joy of being and only needs awakening. Joy is your natural state and doesn't need to be worked on; it is simply the state of who you are.

So, in order to develop a healthy, disciplined mind, you must first understand how it works. The Valeo Method teaches awareness. When you are aware of how your life and your mind works you learn to get out of your own way. God can't work for you if your intentions keep Him from working through you. The journey ahead of you is not as much to teach you as it is to help you find yourself. You will learn to live consciously for a change, and that can create a big "Aha!" experience.

Are you interested in knowing why I kept sabotaging my life and only experienced fleeting happiness? You can find happiness in many ways—through relationships, financial rewards, and personal achievements. But happiness without a foundation of joy, which comes from the soul, never lasts. After much suffering and disappointment in my life, that missing part of my life, joy, was revealed to me.

For many years I had great success in business. Whatever I put my mind, I was able to do well. I felt confident and unstoppable, yet my priorities were skewed: financial success was number one, family was number two, and my spiritual relationship with God was number three. My health, including my exercise regimen (or lack thereof) and eating habits came in around number four, and helping others was number five. In my heart I knew this wasn't right. I chose to reason with myself and to God that I would get around to putting things right later. But first, I had to get enough money, material things, and status so I could provide a good life for my family. Afterwards, I would settle things with God and put things in the right order. Then I would have time to exercise and help others. I didn't realize it at the time but that attitude was a guaranteed ticket to failure. Even though I appeared successful on the surface—I had lots of friends, a great lifestyle, and many accolades—I was ultimately on a collision course.

Great things lie ahead for those ready to make a commitment to change and work with the Valeo Method. I share these thoughts with a deep longing and compassion to serve you and help you heal your mind and ease your time. As you begin, I say to you, no matter where you are on life's journey, be encouraged; things can change, and they will change. I am here to be your helper, your coach, and your friend. I wrote this book to teach you this method, but more than that, I wanted to offer you the tools to find something special in yourself, for yourself.

The Valeo Method teaches more than inspirational tips, motivation, motivation tactics, or philosophy. It hones the participant's dormant skills that were always there to begin with and allows them to hammer this newfound power toward real-life challenges. Those who finished this course and learned the Valeo Method were more confident and knowledgeable. More importantly, you gained a new passion for living life to the fullest.

Ming

PART II

THE VALEO METHOD

Chapter 6

What is the Valeo Method?

Every new beginning comes from some other beginnings end.

Seneca

The Valeo Method is a five-step process designed to teach you how to achieve lasting change. It is a simple yet thorough system aimed at addressing life's challenges and roadblocks to wholeness. When you find wholeness in life everything else falls in place; you have arrived.

"Valeo" is a Latin word that means "to have power, influence and to prevail." I chose this word for this course because it fully describes the results accomplished by using and applying the methods. To me, "valeo" meant having courage and being brave. It meant overcoming what at the time seemed insurmountable odds in almost every area of my life. I decided to put it to the test against huge personal obstacles at a time when my own self-esteem and personal power was at a lifetime low. I thought if what I had been teaching and developing all that time had worked to get me back on top after the mess my life was in, I would have to teach it to the world. Well, it did work, and now I am on a mission!

The "power" part of the definition means having the courage and power to overcome weakness and fear. It does not represent power over others, but power over yourself and the power to gain control of your thoughts. It also means that you have the power to do *whatever it takes.* Only then can you achieve your dreams and feel happy and fulfilled. It means having the power to put yourself on the line *every* single day.

The "influence" part of the definition means having the ability to influence others by your example. It means walking your talk and not stumbling your mumble. It means living a life of influence, full of goodness and intentions that create the respect and admiration of your peers and attract God's blessings.

If you live your life in a way that positively influences others, you set yourself up to receive good in return. The universal Law of Attraction demonstrates that what you put out comes right back to you (good or bad). Your thoughts leave your mind and go out into the universe seeking their reflection. Your thoughts literally attract similar thoughts, situations, and energies into your environment. This also means that when you give of yourself you create a vacuum, and God's universe seeks to fill it up.

The last part of the definition is to "prevail." To prevail here means to overcome your challenges, limiting beliefs, childhood wounds, and lingering pain from past negative experiences. It means to conquer whatever is keeping you from living your purpose and realizing the dream of your soul. It means freeing yourself from the shackles of yourself, once and for all. It means being a victor instead of a victim.

Chapter 7
Which Dream Are You Living?

Dreams are illustrations from the book your soul is writing about you.
Marsha Norman

You are living in a dream. It is either the dream of the soul that you were created to live, or the dream of the ego. You might say, "I'm not living a dream, I'm living a nightmare!" If you really feel that way you are definitely living the dream of the ego. Whatever is happening in your life is there for a reason. It did not just show up. Every event, even those that seem insignificant, plays a role in where you are today and where you will wind up tomorrow. Every event is rooted in a prior thought which triggers another universal law—cause and effect.

You will learn from the Valeo Method that your egoic mind, the false self we all struggle with, deals in causality and imperfection only, while the spirit self, the authentic part of each of us, deals in reality and perfection. The quality of your life is based on which force dominates your soul.

I will use the mnemonic D.R.E.A.M. to help you remember the five main steps of the Valeo Method. Although each step is powerful on its own, it is much more effective to follow the steps in order. This way you create more synergy and momentum with your efforts. That doesn't mean you can't open the book anywhere and get a benefit. It just means that if you are going to read it, and you are sincerely seeking change, why not get the most out of it?

When you learn this information as a process you will develop extremely valuable skills to maintain lasting change, and this will enable you to teach it to others. There is something powerful about understanding why things happen in your life. It is difficult to fix something if you don't know why it is happening.

If you are sick and tired of being sick and tired, and if you are tired of missing the mark and falling short of where you thought you would be at this point in your life, you are at the right place. If you are ready to go to a whole new level, if you have desire, teachability, and the willingness to do a little work, congratulations. You have a great opportunity for positive change ahead.

The D.R.E.A.M mnemonic breaks down as follows:

DISCOVERY

RELEASE

EMBRACE

ACTIVATE AND ATTRACT

MANIFEST AND MAINTAIN

The *Discovery* step is the foundation of the Valeo Method. This is where you will learn how the egoic mind uses your thoughts and beliefs to create emotions, which in turn create drama in your life. Drama is a tool the ego uses to get control. Left unchecked when the ego is in control, sometimes your life can seem like a runaway freight train of emotions and uncertainty. Through the *Discovery* process you learn how to switch tracks before it is too late. Psychologist Rollo May was quoted as saying the definition of insanity is doing the same thing over and over and expecting a different result. Most people spend their entire lives living unconsciously and just showing up to see what hits them next. This is a painful, unpredictable, and unfulfilling way to live.

Millions of people drive a car every day without having a clue how a combustion engine works. If it breaks they take it to a mechanic who knows how to fix it. But when something goes wrong in your life or when things aren't moving smoothly, most of us don't know why this is happening and therefore we don't have a place to get help. We just live with it or mask the problem with unhealthy options. The *Discovery* process reveals why things are happening in your life so you can learn how to repair the undesirable situations and results immediately.

The *Release* step reveals how to get to the source of your burdens and the weight that you carry unnecessarily on your back but can't seem to get rid of. This could include guilt, regret, poor self-esteem, limiting beliefs, negative internal dialogue (self-talk), or confusion about what to do next. In addition (and this may be hard to believe at first), everyone carries the guilt and pain of their childhood wounds. No matter how perfect your childhood may seem to have been, working with the Valeo Method will reveal you have unresolved issues. Even Superman had issues—I mean, come on, something is wrong with a guy who wears his underwear on the outside of his pants!

These issues beg to be addressed and resolved because one way or the other, they will release themselves into your life (if you don't get to them first). You will learn to recognize locked-away beliefs that are quietly and systematically stealing your life source and blocking the way to that which empowers you. Only then will you be able to free yourself from the prison of your distracted mind and gain control of your life.

The *Embrace* step will evolve naturally from the healing of the *Release* step and take you to deeper, more enlightening "aha" experiences. When your thoughts, fears, and limiting beliefs that are holding you back finally have to loosen their hold, something amazing happens: you begin to experience your hidden, sensitive self and your true purpose. You will begin to open the door to your authentic being—that essential part of you that may have been buried for a long time. As you discover and embrace this sensitive, empowering part of yourself, you can't help but expose your special gifts.

Remember, each one of us is unique. We all have our own special talents and abilities. Sadly, many gifts are never discovered because they are smothered by our past pain, doubt, and fear.

This process teaches you to search out and *embrace* your own innate goodness. This is the key to finding and living your life's purpose and becoming whole as a person.

You will uncover a simple way to face and control emotions like anger, grief, and regret. You will acquire the ability to conquer undesired habits and addictions that you have used in the past to mask your pain and keep you from embracing your authentic self.

When you start the *Activate and Attract* process you will have arrived at a point in the Valeo Method at which you have experienced a kind of mental cleansing. You can now begin to replace disempowering, toxic thoughts and energies with the opposite, and invite new beliefs, expectations, and confidence into your heart. It is time to *Activate* your God-given ability to co-create your reality.

Here your focus will be on understanding God's gift to you of free will. You will explore and understand how cause and effect works in your life. You will open up your life to experience conscious living vs. unconscious living. This will empower you to live your life with certainty and confidence.

In fact, this step reveals why the Law of Attraction, which has gotten so much attention in recent years, doesn't work for most people.

Let's put it this way: You learn how to harness the power of cause and effect, built on a foundation of faith, to *manifest* success in all areas of your life. But whether you create a life of misery or joy is based on your thoughts and efforts. You do have a choice and this step teaches you how to create your life on purpose instead of by happenstance.

When you enter the *Manifest and Maintain* stage you're really going to be ready to receive and accept your personal truth. Most of us believe there is some Divine, Omnipotent, Omnipresent, and Omniscient Power that permeates humanity, but many people are not sure how to experience this Presence in daily life.

Most people find it easier to envision God in some starry heaven floating on a cloud than to accept the Divine that dwells within themselves. Freedom, peace, and wholeness are not dependent on assets, achievements, circumstances, or fame, but on inner peace. The Valeo Method will help you find that place of inner peace. Manifest and Maintain is the point at which manifesting all things you are meant to have becomes an exciting and rewarding reality in your life. You will no longer have to work for it because you are now in the flow and experiencing the power of alignment with your purpose, the dream of your soul.

This doesn't mean you have to sacrifice parts of yourself or enter a state of martyrdom. Far, far from it. It means living your dreams on purpose, whatever they are, with confidence and intention, and with God's blessings which are built on a solid foundation.

Do you know someone who seems to have it all but is miserable? Do you know someone who has little in the material sense but is full of joy? How could that happen? How can a person seem to have it all in outward appearances and yet lack peace of mind? Easy. I was that person! We were all cut from the same cloth. It is not about background, education, or personal history. What gives some the edge? The Valeo Method will unequivocally give you that answer.

God promises over and over in the Scriptures that He wants to bless you. I believe a person deserves to have abundance in their lives, brought about with good intention, if they are willing to work for it. Is all the money and success in the world worth it without peace of mind?

Have you ever seen a moving van behind a hearse? You aren't going to take it with you. When God tells us, "The gold and silver are mine," that's a clue. Isn't it about time to figure out a way to be happy while we are here at Earth School with the time we each have been granted? None of us has a lease on life.

Whatever your religion is, if you don't have an intimate relationship with God life can be pretty empty and often painful. In this part of the process you'll focus on getting God's seal of approval—His sacred blessings on your thoughts and efforts for guaranteed good results. There is no sense in living the hard way without grace if you don't have to.

This book is not about religion. It is about aligning with the power of God and the power that created everything we see out of nothing. It is also about learning to take advantage of His intentions for good and abundance in all areas of our lives. It's about claiming the life of good we were intended to live now and not miss out on another day.

There is an extra bonus from learning the Valeo Method. Remember, the skills you develop can be duplicated and used to teach and encourage others. If you help someone else meet their needs, God will help you meet yours. So don't give up and don't stop until you finish your journey through this book. Those around you need you—your friends, your family, and people you haven't even met yet. How do you know that? Because if God didn't mean for you to be here, you wouldn't still be here. You're still around because you have more to do, accomplish, and enjoy. And yes, there are people you are destined to affect positively with what you are about to learn. The best way to get what you want out of life is to help other people get what they want out of it. All of humanity needs you to spread your powerful, newfound enlightenment into the universe and let your inner oneness connect with another. Together, everyone achieves more.

If people in the unfortunate circumstance of being in prison can not only change themselves and get excited about the future, but also help and encourage others, what could learning this process for change do for you? This opportunity to change is right in front of you. How seriously you take it is up to you. You could treat it like a buffet line—take what you want and leave the rest. In fact, if you do approach it that way you will get a lot out of this book. Or, you could get really serious about following a proven plan of action and change your entire life. I challenge you to see it through. Don't get discouraged and throw the baby out with the bath water. Lasting positive change is not always easy, but it is always worth it.

Over my many years of seeking self-improvement, I realized all the seminars I attended and all the information I listened
to in audio programs didn't have a lasting effect. Within a few
days or weeks I was right back where I started. I wondered
what happened. Was it my fault? I wasn't sure, but in creating
the Valeo Method I was committed to create lasting change and
not just a temporary fix. I went through enough of those experiences myself to know how to provide more than a temporary
fix; this process will provide you with rock-solid lifetime skills.
This way when your life veers off track you'll know what to do
to get right back on.

It takes practice to learn how and when to make necessary
changes. Repetition is the mother of skill. Small efforts add up
to big results over time. What you are looking for is a measurable amount of progress in a reasonable amount of time. It's
about getting a little bit better every day. This kind of effort can
produce a tsunami of change over time. Bad habits may seem
inconsequential but a pattern starts to develop in the wrong
direction. All of a sudden we can't believe we are in a place
we really hate! For example, when I wound up eighty pounds
overweight I was lethargic and tired. I looked at a picture of
myself one day and said, "Who is that? Oh, my God, what
have I let happen to me?"

You don't go to the gym, work out one time and say,
"Whew, I'm glad that is over; now I'm fit for life." It takes
constant attention, intention, and effort. By following the Valeo
Method you will be able to stay on a steady game plan. You'll
get what you want without second-guessing yourself. Look,
you've already done the hardest part—you are at the gym. Isn't
the hard part just getting there? After that, the working out
part is not so hard, right? You are working everything out right
now as you continue to read these words.

I recommend you use this book as a study guide and re-
read it until you master all the steps of the D.R.E.A.M. formula.
May God bless you and open your mind to understand, learn,
and grow. Then you will discover and enjoy the endless possibilities ahead in your life.

Now let's summarize the five steps. You are going to *Discover* what is causing your problems in life. You will understand why and how you sabotage your success and don't reach your potential so you don't ever return to the place you were before.

You are then going to *Release* the things holding you back. You are going to free up your potential for the future. You will permanently release painful, toxic thoughts, lingering emotions, and limiting beliefs.

Next, you are going to *Embrace* your potential for the future. You will learn how to seek and find your hidden gifts. You are going to learn to embrace your authentic self so you can be the person you were created to be.

You are going to learn how to *Activate and Attract* the personal power, creativity, and strength that is waiting to be unleashed within you and attract the energies, people, situations, and courage you need to realize your dreams.

Finally, you will take the most important step by laying a solid foundation underneath every thought and action you take. You will *Manifest and Maintain* what you want in life. We've already established that life is too short to do it the hard way, especially when you don't have to, my friend. This last step will teach you the two secrets to manifesting greatness in all areas of your life with confidence. You will learn to maintain your new success on a continual basis.

Chapter 8
Memorialize This Experience

Discipline is remembering what you want.

David Campbell

I know every self-help author or Life Coach worth his or her salt tells you to keep a journal. Please indulge me here. You will be going through some major thought-provoking and sensitive, emotional issues in these next pages. You will experience some breakthroughs and revelations regarding how you got where you are in your life today. This is just too powerful and too potentially life-altering to *not* get the most out of it.

If you really get serious and get this I promise you will have the opportunity to be a human catalyst for change. I am serious. I am speaking from experience and I can prove it. This method can and will change your life, and you can use your newfound knowledge and skills to encourage and help others on a major scale. You could be changing lives in no time.

So, I strongly recommend you keep a journal or at least take notes of your progress while learning and implementing the strategies ahead. It is always good to keep a journal to record the significant events, lessons, and memories of life. This is no different. My experience with the Valeo Method indicates that keeping a record is a great reminder and measuring stick for your progress while going through the five steps. It will also be encouraging to you as you approach the end and look at the strategies for Team Building.

I started keeping a journal more than twenty-five years ago and the experiences have been fascinating. When I look back today I am amazed at the twists and turns, ideas and revelations I experienced. I saw how I achieved what seemed like impossible goals. Often, I was lost and totally off track.

There were things I thought I had to have and do, but when I received them they weren't what I expected. There were heartaches and victories. Many times when I was searching for why things were the way they were in my life, my journal gave me perspective and answers.

Your journal emphasizes the importance of "you." It is a tool to measure growth. Here is the point: Gradual changes can go unnoticed over time, especially if they are not documented. You can drift into bad situations or miss out on opportunities to make progress. You need to recognize your good changes and celebrate them; plus, you need to catch yourself before you go off course. Journaling will help keep you in the present moment.

A journal lets you document your life story. In many ways your journal is not just for you, but a way for you to leave a legacy of your life. The journal doesn't have to be fancy or leather-bound. It can be as simple as a spiral notebook. The key is to keep a record and document the Valeo Method progress in your life. You'll be glad you did.

EXERCISE

Documentation beats conversation. This exercise helps you be aware of and keep up with your progress. The worst thing you can do if you are seriously seeking change is to get discouraged or lazy and give up. This exercise provides a way to help you keep up and pay attention to change and your progress.

It's hard to get to a destination unless you are aware of your starting point. When you are clear about where you are today and focused on where you are going, you invite great things to start happening. Miracles happen every day under the right circumstances. In fact, I believe God has a miracle with your name on it waiting for you right now. Are you ready for a miracle in your life?

Seven areas of potential growth are listed here. Rate yourself on a scale of one to ten in all areas of your life, with one being the lowest ranking and ten the best. Next, write down in the space provided where you would like to be in ninety days and then after one year. There is also a place to write in your results later, when those dates arrive.

Maybe you are already satisfied with some areas of your life. Perhaps you are in great shape physically and are not seeking to change but only maintain. You will just work on the areas you want to change. It is hard to hit a target you cannot see. This exercise gives you a way to work toward those targets. Remember, it's not how you start but how you finish that matters. As Saint Paul said, *"Don't you realize that in a race, everyone runs, but only one gets the prize?"* So run to win!

	Rank Today	90 Days Goal	90 Days Actual	1 Year Goal	1 Year Actual
Today's Date _____					
Emotionally(Balance)					
Attitude (Future Outlook)					
Physically (Condition)					
Financial (Standing)					
Relationships (Fulfilling)					
Confidence (Courage)					
Spiritually (Connected)					

Because of the instruction and guidance I received from the Valeo Method of healing, my life has literally been transformed. I have learned to bring out hidden potential from inside myself. I learned that the only source of real power is from God. The mind is a mysterious instrument of creation. If you are unaware of how it operates, it can cause you a lot of pain and suffering. However, if used intentionally, it provides the means to achieve your dreams. Above all, learning to apply the Valeo Method in my life has given me an understanding of my purpose and a last-ing peace of mind.   *Frank*

PART III

DISCOVERY

Chapter 9

Know Thyself

It is not the mountain that we conquer but ourselves.

Sir Edmund Hillary

I know you are probably thinking, "That sure was a big buildup to the first step!" Yes, it was, because it is important we start out with a good foundation. Did you know that when a tall building is built as much as a third of the total height is underground, in the foundation, before they even start to go up? They have to dig down to the bedrock. That is what we just did here.

The magic of the Valeo Method is the order in which it is taught and the synergy that comes when it all adds up together as we tap in and activate our winning spirit.

In order to know what you should be doing in your life you have to focus on what you want to be. Whatever is going on in your life today, good or bad, did not get there overnight. There is a reason behind everything you are experiencing, even down to your simplest thoughts.

It is good to know and to understand others—this is wisdom. However, to know thyself is true enlightenment. You must seek the insight to gain the outlook necessary to discover your intended path, for only then will you find your bliss. If you don't go within and find out who are and what is your purpose, you go without the joy life holds for you.

The prefix "dis" means "un-," or to stop; reverse. In the *Discovery* step you will uncover the ways in which you got stuck or off track in your life and then stop and reverse the unintentional thinking that has taken you where you no longer desire to be. Alternatively, the prefix "re-" means that which is done over and over again, and in this case it represents issues that keep rearing their ugly, undesirable heads until you either address them or give up and accept them (like too many people do).

What is the dream of the soul? It is your purpose, your calling. For example, I serve you best not by *teaching* you as much as *helping* you discover this Divine part of you in yourself. The greatest gift I can give you is to wake you up and remind you who you are. The most important part of life's journey is to always remember that God's greatest gift is unconditional love, and that His greatest promise is unlimited potential.

Maybe you are not living the dream of your soul and as a result you feel unfulfilled and lack wholeness. Why? Because you are living another dream—the dream of the ego. This dream can be a nightmare! This dream steals your life and blocks the truth and your destiny. The Valeo Method offers a solution, a permanent awakening, and the joy of living your purpose once and for all.

Chapter 10
The Awakening

*Live as if you were going to die tomorrow
and learn as if you were going to live forever.*

Mahatma Gandi

There are two foundational tools to the *Discovery* process:
awareness and clarity. The outcome we seek here is to discover
why you are where you are in your life right now. Therein lies
the key to your future and the answers to lasting change. This
is how you find out why undesirable things happen in your life.
Only then will you be prepared to take control and create a
future that is compelling and fulfilling.

Actor Robert DeNiro starred in a 1990 Academy Award–
nominated movie called *The Awakening,* with Robin Williams.
It was a true story about a man, played by DeNiro, who was
tragically affected by severe encephalitis. He spent many years
in a catatonic state. He was awake and totally conscious but
had no motor skills and was not able to use his body in any
way except to eat. There was no outward indication that he was
coherent.

For many years he lived in a psychiatric hospital. His mother would visit him and as she spoke to him her mother's instinct told her he understood.

Robin Williams played the role of a doctor who had discovered an experimental new drug and received permission to try it on his patient. As a result, DeNiro's character was able to gradually come out of the cationic state and function on a near-normal level.

For the next few months he was elated as he prepared for his re-entry into his new self and his new life. He began to ease back into reality and even met and befriended a lady who came to visit a relative at the hospital. Then, sadly, the medicine began to lose effectiveness and he gradually slipped back into his previous state. His doctor (Williams) filmed his sad and gradual loss of physical awareness. DeNiro's character insisted on the documentation in order to help the doctor seek a future cure for others.

I share this story because it parallels our own lives in many ways. We start out full of dreams, possibilities, and hope. Then we slip into a kind of trance, controlled by the false self, and we forget who we are and the dream of our soul.

What would happen if you got an opportunity like this man? What if you could start fresh? What if you could step away from your limiting beliefs and negative emotions, such as doubt and fear? What if you could experience a period of time in which you were unstoppable, limitless, and full of courage and confidence? How would you react? How would it feel? Just take a moment to think about it.

Now, what if you had this experience for a few months but then you started to gradually lose it—somehow it just slipped away? Can you imagine the pain? If you are not doing what God intended for you to be and do, I must ask you a question I had to ask myself: What are you doing? What are you missing? Aren't you living a life where you are missing out?

The Valeo Method allows you to come out of the trance, gain awareness and clarity, and know the truth. You are unlimited and unstoppable. That is the way God created us all. We just let our human-ness get in the way of our dreams, and the dramas and traumas of life cause us to forget who we are.

You don't need to take medication to find yourself. However, you do need to be willing to learn some strategies and simple skills. Is it worth it to experience a gift like the DeNiro character and wake up and realize the desires of your heart?

In the movie the medication stopped working no matter how much the doctor increased the dosage. If we wait too long our options get scarcer, too. The good news is with the journey you are taking there is no reason to lose yourself once you discover the truth. The real you is always ready to wake up and come alive with purpose; it is just waiting for you to take the first step.

If an airplane leaving New York City and going to Los Angeles was off course by just one degree that shouldn't make a lot of difference, right? Wrong. Actually, the plane, depending on the wind, could end up in Seattle. Small, wrong decisions compounded over time bring disastrous results. You look up one day and say, "How did I get here?"

In these pages you will learn how to quickly recognize when you start to get off track and how to get right back on before it gets out of hand. With practice and conditioning it will get easier to achieve what you desire. You will learn to control what you can control and how to get yourself to do what is uncomfortable until it becomes comfortable.

There is no reason to ever miss another opportunity to experience the joy of living in the truth, connected to your original essence and the Real You. It's time to loosen the shackles of the self and free yourself from the invisible prison of a distracted mind.

In working with thousands of people over the years in my seminars and coaching sessions, I noticed something interesting. The people who are unhappy and struggle with fulfillment in their life have one thing in common: they all have a string of incompletion threaded through their lives. This ranges from relationships to careers, to raising a family, to physical fitness, to abandoned businesses and personal pursuits. When the going gets tough (sometimes not even that tough), or they are not sure what to do, most people just give up. They lack what it takes to keep them going. A major, contributing factor to this problem always turns out to be a lack of awareness as to why things are the way they are and a lack of clarity and vision about what to do next.

Chapter 11
The Power of Awareness and Clarity

*I know of no more encouraging fact than the unquestionable
ability of man to elevate his life by conscious endeavor.*

Henry David Thoreau

Life on its own is a beautifully organized dynamic. If we
think of life as a movie, every scene is what it is by virtue of its
role in the movie. Similarly, everything in your life is happening
for a reason and is heavenly guided. The results of your human contributions, positive or negative, relating to your current
circumstances are based on your awareness and clarity.

Awareness puts you on a path to understand your roles and
purpose in life. Your level of awareness determines whether you
choose consciously or unconsciously, which can mean heaven
or hell in your daily life.

What is hell, anyway? Hell can be many undesirable things.
Hell is one thing for sure—it is the pain you suffer from wrong
thinking. Hell is missing out; it's being unfulfilled and reject-
ing who you are as a person. Hell is the opposite of peace and
happiness. Some people think God sends you to hell if you
don't do what is right. God doesn't send us to hell; we do a fine

job of getting there on our own. Seeking awareness and clarity leads us to truth, when we find out the truth about who we are we find out how to leave hell permanently.

Awareness gives us the ability to recognize why things are happening so we can make conscious choices that help us on our desired path. When we live unconsciously we just get up and see what life throws at us every day, then we react and try to deal with it. We stay off balance and out of control. This way of living can be brutal. Things can come at you so hard and fast you can get overwhelmed and discouraged easily. It can be like trying to hold back the flow of a river. If you can't hold it you will get overwhelmed by it, and you will be tempted to reach for a way to escape it. The same things happens in reality. This is when we try to mask the pain in unhealthy ways.

To develop a healthy, disciplined mind you have to be aware of how it works. You need to know what supports and strengthens the mind and what weakens it and tears it down. This doesn't require a psychology degree and it's not rocket science, either. The skills to be mentally focused, emotionally engaged, physically energized, and spiritually connected are available to anyone who is willing to do a little work and self-analysis.

Clarity is simply focused awareness. Clarity gives you the power to see the perfection in every situation as part of your life's journey. When you have clarity you perceive with wisdom. It's hard to hit a target you can't see. Clarity allows you to see through the illusions and antics of a distracted mind and allows you to experience the force of the spirit-powered immortal soul. Then you are able to see how you sabotage the natural force of the Real You, which is always seeking to do, be, and have the dream of the soul.

Amazing things happen with clarity because you are able to choose confidently through wisdom instead of fear and doubt. You learn to recognize and remove unwanted emotions that cause lack of forgiveness and judgment and replace them with compassion. Clarity also releases the natural flow of energy from the heart and soul. Clarity helps you do more than just recognize the force behind your predicaments. It helps you conquer them with intellect and allows you to stop being a victim. When we have clarity we have vision. When we have vision, things happen in our lives. If we don't have vision there is nothing to tie our objectives to. When we have clarity about our vision there is a natural pull toward it, which creates a string of opportunities and connections we can follow.

Chapter 12
You Can't Stop the Clock

Tomorrow, and tomorrow, and tomorrow creeps
into this petty place from day to day.

William Shakespeare

The reason you need to get busy and master awareness and clarity in your life is simple. Time is moving; we can't stop the clock. Most people are so busy just living that they let life slip away—they take the express lane of life. Then they wake up one day and say, "Oops, is this all there is?" Time can be a gift, but it can also be a thief.

People spend millions on cosmetic surgery, human growth hormones, and skin treatments every year to look and feel young, to prolong life. At the same time, most people let weeks and months go by without really enjoying the gifts life is trying to offer. Isn't it time to focus on nurturing the quality of your life at least as much as how we look as we go through it?

I like to think of life like instant coffee. When I open a new jar I am very generous with the spoonfuls. As the jar gets half-full I start to round off the spoonfuls a little more. By the last quarter of the jar I'm downright stingy and real careful not to waste any. Isn't life the same way? That's why awareness and clarity of what is happening to us every minute is so important. We can't afford to waste one moment of precious time in our lives.

Institutionalization

When people go to prison, in about ninety days or so they become legally and psychologically "institutionalized." Sounds awful and it is. They become robots in a set system and schedule. Everything is done at a specific time in a specific way with mind-numbing redundancy. They become like gerbils on a wheel, told when to get on and get off. It takes serious discipline and awareness to take control of their thoughts and make positive mental progress in that environment.

When a person is released back into society, it takes months and sometimes years to readjust. The mind craves the routine and the comfort zone of the prior conditioning. Emotions of fear and doubt dominate the unprepared and unconditional mind. A 2008 Pew study indicates that one in three inmates in America returns to prison within three years after release. How could that happen? Some people never adjust to life outside of prison. They literally crave institutionalism. It is hard to imagine someone could feel happier in the prison environment than in a free society, but it is true.

Are You Institutionalized?

A person doesn't have to be in prison to be institutionalized. When I was in prison I started to pay attention to my family, friends, and business contacts and how they lived their lives outside prison. I noticed something quite common among them.

Most people live boring, routine, and uneventful lives. They are like robots. They go to work, come home, and just exist. They cope with their boredom by numbing their minds with television, and if that is not enough they turn to food, alcohol, drugs, or other habits to anesthetize themselves. Not everyone is this way, but we can all relate to it. People are always searching for a way to mask their uncomfortable feelings about their unfulfilled, routine lives. They could be bored at and tired of a job they hate or that provides no challenge. They could experience self-loathing over a personal problem or physical condition. They could be in empty and unfulfilling relationships with a spouse or significant other. They could be in emotional pain due to financial problems. Possibly, some or all of these things arose from the feeling of poor self-esteem that creates a life that lacks purpose or direction.

It's safe to say that at one time or another most of us find ourselves in a rut in our lives. But isn't a rut just a grave with the ends kicked out? People in a rut are institutionalized, not by choice, but by not knowing what else to do or having the inspiration or the motivation to make things different. They are locked in the self-imposed prison of a distracted mind. They are wasting the opportunity to be who they are meant to be. They have lost contact with their authentic self. What follows is a lifetime of missing out.

God never intended for any of us to live this way, and neither did we. The Bible tells us, *"To those who use well what they are given, even more will be given, and they will have abundance. But from those who do nothing, even what little they have will be taken away."* That verse is worth re-reading a few times. Are we missing out on what life has been and currently is offering us because we are in a trance?

Even organizations and businesses become institutionalized. They get so caught up in their identities that they are inflexible to change. But some groups take on new attitudes that are exciting and welcome possibility. They will do whatever it takes or whatever works. This brings great freedom and possibility in a growing and ever-changing environment. Over time, success brings rules, procedures, and roles. When this happens the excitement and spontaneity that come with taking risks are smothered. The identity of the group becomes institutionalized just like the individual, just like the inmate. There is little difference. As long as you remain institutionalized you will never be able to live the dream of your soul and really live and experience your true calling.

Chapter 13
Healing the Mind

It is reasonable to expect the doctor to realize that science may not have all the answers to the problems of health and healing.

Dr. Norman Cousins

The secret of progress is self-analysis. Most of us are "pregnant" with the best person we could ever be, if we could just give birth to it!

In life, we have only two choices: do nothing and just let life unfold and die wondering what we could have been (a painful option); or give birth to a bold, not new but *authentic* you—the Real You—and build a life on that foundation from this day forward.

Committing to do what it takes to take charge of our lives instead of letting our lives run us can be like going to the dentist. Sometimes we put it off till we absolutely have to and hope it's not too late. For example, I believe God lined things up in His universe in such a way that you would find this information today—right now. Acknowledging that everything has a purpose is a huge step toward living consciously and we will address this and its many aspects as we go through the Valeo Method. When I finally learned these concepts myself I was amazed at what was right under my nose screaming for my attention, yet I couldn't see it.

Have you ever looked at one of those photos where something was hidden and you couldn't see it to save your life? Then all of sudden you saw it and when you did you couldn't even look at the picture again without it just jumping out at you, right? That is the way life is; there is so much to see and when we do wake up and see it we can't believe it was there all the time. The process ahead will help you permanently unlock that code.

Underdog Champions learn how to see things they missed before and be sensitive to what God's universe puts in front of them daily. They learn to constantly ask, "What does this mean?" "What is the message here for me?" and "What am I supposed to learn from this?"

Making Our Choices Count

One key to healing our minds is understanding how we make choices. The most important decision you can make here and now is to live consciously instead of unconsciously. That may sound overly simplistic, and you might even say, "What is this guy talking about? I am not an idiot; I can see what's going on in my life!"

Of course you can. But are you just showing up for life? Let's look at it a little deeper. When you make the choice to live in conscious awareness, you are controlling the engine of the evolutionary process. This is what gives your life balance between joy and suffering. You may say you will never take anything in your life for granted ever again, and that's great. But if you are too laid-back and unconscious about your choices, life can seem confusing, unfair, and unpredictable. A person can find empowerment unconsciously but it can be a long and painful process. When you become aware that you can choose conscious living, you can tap into authentic power very quickly. If you choose to do nothing and live unconsciously, you invite fear and its partner, doubt, into your life, which can cause a steady loss of energy, power, and control.

A Warning or an Example?

Something I learned from working with a wide variety of people with many individual challenges is simple but profoundly effective at creating positive change: People will do more to avoid pain than they will to gain pleasure.

Have you ever known someone who stayed in a bad relationship because the fear of change was too much to face? What about people who stay in a job they hate because the pain associated with the fear of change paralyzes them? Why are people so afraid of change?

What if you took this human dynamic and used it to your advantage by turning it around? For example, what if you began to associate massive pain with the things you want to avoid—is your life going to be a warning or an example? If you could fast-forward to the closing scene of the movie of your life, do you think looking back would make you proud? Would others looking back at your life think you set an example of how to live happily, conquer challenges, and succeed? Or would they say something like, "How could she have let this happen?" or "Son, let that be a warning to you; don't wind up like him."

Thinking about things in this manner is not easy. It's much easier to just go back to living unconsciously, right? Or is it? It takes work, and sometimes it is downright painful to change. Mohammad Ali said, "I hated every minute of my training. But I said to myself, suffer [and] pay the price now and be a champion for the rest of your life." How would it feel if you associated massive pain with leaving your life the way it is now, and massive pleasure with the feeling of creating a comeback along with your very own Underdog Champion story? The truth is, you can. Everybody loves a comeback, and everybody loves an Underdog Champion.

The past does not equal the future. All that matters is your attitude right now. The past is history, and the future is a mystery; that's why we call the gift of the moment "the present."

Doesn't it make sense that a loving God would send you forth with the intention to be happy and successful? Within the seed of your creation God planted the instructions for your life, which contain the dream of your soul. You are programmed for success. Just like God created each plant and animal with a set of instructions and instincts for success, you were created with a blueprint for success. This is your purpose, your destiny; this is what God created you to do, be, and have in your mortal life. He sent you on life's journey with a gift of free will to be used wisely so that in the end, you will return to Him. He doesn't force you to follow His instructions, even though He could (He's God, for goodness sakes!).

It is up to you to use your free will wisely and effectively to complete your unique purpose that is meant for you alone. But even if you don't use all you were given, He is always watching. He is ready to help. The Lord speaks through the prophet Isaiah and says: *"Then you will call, the Lord Will answer. Yes, I am here, He will quickly reply."*

The plan for a successful life is really pretty simple and it is meant to be a win-win situation. Problems arise when we allow our human ability of free will, which I refer to as humanness, to mess things up. We let our choices throw us off balance and get lost on our journey. Then the worst thing happens: we ignore our internal guidance system which is constantly communicating to us through our intuition (as in the Creator speaking to the created). Because we are basically unconscious, like a kid ignoring a parent calling him to dinner, we miss the message of our purpose and our instructions which carry the imprint of God. Even worse, we get the instructions (like a feeling to change course, pay attention to something, or a feeling of certainty about something), but the ego snaps into action and distracts us with negative self-talk or by manipulating our feelings and causing us to ignore or forget what we should have been doing.

You might be thinking this is a little dramatic, but your egoic mind is dead-set on running your life with fear-based emotions and keeping you from love-based emotions and the Real You. How long will you let it go on before you say, "Hold it, whose life is this anyway?"

This is a major source of pain and suffering in our lives which leads to unconscious living and the birth and dominance of the egoic mind. Living a life dominated by the egoic mind coupled with our unconscious thoughts will guarantee a life of pain, suffering, and doing it the hard way. It is a ticket to chaos and a steady flow of drama, missed opportunities, and suffering. Isn't it time to uncover your original instruction, control the egoic mind, and co-create the life of your dreams? No more doing it the hard way for those who follow the Valeo Method!

Bundle Of Joy Begins

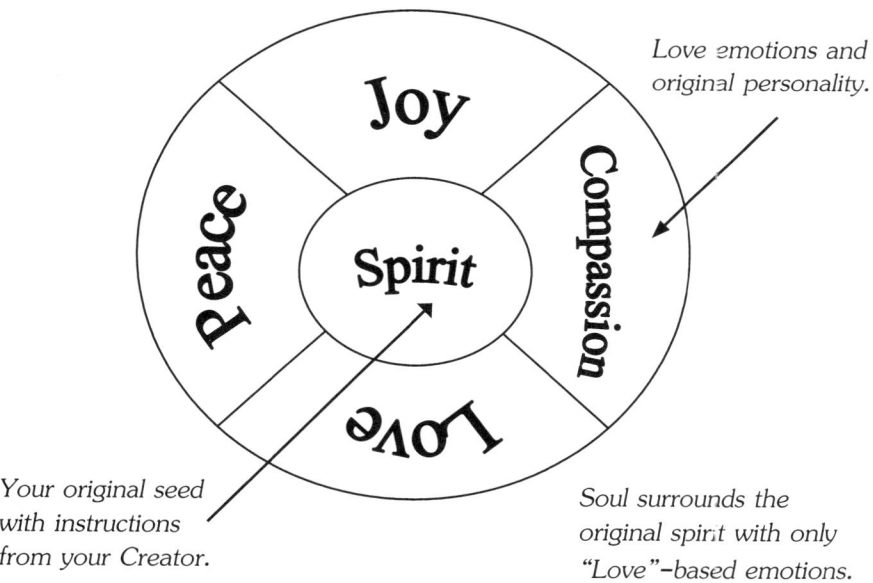

Love emotions and original personality.

Your original seed with instructions from your Creator.

Soul surrounds the original spirit with only "Love"-based emotions.

When we are infants we are pure energy and joy. In fact, that's why they call us bundles of joy. We manifest unbridled emotions of pure love. During your first few years your primary function is emoting, or putting out emotions. Since all we know are the love emotions of our original spirit, we give and receive much joy.

Usually by age two we begin to link words to things we want. This is also when we begin to link emotional energy with our physical reality. This is when the terrible twos come along—we are introduced to the word no for the first time, which triggers an emotional (feeling) response. This is also our first small experience of our free will and the awakening of the egoic mind.

Our curiosity and the natural pull into our evolving lives invite us forward with our *attention* and is followed by our *intention*. Our inner thoughts and choices begin to create our outer behavior and our view of the world.

The imprint of our God-given personality traits are embedded within our original instructions. These are all pure, contained, and grounded in unconditional love. This is where we get our individuality as human beings. Even at a very young age, identical twins display different spirit-inspired personality traits, such as eye movements and their unique reactions to humans. You could say that these traits carry God's fingerprint on each individual soul. When we make decisions through our free will this becomes our individual, personal fingerprint of the soul.

Chapter 14
The Emotional Body

*The emotions aren't always immeaditely subject to reason, but
they are always immeadiately subject to action.*

William James

Beginning with the early baby years and continuing through
age six to seven is the development period of the emotional
body. The emotional body holds the key to your future joy and
happiness. This is a relatively small amount of time compared
to the average life span and is unprecedented in its ongoing
effect on a person's life. It may be hard to conceive that as you
grow as an individual, your emotional body's maturity does not
exceed these early years, but it is true. You will find out more
about how this discovery affects the quality of your adult life
in the Embrace step. You will learn that this is the reason this
sensitive part of you needs constant nurturing throughout your
life in order to maintain healthy emotions. You will understand
why emotions, the language of the soul, play such a dominant
role. Your emotions affect every thought, every decision, and
every good or bad thing that happens in your life.

The need to individuate, to expand and grow into your own
unique identity, forces your developing mind to evolve. We
instinctively adhere to the laws of nature and we explore and
learn. We create situations and adapt to our environment. In
other words, through these processes we become who we are.
It is a grand and beautiful plan, and this is where it starts to get
fascinating.

Let the Story Begin

Through our preschool years we learn to link words to basic needs. Our emotions, displayed through crying, screaming, and pouting, serve us well in getting what we want, and sometimes more than we want. A sad face yields an assortment of benefits ranging from food to a change of pants to entertainment.

Upon reaching school age we must learn to adapt to other children and adults around us. We shift our focus from just getting what we want to trying to fit in. This is the beginning of the shaping of each individual's False Self. It is also the beginning of a lifelong battle with the original and authentic self (the spirit), which has been mostly running the show up until this point. This is also the point at which the false self starts to overshadow authentic self, which is really just an illusionary, character-created ego. The ego takes on the starring role in the story of your life.

The more we are around other children, especially in school, the more we are apt to change. The original bundle of joy persona takes a back seat as the ego uses the power of free will to craft this new and emerging imaginary self.

This is a time when we, as children, are very sensitive and impressionable. The need for approval and loving attention from parents and adults is paramount. I love the story about the young boy who said, "Hey Dad, let's play darts. I'll throw the darts and when I hit the board, you say, 'That's wonderful, Son!'"

The Basis of Your Story

God used the beautiful background of a starry night to show Abram (later called Abraham) how many descendants he would have, with each star representing a person. To get an idea of how we create the stories of who we are and how we relate to other people and the environment, picture a clear, beautiful evening sky with millions of stars sparkling. Just imagine yourself as one of those specks of energy in God's vast universe.

The Ego is Born

Soul

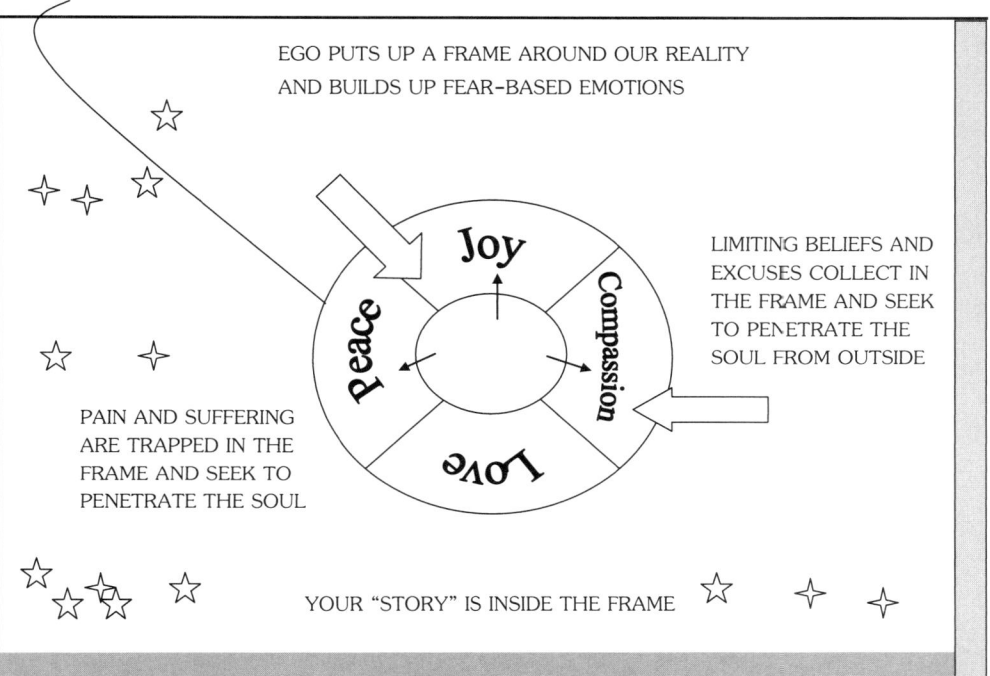

EGO PUTS UP A FRAME AROUND OUR REALITY
AND BUILDS UP FEAR-BASED EMOTIONS

LIMITING BELIEFS AND
EXCUSES COLLECT IN
THE FRAME AND SEEK
TO PENETRATE THE
SOUL FROM OUTSIDE

PAIN AND SUFFERING
ARE TRAPPED IN THE
FRAME AND SEEK TO
PENETRATE THE SOUL

Joy
Peace
Compassion
Love

YOUR "STORY" IS INSIDE THE FRAME

SPIRIT PROVIDES THE PERSONALITY WITH EMOTIONS OF LOVE
THE EGO CREATES THE EMOTIONS OF FEAR
THE EGOIC FRAME KEEPS YOU FROM CONNECTING WITH THE LIGHT AND
THE SOURCE OF LIFE. IT KEEPS YOU TRAPPED IN "HUMANNESS"

Visualize the freedom and uniqueness of each star. Imagine how each has its own significance in the scene as a whole.

Now picture yourself—your own energy—as one of these stars. This is metaphorically how we begin as human beings: just a speck of freedom and energy among an endless vista filled with other human beings.

Now pretend you can look up and pick one of the stars to represent you. Let's imagine God as the source of light and you as a reflection of that original light, just like the stars. As Saint Paul tells you, *"For once you were full of darkness and now you have the light of the Lord. So live as people of light! For this light within you produces only what is good and right and true."* The light of God is truly in every one of us; it is what sustains us.

The next step is to visualize a frame around your star. This illustration is an example. Within this individual frame is where you create, build, and maintain your individual and very personal story of who you are and what you stand for. The closer you remain connected to your original source of life, the less you will suffer.

As years go by, you continue to individuate as you interact with others in your environment and strive to fit in. It is a natural part of growing up. This is also when life is breathed into your ego, the false self that is waiting, ready, and happy to take control. At this point the ego is not all bad; in fact, it actually appears to be supporting you as you adapt to your world. It takes the dominant role in directing your life.

This doesn't sound like such a bad deal so far. The egoic mind creates an imaginary self to represent you through life. But the true challenge arises when the ego gets out of hand, when its motives and influences create less than desirable experiences and situations in your life. This is when you need awareness and clarity as to how the ego gets its instructions and ideas for controlling your life.

Within the framework of your evolving life, the ego stays busy, accumulating beliefs and creating instructions of its own. It prefers to ignore all instructions from the authentic self and even deems them unnecessary. Does it sound crazy yet? It gets worse.

Combined with your spirit-based personality traits and gifts from God are the developing and learned personality traits of the ego. What results is what we call your emerging mental body, or the soul. The soul is the sum of all the energies and emotions of these two dynamics. We will address this in much more detail later in the book.

The next illustration also shows how the mental body wraps around your spirit and interacts with it. Picture the soul or mind like a doughnut wrapped around your original spirit. The spirit fills the soul with love emotions from the center. The ego, which resides outside the soul, seeks to fill the soul with negative, fear–based emotions. The cunning ego puts a fence up around the soul to trap its energy and block out the light, power, and truth from your original source. Your ego–driven individuality resides within this fence, and this is the "self" most people believe they are. When we die, this "self," the ego, dies; the authentic self in the center keeps on going.

This is why it's so sad to see how many of us live our entire mortal lives ignoring the only real part of who we are. We are literally living with and serving a false identity. Our soul becomes the container for our pain and suffering. The spirit fills the soul with thoughts and feelings of love from within. The ego adds feelings and emotions of fear from outside, and the strongest emotion dominates. The result is either who we think we are or who we are authentically.

I know it sounds a little tangled, but hang with me. This positive and negative energy dynamic fuels our lives. Your life story might seem to come from your authentic self, although it does not; it is an illusion created by the ego. This is where the foundation of all your challenges to live a happy and peaceful life begins.

Your parents or caretakers are your earliest influences in most cases. Usually they do the best they can to teach you and instill within you what they believe are good and supportive beliefs. Take my situation, my parents did a wonderful job giving me love and support. However, they were only seventeen and nineteen years old when I was born and they had their own challenges, like figuring out life as young parents.

Many times parents unwittingly drain a child's energy and set children up for failure in their adult life. They allow their own deficiencies or failures to create future drama and trauma for their children. Some parents might even blame their children for their problems. They might say, "If it weren't for you, I could be pursuing my career." Other parents create blame by suggesting that the child doesn't help enough. Some parents create an uncomfortable environment of intimidation or fear.

Then there is the worst; violence and abuse from unbalanced behavior, spurred on by the parent's own pain and suf-

fering. All these circumstances are major contributing factors to
the foundation of your life. Your "personal story" is grounded
in these early and sometimes totally locked away childhood experiences. A troubled and pain-riddled childhood often leads to
being misunderstood and causes struggles later in your adult life.

Your goal with the Valeo Method is to discover what made
you the way you are, and release the thoughts and beliefs that
hold you back. Everyone's history and story is different so only
you can sort this out. Don't worry—you will know how! Only
then can you discover your gifts and build a future on them.
Don't beat yourself up through this process; we all have issues
that need to be addressed.

Chapter 15
The Rule Book and the Play Book

One might as well try riding two moving horses in different directions as to try to maintain in equal force two opposing or contradictory sets of desires.

Robert Collier

The ego is busy in your early years collecting beliefs, assumptions, and opinions from your outside influences. It then uses this information to create what we will call the Rule Book. This imaginary rule book becomes your instruction manual on how to live. The first rules come from your usually well-intentioned parents and closest family. When you begin to attend school you adopt more beliefs from your teachers, friends, and peers. In addition, you begin to be influenced by the voices of society and the collective consciousness of your environment.

The ego accompanies you through life and collects beliefs to go in your rule book, your ego's operating manual and the source of your life story. The ego selects rules from this rule book to direct and influence your way of life.

But hold on a minute. Where did all these beliefs come from? Don't you get a say in this? Remember, the Real You fades into the background as the ego steps up. It is inevitable that you will begin to identify with your false self to interact with others. Keep in mind, though, that the key through all of this is to recognize what happened in your past to get you where you are today in your beliefs, and where the ego controls your life.

Your beliefs came from the person or people who taught them to you or from whom you heard them, right? Not necessarily; in fact, the answer is probably no. Where did your parents get their beliefs? From their parents' friends and their contacts in life. So if your parents got their beliefs from their parents, where did your grandparents get their beliefs? Do you see where this is going? Somebody had to make all these beliefs up. This means these beliefs are just another person's evaluation or opinion, which was probably based on their interpretation, or worse, their judgment of a particular, unique life experience. Does this mean it is best for you today? What if the beliefs you are operating on go back centuries? How can they make sense today? I know this is an extreme example, but the point is, you must become aware of what the ego, your false self, is doing with your inherited beliefs. They can take control of your life.

So think about it; your life may not be exactly what you want, but the foundations of where your life is today, at this moment, are the sum total of your beliefs. So let's look at the reality of the situation. Your rule book is a hodge-podge, unorganized collection of beliefs from multiple sources. This makes it easier to understand how life can be complicated and seem out of control and even hopeless sometimes. When I first began to understand this information I was really taken aback. I had to sit down and think about it. I felt taken advantage of by my own ego! I wasn't happy with what I had allowed to happen. But thank God the cat was out of the bag. No wonder my life had been such a roller coaster of extreme highs followed by painful lows. There I was, living from a crazy rule book created by my even crazier ego. I was living unconsciously, allowing that ego to influence my every move. Plus, it was based on a disorganized puzzle of beliefs that had been largely created by other people, many of whom I didn't even know! The good news was this was something I could fix. I had acquired awareness, and so can you. It is time to stop the madness in your life!

To create lasting change you have to fashion a kind of mental potion. Envision a clear, quart-size mason jar with a brass lid. Then fill it three-fourths with water and one-fourth with oil. The water represents your authentic self, or the Real

You. The oil represents the negative beliefs and emotions in your life that you have collected and created by your ego (the false self). Then watch yourself go through life shaking the jar non-stop while at the same time trying to see clearly what you should be doing to try to enjoy life. What happens? Your life becomes a cloudy mixture of confusing thoughts mixed with emotions. So, you wind up living unconsciously because you have unclear thinking—thus, you lack clarity.

Now, by using the Valeo Method, see yourself putting the jar down and stop shaking it. You will let the mixture settle down; the oil will float to the top, and the water (clarity) will remain on the bottom. Now it will be easier for you to dip out the junk in your life, one scoop at a time and once and for all. Finally, you can see clearly who you really are and where you need to go.

Conflicting Beliefs

You have conscious beliefs you are clearly aware of in your rule book. You also have many unconscious beliefs, and the two create some interesting challenges and dynamics. Your conscious beliefs and thoughts are on the surface. You are always aware of them and they constantly influence you. Your unconscious beliefs are stored away, sometimes very deep in your soul, and you tend to forget they are even there, although they still influence you in many significant ways.

Have you ever started to do something and then lost interest or motivation and didn't know why? It could be your unconscious beliefs colliding with your conscious ones. It can even get more complicated when you have conflicting beliefs about the same subject. Then, to make matters worse, both beliefs could be unconscious ones, or one could be conscious and the other, unconscious!

Here is an example to illustrate this scenario: Let's say someone you admire and respect gave you the belief, "Look before you leap." Good advice, right? Most of you would take that to mean, "Be cautious, don't make hasty decisions, and take your time."

Now let's look at it from another perspective. Someone you have equal respect for gave you another belief: "He who hesitates is lost." This is also good advice. That could be taken to mean, "Take advantage of opportunities when they present themselves and don't be afraid to act quickly."

Now let's consider the potential challenges that could arise from these two beliefs. Let's assume both beliefs are conscious and you believe strongly in each one. You are about to see how drama is created in your life.

These two beliefs are conflicting, right? Simply put, one says "go ahead" and the other says "stop." Can you see how the drama could intensify if one belief was conscious and the other unconscious? Either way, a conflict in thinking is inevitable. The emotions associated with indecision, confusion, and avoiding taking action are palpable. No wonder we get confused about what to do next and make wrong decisions about our lives!

The purpose of the Discovery step is to establish awareness and order in your beliefs so you can take control of the ego and your mind. This takes some work. It won't happen overnight but it will happen if you are committed, and it is so worth the effort. Remember, you have momentum in your habits, thinking, and way of life. You did not get where you are overnight. In some ways it's like turning the Queen Mary 2. She is a big ship and it takes about a mile to turn her. But once she gets on the right course it takes a lot of effort to move her off course. As Dr. Martin Luther King, Jr., said, "Don't look at the whole staircase; just one step at a time."

The rules you fill your rule book with determine if you feel like a winner or loser, success or failure, and victor or victim. The key here is to be able to recognize your hesitation in making decisions and to notice the repetition of pain and suffering. Then you are able to say to yourself, "What beliefs are behind this situation? What is causing me to feel this way and have disempowering thoughts or repeat my unproductive behavior?" Rules are good when they empower or protect you. The challenge is that most of us have more rules that limit us and fewer that protect us. Please understand the Valeo Method does not promote throwing out rules that protect and help you; only the ones that take away from your quality of life.

The Playbook

What comes to mind when you think of a playbook? How is a playbook different from a rule book? Rules, although necessary, can get out of hand, especially when they are created by an enemy like your own ego. Even though they are self-created you will discover they are not your friends. A playbook brings up thoughts of a coach on the sidelines, a military strategist hoping to conquer an enemy, or a corporate boardroom meeting where a future growth plan is laid out. A playbook represents action, goals, strategy, hope, confidence, and leadership—all good things.

Most of us become victims of the negative beliefs in our rule book. Since we don't know any better we identify with them and take the consequences that follow. This is why people keep winding up in circumstances they don't want.

There is a better way. When you become aware that you can create a playbook to follow and focus on, this will empower and inspire you. You will begin to change your negative, disempowering beliefs (rules) to empowering, positive beliefs (plays) to fill your playbook. This is also a great opportunity to write in your journal and create your own playbook of life.

OLD RULE BOOK

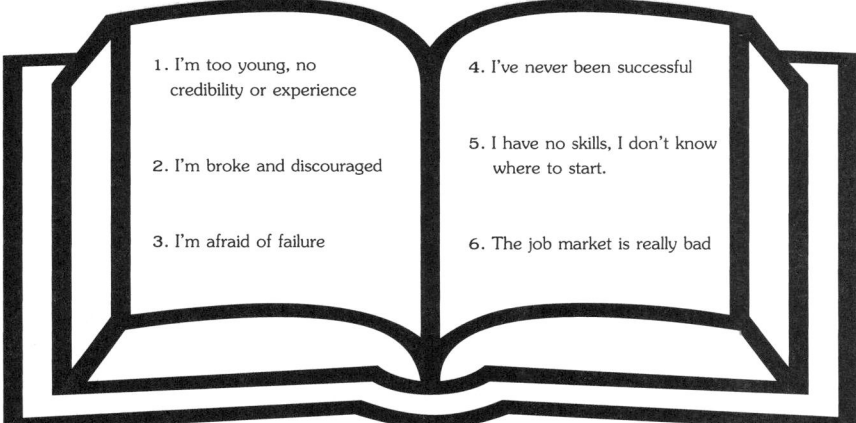

1. I'm too young, no credibility or experience

2. I'm broke and discouraged

3. I'm afraid of failure

4. I've never been successful

5. I have no skills, I don't know where to start.

6. The job market is really bad

NEW PLAY BOOK

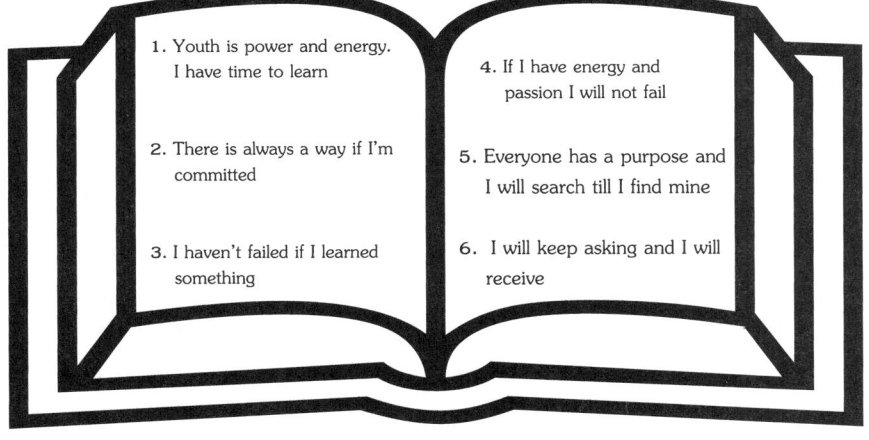

1. Youth is power and energy. I have time to learn

2. There is always a way if I'm committed

3. I haven't failed if I learned something

4. If I have energy and passion I will not fail

5. Everyone has a purpose and I will search till I find mine

6. I will keep asking and I will receive

EXERCISE

•Write your rules in your journal or notebook. At the top of the page, write "RULE BOOK."

•List at least ten rules (limiting beliefs) that have been holding you back.

•After completing the Discovery step of the Valeo Method, go back and create a "PLAY" to replace every RULE, as shown in this example.

When changing a limiting belief to a new, empowering belief, ask yourself: Is this belief moving me toward my goals and dreams in life or away from them? Is this belief causing me pain or pleasure?

Beliefs are not easy to release. The ego is stubborn and proud of the limiting beliefs it has created, so these beliefs may not go away without a fight. Understanding more about the different types of beliefs and how you attain them will give you the leverage to change and control them.

Current and Core Beliefs

As you learn the Valeo Method and understand more about how your rule book was formed, you will also learn that there are three basic types of beliefs: current beliefs, core beliefs, and locked-away beliefs. You will learn to break your beliefs down so you can control them.

We will address the first two beliefs now and save the locked-away beliefs for the Embrace section of the Valeo Method.

Current Beliefs

Current beliefs are based on events that take place in your life in the present moment. The more out of control your life is, the more your current beliefs will affect you. These beliefs are constantly evolving and subject to change. As your immediate world changes, you adjust your beliefs to fit your needs, desires, and distractions. Your beliefs today are most likely quite different than they were even two years ago. If you look back you can pinpoint certain things that were very important and even urgent then, but which mean very little today. These beliefs were significant to you at the time because most of us live in a moment-by-moment reality. We spend little time thinking about or planning for what happens next.

Things that affect our current beliefs are relationships, family, finances, religion, economy, peer pressure, school, job, career, or business. Groups or organizations you belong to affect your beliefs. An extreme example would be gang membership, which is strongly influenced by current beliefs about control and fitting in.

Current circumstances dictate current beliefs. For example, if you have a present financial crisis it dominates your thoughts, which in turn affects your beliefs. If you have a bad habit it can dominate your life. Problems with children, spouses, or significant others will also dominate your current beliefs. If you are not well-grounded, confident, or emotionally strong, your current beliefs can wreak havoc on your life. Think about some decisions you made while on a rebound from a relationship or rejection in a relationship, the loss of a job, or any other major disappointment or failure. Your current beliefs contribute to your decisions to drink and drive, use drugs, accuse and blame, react instead of respond, and do things out of good character. This is where the ego loves to step in and justify wrong actions, which rarely result in long-term, positive results. If you are struggling with a life that is out of control, your sense of confusion and living unconsciously is giving your ego a blank check to buy into the passing beliefs of others while you seek relief. The ego leaps at the chance to keep you confused and off-balance. Doesn't that sound crazy? It is, and it's true. This is how it protects its identity and existence. We will explore this crazy ego and its characteristic traits in the next section on Release.

Current beliefs can be a strong influence on children of all ages, and they hit a crescendo during adolescence. The beliefs related to fitting in are powerful and drive many youths into bad situations. They relate to their beliefs about fashion, physical appearance, music, ethnic trends, their neighborhood environment, and even their parents' economic situations. Peer pressure to dress a certain way and experiment with hairstyles, body piercing, and tattoos are influenced by the group dynamics of current beliefs. Of course, the most dangerous are the beliefs about drugs, alcohol, and sex.

Current beliefs create compelling desires to fit in and be cool, no matter what the cost. Today's adults learned as adolescents to live by current beliefs and developed bad habits while also making bad decisions. Current beliefs can create shallow thinking and decisions to fulfill instant gratification which supports a victim mentality. The ego justifies current beliefs with, "What else am I going to do?"

Quite often there seem to be very few choices for youths because of their environment. A book and audio course for teenagers will follow this publication, using the Valeo Method and geared to educate and prepare this impressionable group to take control of their lives by learning these life-changing concepts and strategies.

The ego is quick to validate thinking and behavior that produces less than desirable results with more justifications like, "You have to do this, what other choice do you have?" "These are the cards life has dealt you." "This is what your friends are doing." Sadly, the ego wins many of these battles. When we grow up and become adults without getting a handle on how our current beliefs affect our lives, we are destined for a future full of pain and struggle. Prisons and treatment centers are overflowing with people who are living the consequences of their negative current beliefs.

You might be thinking, "This is kid stuff; I don't let current beliefs affect me—I'm in control." If you are, that's great; just remember, this step is about Discovery and awareness. It is about paying attention to your current beliefs because they have a way of finding a home in your mind, with or without your permission. Then they can become deeply embedded and you'll forget about them, but they are always just under the surface, waiting for the right trigger to pop out. These types of beliefs can use your ego to steer your direction.

As a teenager I had two friends whose parents were well-off financially. I didn't suffer for anything as a child, but because I grew up with three younger siblings and my parents worked blue-collar jobs, I was able to experience the great lesson of what it is like to live on a tight budget. When my friends were able to do things and have new motorcycles and big allowances without having part-time jobs, I felt left out. Teenagers can have a heartless way of rubbing things in, as well, which made me feel even more inferior. It created an unhealthy, "I'm going to show you someday" attitude.

Years later I ran into these guys and reveled in showing them how much more successful I was than they were. It was so important to me to prove something. This attitude was the result of an unhealthy belief that I had carried around for years. But something later on taught me a valuable lesson.

One of these guys was my former college roommate. We had been in touch on occasion and I thought he was living well and happily. Then I received word that he had phoned his father, with whom he was always fighting, and said he needed to come over and talk. As his father walked in the door of his home my friend shot himself in the head with a .357 magnum pistol right in front of his father. He died in a pool of blood at age thirty-eight. He was one of the guys I wanted to impress.

Events like that can cause you to do some real soul-searching. That was a major opportunity to think about my beliefs because I always thought this guy had it better than I did, but on the inside he was suffering unbearably.

Are you trying to prove something to someone or yourself? Are you holding on to an old belief that you can't let go of and the pain is affecting your beliefs today? Are you holding a disempowering belief over some issue that is over and finished?

Core Beliefs

Our core beliefs establish the foundation of who we are. Core beliefs are deeply rooted and hold intense feelings related to our principles, morals, and character. Core beliefs are strong and less likely to change than current beliefs.

When someone challenges our core beliefs the alarms go off. We might say, "That's it! This is where I draw the line!" It's like that song, "Don't mess with Texas" or when Popeye the sailor says, "I've had all I can stands, I can't stands no more," and out comes the can of spinach. We will throw off the gloves and get ready to fight over core beliefs. We'll say things like, "Don't insult my Momma!" or "Don't you dare lay a hand on my kid." We mean business about our core beliefs.

We are raised by parents or caretakers who pound core beliefs into our heads. They say things like, "Good people don't act this way," "God will punish you for this or that," or "If you do that, you will ruin your life," or how about, "Only losers do that kind of job," or "You'll never amount to anything; you are just like your brother." "Nobody in our family ever gets a break."

Core beliefs are important because they define who you are; your heritage, your race, your religion, your integrity, and your self-worth. Beliefs about family, country, and God are core beliefs. The Valeo Method is never about changing any em-powering or healthy belief. The reason we address this strongly is simple—you must learn to become an expert at analyzing and selecting the beliefs you allow into your life. In addition, you must be an expert at recognizing and interpreting the beliefs of those in your circle of influence, including those who need your help and who can help you.

Let's think about the source of your core beliefs. Just like current beliefs, they come from somewhere but what is the source? Did you make them up or adopt them? What if a per-son had a great-grandfather who looked down on women and abused them mentally and physically? Could that trait be passed down from son to grandson till someone very close to you is deeply affected by the old belief? You bet it can. Add in alcohol abuse and it really gets complicated.

There are many situations where negative core beliefs continue for generations without resistance. Can you think of someone who has experienced this situation? Where does this wrong thinking, with all of its negative results, end? Discovery is about having the awareness and clarity to recognize how passed down core beliefs can affect your life. It's about having the courage to stand up and say, "I'm not going to live this way anymore!"

These examples are serious and dramatic, and that is exactly why you must pay attention to how they could be affecting your life. It doesn't have to be mental or physical abuse, either.

How many times do people go into a profession to follow a parent's footsteps or take over a family business because it is expected of them and they wind up miserable? These people miss the opportunity to live their calling and realize the cream of their soul. Their core beliefs drove them away from it. Even though these people might be totally miserable they can't bring themselves to make a change because their core beliefs have control of their life. Many times this is the reason for a person's unhappiness—core beliefs that conflict with the authentic self and its true purpose.

Two Ways to Learn

How long do you put up with this kind of thing? How long can you continue to let your limiting beliefs control your destiny?

The answers lay within the reasons we suffer challenges, disappointments, and failures in life. One of the main answers is due to belief systems that you create like a junk drawer. Do you have beliefs you need to change? Unless your life is perfect in all areas, you do.

Just as easily as you collected and adapted to your existing beliefs, you can replace them with new ones. You just have to find beliefs that serve you and eliminate the old ones that hurt you. Always remember: Your *attention* and your *intentions* are strongly influenced by your beliefs. If you are not getting the results you want out of your life, you can backtrack. What is your intention in any particular situation? What brought you to this particular point? What influenced you? Then you can ask yourself which belief (current or core) influences your attention, intention, and actions. Change the belief and the attention, and the intention and the result have to change, too.

Another source of your beliefs is from your own life experiences. As I said earlier, you can learn two ways: from the school of hard knocks or by modeling successful people. The school of hard knocks can teach you and serve you well, and although it is not the best way to learn, it certainly works. It is much easier to model successful people if you seek out those who are getting the results you want in your own life. You can use their experiences to avoid the knocks they have already encountered and concurred. You can also do another thing which can be valuable: compress time. If you have wasted time going in the wrong direction in the past, this is a way to make it up.

Sounds pretty simple, right? It is!

Four Steps to Model the Success of Others

1. Find someone who is getting a result you want. It could be a career, relationship with significant other or marriage, skill, income, talent, business, or profession. It could be a good parent, teacher, or kind person. It could be some one's spiritual walk with God.

2. Find out what their beliefs are in detail, and how they put these into practice in their lives. These should be their cur rent and core beliefs.

3. Find out the whys behind what they're doing. What are the compelling reasons behind their actions? What is their burning desire or burning discontent? If you discover the whys, the hows will come easily. Compelling reasons are just goals with emotion behind them. Emotion creates mo tion, which fuels action.

4. What are the strategies they use for success? Strategies are like recipes. What ingredients did they use, and how much of each? How long did it take, and what was the order of the ingredients? What did they do first? How many times did they have to repeat their actions? The more details, the better. Clarity is power!

If you are serious about what you want, you will need leverage from being sick and tired of a certain situation and the passion to change; then, the possibilities are limitless. Most of us spend our lifetimes asking others for their opinions and letting that be our guide. It's time to put some careful thought into choosing the beliefs we allow the ego to make for us. No matter how big the obstacle appears to be, someone else has already been there and achieved something great.

These people are the backbone of our society. There are many of them and we need a lot more, especially during challenging times. God gave us something in our nature that gets stirred up when we see someone else getting a result we want. We can tap into this attitude and let it give us strength because someone else has created a model and now we know it can be done. This is how average people accomplish above-average results. Their doubts are subdued and their confidence is raised because someone else got there first and set the bar.

People had been trying for decades to break the four-minute mile until 1954 when Roger Bannister did it. Then, within two years after he broke the record, more than one hundred people did the same thing! By our nature, we work better when we have an example of a success story to follow. Thank God for the trailblazers and those who go first. But there are many of us out here who have the ability—we just need the willingness and the desire. Without modeling someone else who did it first we might miss out. This is a good reason to become a master at modeling success.

Try to find someone who is not only successful and getting the results you want, but also find someone who was down, but not out. Find someone who overcame the odds and achieved their dream. If we become sincere seekers of excellence and success, the Activate and Attract step of the Valeo Method will show you how to co-create amazing things in your life. You will learn how to free yourself from the Law of Human Limitation and activate the Law of Attraction so that God's universal laws will consistently bring energies, people, and situations into your life to manifest your dreams. You are about to see hope turn into reality.

Chapter 16
Documentation Beats Conversation

The palest ink is better than the biggest memory.

Chinese Proverb

Stories of success are powerful and encouraging. They help us empty our minds of limiting beliefs so we can fill them up with empowering beliefs. We need to hear about and read success stories to strengthen the foundations we are building. The Master Teacher, Jesus Christ, used stories (referred to as parables) to teach His disciples and followers.

Role models are helpful and can advance your momentum. Begin to think of what you desire, and remind yourself that you are driven by the same Divine source that gives you every heartbeat and every breath. We all have access to that same source, and remember—God does not play favorites.

My First Experience of Modeling Success

At the end of my senior year of high school I married my high school sweetheart. We were kids in love and determined to be married even though my wife still had to finish her senior year. I went off to college in Memphis, ninety miles away, and she stayed with her parents and completed high school.

After my wife graduated I was still in college and my folks were helping us up until the point at which I could finish another year to get my degree and find a job. I felt guilty taking money from them, especially with three younger siblings still at home.

I decided to drop out of college, get a job, and finish later. I answered an ad in the newspaper from Church's Fried Chicken which was hiring manager candidates for six new stores they were opening in the Memphis area. More than one hundred people applied. I figured it was a long shot since I was not even nineteen yet and had no experience.

The company planned to hire twelve candidates who would go to a thirty-day boot camp training store in San Antonio. From the twelve candidates they would select six managers for the new stores. The rest would be assistant managers in the same stores.

I hit it off with the regional director who interviewed me and pleaded with him to give me a chance. I promised him he would not be disappointed. He was an Underdog Champion himself, which worked in my favor. He was the first black regional director in the company. He had started at the bottom, as a cook, and worked his way through the ranks until he was at an executive field position overseeing twenty-seven stores. He decided to take a chance on me. This became my first experience at having a mentor and modeling a successful person.

My mentor was impressed with my eagerness and enthusiasm (amazing what being broke and jobless can do for you). He said I reminded him of his beginning with the company. He spent time with me before I headed off to training school and shared his beliefs and strategies for success. I was determined to be a manager of one of those new stores. All the other candidates had restaurant management experience or college degrees. I *really* felt like an underdog!

My mentor told me what I had to do. He said he had gotten his own store by doing the basics better than anyone else. He said he decided to learn the basics of running a store and be the best at those three things. The three basics were cooking chicken, cutting chicken (while standing inside a forty-five degree cooler), and selling additional side items to customers (a big profit center for the stores). He told me if I was the best in all these areas, my age and lack of experience would not matter.

I decided to strive to do my best and model my successful mentor's game plan. It was encouraging to have someone believe in me. He told me the company was looking for people who could lead from the front and set an example. He continued to assure me that if I modeled him (beliefs, compelling reasons, and strategies) and mastered the basics, I would get my own store.

The other candidates were friendly but talked to me like I was a kid. They told me it would take me a long time to get my own store. I got discouraged but I kept thinking about what my mentor had told me.

Thank God I listened. I was awarded the top trainee award by the instructors at training school from more than forty attendees. I out cooked (fastest), out cut (precision and speed), and outsold side items of them all. We all left school hopeful and anxious to see who would step into the first new store manager position which would open in three weeks.

Soon after returning home the regional director announced I was getting the first store. Two guys who went with me to training school became my assistant managers. At first they were jealous and kind of resentful toward me, but after the shock had worn off we became good friends.

I tell you this story to illustrate how I first learned about the power of modeling success vs. doing it the hard way. I actually surprised myself with the results!

The Rubber Band Story

When you stretch yourself beyond your normal comfort zone an interesting dynamic takes place. You create a permanent reference point. To illustrate, just think of an ordinary rubber band.

Think of (or pick up) a fresh, new rubber band and wrap it around each thumb and pull it as tightly as possible without breaking it. Hold it that way for at least two minutes. When you release the rubber band it will never be the same as its original size again, not ever.

This is a powerful illustration and I wanted to share it to follow up with my modeling story. Once I had experienced positive results from my actions it created an empowering mental anchor or reference point for future success in my mind. I permanently stretched my mind like the rubber band. All your life experiences create reference points (anchors). Here is the key: If you aren't committed to constantly stretching yourself, the rubber band (your life) stays the same and even rots. Your experience becomes your reference point for future progress, either keeping you limited and bound or releasing you so you can stretch, learn, and grow even more.

Two Sons

This is the true story of two sons, born eleven months apart. The father of these two sons was a man with a disappointing life; he had spent most of his adult years in a losing battle with alcohol and drug addiction. He abandoned his family and became a petty thief to support his habits. He shot and killed a man in a botched drug deal over a few dollars. He is currently serving a life sentence in prison.

His sons took totally contrasting paths. One followed in his father's footsteps and is serving a twenty-year sentence for shooting a man during an attempt to rob a liquor store to get money for drugs.

The other brother is a college graduate. He is happily married with three well-adjusted children. He has a beautiful suburban home. He also has a good job and a promising future with a major national company.

Here is the interesting part: The two sons were interviewed and asked, "Why do you think your life turned out the way it did?" Ironically, their answers were almost the same: "How could I do anything different with a father like mine?"

So here we have two totally different outcomes from the same childhood circumstances. One brother chose to follow in the footsteps of his father and use it as an excuse for failure. The other brother decided to stretch himself and avoid the pain he witnessed in his father's life and use it as a reason for success. How many times have you had a choice of beliefs and made the wrong decision? One thing is for sure; for things to change in life, we have to be willing to change. If our beliefs limit us and rob us of our future potential we have to change or pay the price—the higher price of missing out.

Mentoring Never Ends

After more than a year of working at Church's Fried Chicken the store wasn't producing the volume the company had projected. As a result, my income was substantially less than I had expected. While visiting my in-laws one day I ran into my wife's uncle and told him about my disappointment. He suggested I get into the insurance business with the company where he worked. I asked how much money he was earning, and I was surprised to find that it was more than three times my present income. That was enough to get my attention. He explained he was one of the top salesmen in this company of more than six hundred. Then he showed me his presentation and how he made his sales. I knew immediately that I could model what he was doing.

I had continued to read self-help books and around this time had just finished an amazing book called *The Power of the Subconscious Mind* by Dr. Joseph Murphy. He talked about the power of focusing on what you want by visualizing it in detail and how to attract the life you want by getting control of your subconscious mind. The book was filled with story after story of ordinary people getting extraordinary results. After my previous (stretching) reference of getting the management job with Church's, the encouraging ideas in the book gave me even more confidence to explore this new career possibility.

I asked the uncle if he could help me get an interview. He had been a top producer for the company for the previous seven years and he was confident he could help me set up an interview because of his position and success with the company.

The day of the interview finally arrived and I was excited. It went well until the manager asked my age. When I told him I was nineteen (but that I would be twenty in two months) he said, "Son, I'm sorry. I appreciate your enthusiasm, but we have never hired anyone under twenty-one in the seventy-four year history of this company. You're just too young."

"But you don't understand," I pleaded. "I can do this job and do it well; all I need is a chance." Our conversation continued and I could tell I was making progress in winning his confidence. I wanted the job so badly I could taste it. I could already see myself selling insurance and the money rolling in.

I even shared my Church's story and how I got my own store and beat out all the other candidates. Then I went for broke. Without hesitating I said, "Sir, if you give me a chance, you'll never regret it. The first year of working for you I will be your number-one salesman!"

I'll never forget what happened next. The manager leaned back in his chair and said, "Son, I have thirty-five salesmen and some have worked for me for over twenty-five years in this office. They have client bases they sell to every year. I'm satisfied you could do well with our company. But you can never be number-one in this office your first year."

I quickly responded, "I've spoken extensively with one of your company's top salesman in another city. He has shown me what he does every day to get big results. I know I can model him and get the same results or better. I just need a chance to prove it."

Then the manager leaned forward in his chair. He put his elbows on the desk and rested his chin on top of his clasped hands and appeared to be thinking deeply. After what seemed like an eon, he looked me seriously in the eye and said, "No promises, but I will try to convince the company to make an exception on your age and give you a chance. I will call you in a week."

The next week dragged on forever as I waited anxiously for the call. Finally it came and the news was good. "You got the job," he said. "Just don't let me down; I really went to bat for you. You start training in two weeks."

I started the job full of excitement, energy, and determination. I had something powerful in my mind: the reference of my past experience of modeling someone else's success and getting similar results. A new sales manager trained me. He was a former top salesman who had been promoted a few months earlier. The timing was perfect; a new calendar year began in just two months so I could get ready for that big year I promised the boss. My sales manager worked with me every day for the first three weeks. I studied and memorized the sales presentation the uncle used in his interviews with prospects. My sales manager gave me what he called a proven success formula to model. It was simple: I would ask ten people per day to listen to my sales presentation. On average, three would say yes. Out of those three, one would buy. He demonstrated the process consistently in front of prospects while he worked with me for the next three weeks.

After my sales manager released me to work on my own something dawned on me. What if I asked more than ten people every day? What would happen if I asked twenty every day? Would I double my sales? I did just that, and you don't have to guess what happened. My sales more than doubled! I told everyone I knew I was going to be the number-one salesman in the office my first year. That really put the pressure on me. But by putting myself on the line like that is what also made me keep going when I got tired or discouraged. Halfway through the first year I was in second place, behind a guy who had been number-one in the office six years in a row. Then something I wasn't expecting happened.

I got to find out the power of the NIOP (Negative Influence of Other People). Most of the other agents in the office were not exactly excited about this aggressive new kid outselling them and making them look bad. They tried all kinds of ways to discourage me, and it worked for a while.

For example, they told me that my territory was over-saturated and had been oversold by a former representative whom I had replaced. He was a top producer who had been promoted, which then required him to relocate. They said the existing clients were loaded with insurance and couldn't be sold any more. They said he had already knocked on every door, talked to every person, and the area was worn out. They said I was going to run out of people to sell any minute. For the first time since I started working for the company I began to worry.

I worried about buyer's remorse. I worried about cancellations. I got discouraged more easily than I had before, and started to go home early. I lost my courage and my motivation.

My sales manager confronted me and wanted to know what had happened to my sales. I gave him a long list of excuses and told him the other salesmen had given me advice. I will never forget the smile on his face when he said, "They got you." I looked at him, confused. He continued, "You have been making them look bad by outselling them. There are two ways to have the tallest building in town. You can build it yourself or you can tear down the other, taller buildings." He explained that there was nothing wrong with my territory. He also had another lesson for me. He said, "It's not the land, it's the man that makes the difference." At first I wanted to keep feeling sorry for myself and making excuses. Then he hit me again. "Are you buying or selling?" I didn't understand. Then he said, "Are you buying their lies, or are you selling insurance?"

I immediately left my pity party and went back to my old strategy. I finished the year as the number-one salesman in the office, and the former leader had his best year ever by chasing me. It truly was the man and not the land that made the difference.

I share the story to illustrate the power of modeling beliefs and following a proven plan of action. By modeling a person who achieved a result I wanted, I got similar results.

It wasn't easy making the top position in the office. I was scared sick in the beginning. I just kept thinking that if I followed the same plan and worked as hard as the top salesman I was modeling I would get similar results. Along with the distractions of NIOPS there were massive rejections, slammed doors, long days, and frequently cancelled appointments. There were always people with buyer's remorse who wanted refunds. In many ways, there were plenty of reasons to give up and lots of reasons to fail.

This experience stretched my mind (like the rubber band) about what I was capable of doing. Here I was, an average person, getting better than average results, not with a special talent or skill, but with better than average desire, teachability, and a willingness to work. The main thing I did to create my success was follow a proven plan.

You can also get the results you seek and achieve your dreams and goals if you model a proven plan. When this happens you create an empowering reference point to rely on and draw from over and over in the future. If you had success once, you can *always* do it again. Your rubber band is permanently stretched!

Chapter 17
Belief and Perception

Reality leaves a lot to the imagination.

John Lennon

What does perception have to do with your beliefs? Have you ever tried to jump from a pile of sand to concrete? It is hard to get a good jump, isn't it? That is because you're not starting from a firm foundation. If your goal is to jump as far as you can, obviously you would achieve more if you began on a solid foundation.

Our perception becomes our reality and the foundation of our beliefs. What we perceive as real affects what we attract and create in our lives, whether we desire it or not, and whether it is accurate or not. If this is true, wouldn't it mean that believing we can model others should bring us similar results? For example, if you perceive that you are weak, lacking talent and ability, worthless, unloved, or a failure, you will attract disastrous consequences. Perception, whether it be true or false, can be an extremely powerful force in your life

Just think about the Hollywood scene. Who doesn't dream at some point in their life of what it would be like to be a famous movie star or performer and live that lifestyle being adored by fans? Yet how many of these people live miserable lives? With today's media access we see this truth every day. Even worse is the sad reality that many have died from drug and alcohol overdoses or committed suicide. Remember Jimi Hendrix, Elvis Presley, Janis Joplin, John Belushi, River Phoenix, Chris Farley, Kurt Cobain.

What happened to these people? Their perception of happiness and success obviously was not what they expected when they achieved it. What appeared to be a dream life not only was unfulfilling, it was so painful they attempted to mask the pain to such a level that the results turned tragic. Something was missing and these people did not know where to turn or where to go to find it. This is why awareness and clarity in our lives are so critical.

We must not only know what we want, we have to know when we are getting it. In other words, are our perceptions of our journey in life filling or draining the soul? What does it take for you to be happy in all areas of life and have balance? Are you kidding yourself and accepting less because you don't think you have a choice? That can be a dangerous place. Ask yourself if you are fulfilling your true purpose. If you are, the dream of your soul, your source of total satisfaction and wholeness, will manifest.

A father got on a crowded subway with five young children. The children were active and bouncing about, annoying other people. The father stared out into space appearing lost in his thoughts and making no effort to control his children. A lady sitting next to them couldn't take the distraction any longer and yelled at the man, "Are these your children? Can you do something to settle them down?" The man replied, "I'm sorry; we just came from the funeral home. Their mother died unexpectedly, and I don't know what I'm going to do next."

Perception is often far different than reality. Sometimes we are not just off base with our perceptions, we are like a lost ball in miles of high weeds. We go on with our lives and build our reality on something that is wrong or unreal. This is why we need to be sure of what we really want and that who we are attempting to model is authentic and the same as our perception of them.

Learning to model others and get results is a skill in itself. The more a person gets to model success the more confidence they will have. I have seen amazing things happen from those who modeled success using all the steps of the Valeo Method. The skills you take away from learning and applying these concepts are life-altering, and not just for you. When you drop a pebble in a pond the ripple continues on.

By paying attention to our perceptions we are always checking in with our authentic self. We simply keep asking ourselves, "Is this truly what I am meant to be, do, and have in my life?" "Is this goal and accomplishment going to give me balance and wholeness in my life?" At the same time we want to use good judgment because if we are so focused with modeling success in one area we may let too many other things go and other areas of our life will suffer.

Beliefs and Habits

Beliefs can create habits. Good habits are just as easy to live by as bad habits. We get in a comfort zone with our habits either way. Our habits become unconscious to us, so much so that sometimes they take control of us and define who we appear to be. We do them unconsciously, without thinking, and ignore the consequences.

Hall of Fame basketball player and coach Larry Bird did a McDonald's commercial in the '80s. His role in the commercial was simple: stand on the free-throw line and miss a shot. Sounds pretty easy, right? Larry had a challenge; he was one of the highest percentage free throw shooters in history. It took him twenty-three attempts to miss a shot. In fact, he had a habit of hitting free throw shots. He was so conditioned to hitting his goal he could hardly miss. What a concept! His perception plus his beliefs became his reality.

What would happen if you had beliefs so strong, so compelling, that you couldn't get rid of them even if you tried? Habits are like gravity; good or bad, they just keep pulling us toward them. Living consciously with awareness and clarity gives us the strength to take control of our habits.

The Power of Belief

Author Dr. Norman Cousins tells a true story that illustrates how quickly and dramatically we can be influenced by others' beliefs. During a college football game the staff doctor treated five spectators for stomachaches, cramps, and nausea. After questioning the people who were sick the doctor determined all five people had drank soft drinks from a particular concession stand at the stadium. To help other spectators an announcement was made to the crowd to avoid drinking soft drinks from that particular concession stand because people were getting ill. This happened near the beginning of the game.

By the third quarter more than two hundred people were reporting the same symptoms. Half of these people were taken to the hospital. Before the end of the game the doctor discovered that the original five people had also eaten potato salad at the same delicatessen on the way to the game.
The problem was not the soft drinks; it was the potato salad. Word went through the stadium quickly and people immediately felt better. The people who went to the hospital were able to go home because their symptoms went away.

This shows how powerful our environment affects our beliefs. Our beliefs are the foundation of our lives. They can be beliefs like those deeply ingrained in the mind of Larry Bird that cause us to create a good habit. They can also be created quickly, like what happened in the stadium. The key is to be aware and conscious of the beliefs you allow to influence your life. Our perceptions become our beliefs, real or unreal. Our beliefs plus our focus become our personal reality.

Gandhi said: "If I believe I can't do something, it makes me incapable of doing it. When I believe I can, then I acquire the ability to do it in the beginning."

Stretch-Stretch-Stretch

If we commit to always stretching like the rubber band our possibilities just get bigger and bigger. Our potential as a human being is only limited by our individual thinking. What we can do as individual human beings is amazing, but what we actually end up doing is often disappointing. How many times do you wait for someone else to take action before you do? When does the day come when we declare, "I can't live this way anymore"?

When you realize your rule book of limiting beliefs is holding you back, then you can make the decision to live by your playbook. That is when you decide what you want, find someone you want to model, and know you are on your way to creating success.

Unlikely Success

C.J. "Madame" Walker was born in 1867 to sharecropper parents. At age six her parents abandoned her and left her to grow up as an orphan. She was illiterate and forced to work six days a week picking cotton and working in and cleaning white households. She married at fourteen, became a mother at sixteen, and was a widow by twenty. Her life was a struggle beyond what most of us could comprehend. When she was thirty-seven and on her knees scrubbing the floor, something happened; she started to think about how she was going to survive when she got older and couldn't continue to do physical work. That day she decided to make drastic changes in her life.

It was 1905, and she took all the money she had (which was just a few dollars) and moved from St. Louis to Denver for a fresh start. She started a business selling hair straightener. Her business grew and she began adding sales representatives. Her company continued to grow until it became a national organization with employees numbering in the thousands. This is not the end of the story. She went on to become the first self-made woman millionaire, black or white, in United States history. Can you imagine in today's dollars what her wealth would equal? So what was her deciding moment? She had one of those days when she said, "I'm not going to live this way anymore!"

Years later she was asked what advice she would give to others seeking to change and improve their situation in life. She said simply, "Perseverance is my motto." She made a decision and never looked back; she never gave up. She took control of her story instead of letting outside influences and discouragement do it for her.

What effect does not having one or both parents around have on a child's potential? An interesting study was conducted in 1989 by New York psychologist J. Marvin Eisentadt. He searched the records of 699 eminent Americans. He discovered that 46 percent of these people had lost a parent before age twenty-one. In contrast, the next two highest groups who had lost a parent before age twenty-one were juvenile delinquents and depressive or suicidal psychiatric patients.

There appears to be a thin line between how a person's life turns out after orphan hood. Some let orphan hood motivate them to overcome their challenges and be successful. Yet almost the same percentage swing to the opposite extreme and let it ruin their lives. There is not much of an in between. What happens seems to be determined by their interpretation and perception of their actual challenges and their circumstances. This signifies how just a little guidance and understanding of the subjects addressed in the Valeo Method can have profound affects.

Most people would never think a thirteen-year-old African-American girl could give birth to a baby girl with no father present and that the baby girl would go through physical and sexual abuse and still have a good future. To make the odds even worse, that same girl gets pregnant herself and delivers a stillborn baby at thirteen. The same girl next winds up in juvenile detention because of her unruliness at age fourteen. But Oprah Winfrey was able to overcome her past and become the only African-American woman billionaire in the world and one of the richest and most influential people in the United States.

One Poor Little Blind Girl

Growing up with only one parent or as an orphan is tough enough. How about growing up with both parents but being blind? How about being blind, deaf, and dumb? Many people would say it is a life not worth living.

When I was in the ninth grade I stumbled across a book in the school library; it was the autobiography of Helen Keller. I didn't know who she was or her story, but that book left an indelible impression on my young mind. Many times in life when I faced challenges I would think about Helen's story and feel encouraged. I never forgot it.

I also realized that not too many people knew the details of Helen's life. Helen Keller, a tragically handicapped person, accomplished some amazing things. Born with all her senses, she was struck with a disease at one and half years old that left her blind and deaf. Her parents were fortunate to find the help of a devoted teacher named Anne Sullivan.

At age seven, Helen started to learn and understand words as Anne wrote letters with her fingers, spelling them out in Helen's hand. She learned to speak and read lips through the daunting process of only the sense of touch.

Helen believed she could accomplish anything in learning and academics that a person without her handicaps could do. She knew it would just take more time and determination. She was committed to succeed according to the same standards as anyone else who could see and hear. Early in her life she took control of her life story which she planned to write and publish. She refused to let her circumstances or anyone else's beliefs about her afflictions affect her outcomes.

Her hands were never free to take notes because they were busy with her teacher, spelling out the topics she wanted to cover in her hand. She had to commit all her lessons to memory until she got home where she typed out what she remembered. Many of her books were printed in Braille and since she hadn't mastered it yet, she had to have them spelled out in her hand also. Helen had her doubts and frustrations just like the rest of us. But she was determined to succeed. She was noted as saying, "Everyone who wishes to gain knowledge must climb the hill of difficulty alone. Since there is no royal road to the summit, I must zigzag it my own way. I slip back many times, I fall, I stand still, I'm running against deep obstacles, I lose my temper and I find it again and keep it better. I trudge on, I gain a little, I feel encouraged. I get back up, climb higher, and begin to see the widening horizon. Every struggle is a victory." It's hard to imagine a determination as strong as the one Helen Keller possessed. Most of our challenges pale in comparison.

She graduated magna cum laude in 1904 at age 24 from Radcliffe College and became the first deaf-blind person to graduate from college. She went on to write seven books. She traveled the world, inspiring millions of people. She met every president from Calvin Coolidge to John F. Kennedy. Hopefully, you can see why this story stuck with me over the years and why I included it here.

Facts inform, but stories inspire. You never know when a story, event, circumstance, or another person is going to dramatically alter the course of your life. My challenges and struggles drove me to develop the Valeo Method which is now helping so many.

What stories and beliefs are affecting your life right now? Are they empowering you or disempowering you? Is your story worth telling? Is it worth modeling? If the answer is no do you realize how quickly that can change? Isn't it about time to start your Underdog Champion story today? Even if you consider yourself a success in your life are you really getting true joy and satisfaction? Have you done your best? What is your legacy? Have you made a difference and a contribution to others? If your life today isn't close to where you thought you would be at this point, and even if your life seems like a warning to others, don't dare settle for less than you can be. You were chosen for greatness. Today is the day you can start being an example for others. You are already on your way by making it this far in learning the Valeo Method. As the late motivation and success philosopher Jim Rohm said, "It is time to stand at the door of your thoughts and pay attention to what you are letting in."

Chapter 18
All Excuses Are Equal

*Ninety-nine percent of failures come from people who
have a habit of making excuses.*

George Washington.

Everybody has an excuse. "Yeah, but you don't know my
story," or "I could've done better but _____ (fill in the
blank)." It's easy to blame some event or some other person
for our shortcomings. Did you ever notice the word blame also
spells b-lame? When we are making excuses we are being lame
and weak. Point your finger at someone else and then look at
your hand—three fingers are pointing back at you.

When conducting seminars and in coaching sessions, I ask
people to write down their most limiting beliefs. The response
can be fascinating. Many times I am surprised because my
impression of the person makes me feel like their limiting belief
doesn't fit my perception of them. In reality, it doesn't matter
what I think of the belief because it is very real to them.

Some people say, "I'm not smart enough; I need more
education." Others say, "I'm too old, I'm too young, and I'm too
shy," or "I have no experience," or "I'm broke." Finally, the

most common excuses people often don't say are, "I'm afraid of failure," or its opposite, "I'm afraid of success."

I once had a mentor I really respected. I was managing a large sales team but sales weren't growing. He was coaching me on how to increase my sales by demonstrating a certain management style. He asked me why I felt performance was not up to par. I gave him a long list of reasons I thought were valid. Then he told me something I will never forget, and it has had a huge effect on my business and my life. He simply said, "You have to learn one thing, but you may not like it." I really wanted to hear it so I said, "Please tell me." I wasn't expecting what came next. He told me, "All excuses are equal."

I was floored because he had patiently listened to me go on for thirty minutes about why my team wasn't reaching its potential. He was nodding his head and I thought he agreed with me. All excuses are equal? Honestly, he kind of hurt my feelings. That was not what I wanted to hear. Then he had the audacity to stand up, shake my hand, and say, "When you have had time to finish thinking about that one, we will meet again." He smiled and said good-bye. I paced the floor and did some real soul searching that day. My conclusion? He was right.

From that day forward I adopted the belief, "All excuses are equal." I urge you to do the same. Just think about it; if you believe you can model other people and get similar results, and you really believe all excuses are equal, then where does that put you? How about empowered and on the way to being unstoppable? Let's keep going—you're just getting started and more good stuff is coming.

Limiting Beliefs Are Just Excuses

We use excuses to justify our failures. We justify our lack of commitment. There is always a reason to put off doing our best, to justify our half-baked commitments, to let excuses keep us from making changes, and to not take action and seize opportunities. Here's the point: Pay for it now by taking control and expending energy and commitment or pay for it later with lack, pain, and suffering. Which is worse?

Procrastination is a dream stealer and the enemy of accomplishment and success. When I decided to lose weight and get my body fat under 10 percent, I knew I needed to lose at least seventy-five pounds which I knew would take fifteen to eighteen months to do in a healthy way.

My belief was that when I reached my desired weight it would be easier to maintain my goal weight than it was to lose it originally. This is exactly what happened, and the longer I stay at my desired weight the more pain I associate with putting on any additional weight. I still have to watch it closely and maintain my exercise regimen, but it is nothing like the effort it took to lose the weight originally.

Are you putting off a decision you know you need to make? People have told me things like, "You don't know my situation. I have no support," or "I've never had success before; how can I do it now?" or "My marriage is on the rocks; I've tried to work it out, and it failed before," or "I don't have any money." All these are just excuses.

One of the best ways to get rid of excuses and problems is simple. Stop telling ourselves and others how big our problems are and start telling our problems how big God is. There is no problem too big for God. Faith in Divine power can do amazing things.

When Moses was helping the Israelites escape from Egypt with the Pharaoh and his massive army in hot pursuit, God got six million Israelites through the Red Sea overnight. I read where a mathematician ran the numbers on that bit of history. He determined that on that night for all those people to get across, God had to dry up a stretch of deep water over five miles wide! It doesn't seem like our little problems should be that much of a challenge if we know how to ask for God's help, does it?

Overcoming the Odds

Ella Fitzgerald lost her mother when she was young. She grew up in a girl's reformatory and sang to escape the pain of her reality. Homeless and wearing a shabby outfit and men's army boots, she entered a talent contest at the Apollo Theater. She sang with all her heart to a packed house. That night a seventeen-year-old homeless girl won first prize and launched a forty year career, selling forty million records and winning thirteen Grammies.

Most people know Sylvester Stallone from his Rocky and Rambo movies. But they don't know how he eliminated his excuses and overcame his challenges to succeed. By the time Sly was eleven years old his family had moved fourteen times. He had a speech impediment as a result of the doctor misusing the forceps during his birth. He was inspired by the movie Hercules starring body building legend and actor Steve Reeves. He went to junk yards to lift car parts to build his muscles. He pursued a career in acting even though he was rejected more than one thousand times at auditions.

Finally, at age thirty-two, he decided to write a screenplay about a fighter named Rocky Balboa. He believed with all his heart that only he could play the leading role. He was so broke his wife gave up on him. He wore his clothes in the shower to wash them because he couldn't afford to go to the Laundromat. He sold his beloved dog to buy food. With only $106 to his name he was offered $75,000 for his screenplay.

He was elated but there was one stipulation he required before he would sign the deal. He demanded that he play in the starring role as Rocky. He knew that no one could convey the character as well as he could. The investors said there was no way so Sly turned down the offer. The investors couldn't believe it so they countered with $100,000. He turned it down again and they offered $200,000. Finally, they offered $330,000 and still he said no. He had a feeling of certainty, a knowing—he had faith and his beliefs were so strong that he wouldn't budge.

He finally got the agreement he could live with and was allowed to play the starring role in the movie. So what was the final deal? Only $20,000 plus a base actor's pay of $340 per week. But his beliefs paid off; he also negotiated a percentage of the profits and the movie went on to gross over $160 million at the box office and won three Academy Awards. Believing in yourself and avoiding excuses is indeed a powerful thing!

Chapter 19
Love and Fear

Restlessness and discontent are the first necessities of progress.

Thomas Edison

It was 1988 and I was facing some challenging times. I went from living well to living well beyond my means. My income had been increasing steadily for years and then all of sudden I got too comfortable and casual (casualness breeds casualties). Things started falling apart in just about all areas of my life.

I had spent the last few years increasing my standard of living while not preparing well enough for slow times or down times, and my expenses had begun to overwhelm me. Have you ever been there before? My relationships, my health, and my emotions were affected by the stress and pressure I was experiencing. I had developed the ability to create all this success and it seemed endless, but somehow my life was falling apart. The worry and pain were almost unbearable. But it wasn't the first time I had been through a tough situation and bounced back so I was determined to discover how to fix it once more. This time I was also was determined to figure out how to avoid ever going through all that suffering again—it was just too much pain to keep repeating.

This was the beginning of the development of the Valeo Method. I was shackled to results and situations in my life that I did not want, and I was becoming very unhappy. The first step of the Valeo Method is about discovering and understanding what holds us back and what causes us to sabotage ourselves, sometimes over and over. If you have had an ailment or disorder of your body what does the doctor do first? He looks at your symptoms, runs tests, and determines what the problem is, right? That is exactly what we are doing here.

For example, have you ever said, "I have mixed emotions," when you are referring to a situation or a decision you are trying to make? I used to say that a lot as a figure of speech, but I didn't really understand what I was saying. Mixed emotions can be a serious problem. We all face them at times in our lives and they cause pain and suffering. They are not something to toss around lightly. Why? Because they can eat your lunch! Having mixed emotions can, in some situations, be like handling dynamite. This is why we to have understand the two kinds of emotions and how to get control of them and not be controlled by them.

There are only two foundational emotions—love and fear. When these two clash it creates a powerful internal conflict which can cause you to become even more confused. When this happens we go into something called negative internal dialogue, and this can result in pain, stress, and even trauma.

Love is a real emotion. God gave us love as the core of our being with our original instructions even before we were assigned our DNA. Fear and fear-based emotions can seem very real and they can cause serious pain, but they are not real. Fear and all the emotions associated with it, including anger, jealousy, hate, doubt, worry, envy, and greed are just illusions created by our egoic minds. I believe that statement now, but for a long time I didn't, so if you don't believe it I don't blame you at this point. I believed fear was real because even though I had a hard time admitting it, fear controlled my life. Fear kept me from doing what I needed to do to turn my life around before it got in such a mess. Fears can even appear to be keeping us safe and protecting us. What it really does is limit us, control us, and keep us from taking action. At the same time, it keeps us in misery, pain, and suffering. The Scripture tells us there is only one true fear we should have, and that is fear of a life without God.

Babe Ruth said, *"Never let the fear of striking out get in your way."* He was a leading home-run hitter but he was also the leader in strikeouts. Every action or choice of any significance you make is based on the emotions of love or fear. Decisions made out of fear are almost always wrong.

Even some of the most powerful people in history have fears. Have you ever noticed how other people's fears sometimes seem silly to you? Yet these fears seem very real to them. Napoleon feared cats. Julius Caesar feared dreams. Peter the Great was afraid to cross a bridge. Socrates was afraid of the "evil eye." Mark Twain was quoted as saying, "I have been through many terrible things in my life and some of them actualy happened."

The key is to get to know fear, recognize it, discover what it really is, and then turn that fear into power. You might be thinking, "Yeah, easy for you to say." I am going to prove to you that it is easier to get a handle on this thing we call fear than you think. What does fear really represent? False Evidence Appearing Real—it *doesn't* mean Forget Everything And Run!

It is a fact that the things we fear and worry about rarely ever actually happen. A University of Michigan study revealed that 60 percent of the things you worry about never happen; 20 percent of your worries are focused on the past and totally out of your control, or they are based on trivial, insignificant things that don't even matter. Out of the remaining 10 percent, only 4 to 5 percent are legitimate fears. All that energy wasted for nothing! A newborn baby has two fears: loud noises and fear of falling. Just think what would happen in our lives if we only kept those two fears and didn't allow our egoic minds to create so many new ones.

Fears make up the very core of our negative, limiting beliefs. They keep us trapped in our self-limiting stories and hiding in our comfort zones. But here is the irony; life begins at the end of the comfort zone. What a great reason to let go of fear! The Scriptures tell us, *"The Lord is my helper so I will have no fear. What can mere people do to me?"* We are also told 365 times in the Bible, *"Have no fear."* Isn't it interesting that there 365 days in a year, also? Hmmm, coincidence maybe?

A little girl who walked home from school every day regularly passed a house with a big, mean-looking dog in the yard. Every day this frightened her, and she would run as fast as she could past the house with the dog pursuing close behind, growling and barking. One day she tripped and fell, dropping her books and papers. In her frustration she jumped up and yelled at the dog, waving her arms in the air. The dog backed off, looking surprised. It was then she realized the dog was old and gray and had no teeth. She had been afraid all that time of this harmless dog. How many times have you realized that what you were afraid of wasn't real?

What false fears are ruling your life now? What false fears are keeping you in your limiting story and stealing your dreams and joy? Fear becomes our jailer because it locks us away from our future, from hope, and from possibility. Fear can wear us down, make us tired, and make us give up and let dreams fade away. Studies show that eight out of ten people don't reach their goals because of fear. The emotions that drain our hope come from fear. The emotions that give us energy and courage come from love. Don't let your fears rob your future for another day.

Some people are afraid they're too old. Ray Kroc was fifty-three when he bought the McDonald's brothers restaurants. Colonel Sanders was sixty-five and broke when he started Kentucky Fried Chicken; ten years later at age seventy-five he had created the concept of franchising and was one of the wealthiest men in America. Clive Chichester became the first British person to single-handedly sail around the world at age sixty-six. Harry Bernstein published his first novel at age ninety-six! Hey, what more do you want? Why didn't fear of being too old or too late stop them?

Just remember the other side of fear is where the living is. Saint Paul tells us, *"God has not given us the spirit of timidity, but of power, love, and self-discipline."* I promise you, my friend, fear represents only one thing in your life—wasted time!

Chapter 20

How Much Pain Before Change?

We must suffer one of two pains: the pain of discipline or the pain of regret.
The difference is discipline weighs ounces while regret weighs tons.

Jim Rohn

Limiting beliefs cause us to avoid the pain of change in our lives. Sometimes pain is good because it changes our direction or makes us strong. Remember, because people will naturally do more to avoid pain than to gain pleasure, the fear of change is powerful and keeps them stuck.

Ironically, a big step towards making a change in your life is to discover what is causing you to stay the same. It takes courage to face limiting beliefs and understand what they are and how you got them—but right then and there, you must change them. Limiting beliefs are like heavy balls and chains shackled to your legs.

Let's pretend you have three limiting beliefs: "I'm afraid of failure," "I don't have any money to start a business," and "I am not smart enough." Now, picture each of these limiting beliefs as a ten-pound ball and chain. Now drag each one of these weights around everywhere you go for the next five years.

At the end of five years double the amount of the weight. After another five years go ahead and double the weight again. Hey, you're getting older, you've acquired a few more wrinkles and lost a little more energy, but the weight and the pain of your limiting beliefs are just getting heavier. Does this make sense in any way whatsoever? Forget it. That is the way limiting beliefs work, so make sure you'll have none of them.

Just think about the pain, the burden of all that weight. The thing to remember is this: Today, change may seem hard, but tomorrow it will be even harder.

The Two Yous

What if you could look into the future and see yourself at a ripe old age? Would you visualize yourself as if you had never given up on any of your limiting beliefs? How would you look? Tired, discouraged, disappointed, or sad? What about your physical body? What physical condition would you be in? Would those limiting beliefs have taken away from your quality of life? Would you leave a legacy?

Now let's totally change focus from that thought. Let's visualize the future of a person the same age as in the prior situation only this time there is a change. This person broke through their limiting beliefs and the fears associated with them. How would this person look? Is there more joy in their eyes and on their face? What is the physical condition of this person? How would they feel compared to the person in the prior example?

Why am I using this illustration? Because it is powerful and it is real. The older you get the more powerful it gets. Remember, we will do more to avoid pain than to gain pleasure as a natural human instinct. When we can incorporate that thinking into our lives we will find the motivation to change. Now is the time to design how you are going to look and feel and where you are going to be emotionally, financially, and spiritually in the twilight years of your life. You can pay the price for change now, or you can pay later with disappointment and suffering— either way, there is a cost.

Is someone holding you back? Has someone told you that you couldn't be, do, or have something? Has a person or event in your life caused you to stop dreaming? Have you allowed a person, event, or circumstance to shackle you and convince you that you don't have what it takes? If the answer is yes, don't beat yourself up about it; it happens all the time. Even people who love you can discourage you because of their own limiting beliefs. They may think they are protecting you from the pain of disappointment by discouraging your dreams. It sounds crazy but it happens. In reality, they are transferring their own fears and weaknesses onto you. This is tragic. It is unacceptable, but sadly most of the people it happens to are so unconscious in their thinking that they don't even realize what they're doing. Can you remember a time when you had a limiting belief and you broke through it and surprised yourself? How did it feel? The Real You, your authentic self, came through for you. That can happen every day all the way through the rest of your life, beginning right now!

It's Time to Make a Move!

Bonnie St. John was the first African-American woman to win an Olympic medal. As a child she went with friends on ski vacations every year. Despite having a handicap of only one leg she mastered the sport. She participated in the 1984 Paralympics downhill skiing competition. At the beginning of the second race she clearly had the gold medal in sight. Then she had a bad break and fell on an icy spot in a turn. She thought her dream was over. She got up and finished the race anyway and was still able to take home a bronze medal. She later found out the gold medal winner fell in the same icy spot as she did, but this girl got up too and won the gold medal

There two lessons here. First, we are always better and more resilient than we think we are. Next, everybody falls down; we live in a fallen world. Winners just get up faster. A powerful step in winning in our lives is knowing when to get up and claim our victories. This means changing our limiting beliefs (rules) to empowering beliefs and acting with our faith and courage and not from our fears.

Gift for You

The best gift I can ever give you and the best gift you can ever pay forward to others is the gift of encouragement. We all need encouragement, no matter how independent, prideful, or confident we are. Encouragement works magic; it brings out the best in individuals, fires excellent thinking, fuels creativity, and lifts confidence.

On display at the Smithsonian Institution in Washington, D.C. are the personal effects of Abraham Lincoln on the night he was shot. The items include a pen knife, a small handkerchief embroidered "A. Lincoln," a confederate $5 bill, a spectacle case repaired with cotton string, and a worn-out newspaper clipping praising his accomplishments as president. The article begins, "Abe Lincoln is one of the greatest statesmen of all time."

Now, why would a man regarded as one of the most influential leaders in the history of America carry around such a news clipping? Could he possibly not realize his worth? The truth was, Lincoln was under constant criticism as a politician. He wasn't always popular. The press was ruthless and critical of him. They challenged and criticized every decision he made. He needed to know his value. He needed encouragement just as every one of us desperately needs encouragement, no matter who we are or what we have accomplished.

Be encouraged as you go to the next step of the Valeo Method. Some of what you are going through here is not easy. Don't skip ahead to the Release step or any of the others until you feel comfortable with the review at the end of each section.

As Saint Paul says in the Bible, *"I also pray that you will understand the incredible greatness of God's power for us who believe Him."* Let us understand that the greatest encourager of all, our almighty God, is there to help those who believe in Him every step of the way.

Progress and Strategies

Before going to the Release step of the Valeo Method it is important to be clear on all parts of the Discovery process.

1. Understand that every one of us has a unique purpose to and assignment for our life. You have a Dream of the Soul, a calling, a purpose that is seeking to manifest itself.

2. Each of us has created a false self, an egoic mind, to allow us to adapt to other humans and to fit in. The egoic mind is not your friend; it is your enemy.

3. When you abuse the gift of free will you will only get your self in trouble.

4. You can change your disempowering rules of life to em powering plays for life and create incredible results, beginning right now.

5. You can model the success of others and produce the same results. You are a creation of unlimited potential who represents the unlimited expression of God.

Summary and Action Plan

1. I will focus on the power of awareness and clarity and use them to empower myself.

2. I will get serious about my precious time and avoid wasting it, or marking time. I will constantly try to get better. There are 86,400 seconds in each day. If that were money how would I spend it?

3. I will break out of institutionalized thinking. I will get out of my own way and out of any rut I am stuck in.

4. I will constantly analyze my actions and always check my course. I will ask myself every day: "Is my ego controlling my thoughts?"

5. I will think, act like, and become an Underdog Champion, always ready to make a comeback.

6. I will ask myself every day, "Am I living consciously or unconsciously?"

7. I will ask myself these three questions every day: "Is my story worth making a movie about?" "Is my life going to be a warning or an example?" and "Is it time to plan a new ending?"

8. I will ask myself, "Who am I modeling?" I will find some one who gets the results I want and follow the four steps to modeling success.

9. I will check the alignment of my beliefs and perceptions. Is what I see in my future unfolding?

10. I will ask myself frequently, "Am I dominated by the emotions of fear or love?"

11. I will ask myself, "Am I encouraging others?" "Am I dis playing strength and courage to others?"

12. I will put a picture of myself when I was younger than six years old in front of myself in a place where I will see it every day. I will reflect on my child self, my authentic self, every day.

Notes

PART III

RELEASE

*The greatest weapon against stress is the ability
to choose one thought over another.*

James Allen

The *Release* step of the Valeo Method is about letting go of anything and everything that is holding you back in life. It is about releasing the toxic thoughts, beliefs, and emotions that cause worry, doubt, and fear. Through *Release* you will learn how to remove the stumbling blocks in life. You will learn to use a process I developed called "Transitional Language." This process allows us to release the pain and suffering we anchor into our psyche by constantly using disempowering words and negative self-talk in our communication with others.

The Release step is not just about releasing negative energies in your life; it is about releasing and launching *positive* energies. It is about letting your authentic, personal power that rests in your soul guide and direct you to your original intent. The same source that makes your heart beat more than **80,000** times a day is ready, available, and patiently waiting for you to activate it.

It is ironic that as children we can't wait until the next birthday, or to finally grow up. We revel in change. We can't wait to become teenagers; then we can't wait to reach sweet sixteen and get our driver's license. Then we can't wait to become eighteen and be a legal voting adult, and then we can't wait to become twenty-one and be free to make any choice we want. Fear of change has little effect on us at these points in our lives.

Then, without warning, we begin to experience a subtle, gradual change in our thinking. Fear of change begins to creep into our lives. Suddenly, we want to stop and hold on to something—we don't want to keep growing up. And the older we get, the more power it has over us.

I realized this process when I was developing the Valeo Method. It was insidious. The feeling of fear of change crept up on me and I started asking questions like, "Why do we lose our courage to face change and life as we get older?" "What is our relationship to time, aging, and fear?" "Shouldn't we be getting braver and stronger and *gaining* power over fear after all of our life experiences instead of *losing* power?"

These questions are the foundations of the *Release* step, and you are about to find out the answers.

Not only does our fear increase as we get older, but our level of patience decreases which affects how we make decisions. As we get older we want to see immediate benefits and rewards from our efforts. We are conditioned by our environment to be impatient. Feeling this way in itself is not all bad, but the problem comes when we expect things before we deserve them. This attitude will create real problems.

Part of this is due to our ever-changing, fast-paced environment, but we cannot blame the fact that our lives are going faster than ever before. Sure, we live in the fast lane these days, with fast food and an overall quick service mentality; that's just the way it is. But we expect to have success overnight. We want an accelerated college degree on a part-time basis. We can't possibly wait to save up to buy a car or furniture so we let the banks and finance companies do it for us, and we agree to pay much more as a result of that fast service. Banks teach college kids how to ruin their credit by issuing credit cards to them they don't deserve, with credit limits they can't handle, and when they don't have enough income to pay them off. It took my son till age thirty to pay off and clean up the debt he ran up in college because of this situation.

Even as expectant parents we can't wait to find out the sex of the baby, so technology allows us to peek and see. This is not so bad but many parents don't even have the patience to let the baby come on nature's schedule. They set a date and induce labor or just cut the baby out. I know I may be getting a little carried away here but I'm sure you get my point. Who have we turned into? Do we like that person? Would you like you if you met you, or are you too impatient to answer that question?

We let impatience run our lives. It's time for a change. The main reason we lose our courage and personal power is because we allow our egoic mind to create mental opposition and sabotage our progress. We allow change to become a threat to our thinking and our future. At the same time we want what we want now, no matter if we deserve it or have earned it. We want our outcome now and our benefits and rewards immediately.

To top it off we live in a society that *rewards* instant gratification. The faster we can get something done, the better for us and everyone else involved. We constantly upgrade our computers because they'll provide faster products and services for us—or for our employers, who will reward us for our efficiency. We want what we want and we want it now. Everything always seems to be getting a little quicker, faster, and better. It's all new and improved, right? When is the last time you ran out to buy something old and slower?

Since we can't wait for our dreams to come true we overextend our finances and bury ourselves in debt for homes, cars, jewelry, toys, and even our vacations. Progress is good but this running ahead of ourselves has a hefty price tag attached to it. We have seen this price across America as we have watched our lives and others' lives around us unravel as so many lose their homes, jobs, hopes, and dreams. Then, in turn, the quality of our personal health is affected adversely by the constant stress, worry, and pressure that accompanies these losses.

We chase after dreams that we hope will reward us with satisfaction to no avail. As we seek *Release* we receive something else; we fill up with pain, disappointment, and uncertainty.

Drug companies capitalize on the pain of people by offering a plethora of anti-depressant drugs like Prozac, Paxil, and Zoloft, among many others. I was floored recently when I saw a commercial by a drug company. The advertisement actually said that two out of three people who take anti-depressants are still depressed. But not to worry, they have a *new* solution—a new drug you can take along with the other drugs that are not working, which also carries the laundry list of life-threatening side effects similar to the drugs you have been taking for years. The list of life-threatening side effects are staggering; from strokes to heart attacks to seizures.

I was upset that these arrogant, greedy companies had the audacity to air a commercial like that. I was also upset because I thought about how many depressed people out there don't even know they have other options and just keep running to their doctors to get a prescription for this pill or that pill. What kind of long-term damage are they doing to do their bodies to mask their pain?

We've become the prime guinea pigs for the medical industry. Depressed people are willing to try or do anything, side effects and all, to heal an aching soul.

The use of anti-depressant drugs as a catch-all for a wide range of symptoms over the years has left us a nation with millions of victims who are physically addicted to these drugs. Even if patients want to come off of them they can't because their bodies have grown dependent on them. For example, some anti-depressants rob the body of the ability to naturally produce serotonin, which is the neurotransmitter essential for the regulation of the cyclic body processes.

If people try to come off these drugs without close medical attention, they face scary consequences starting with seizures, for example, and progressing on to violent and even suicidal tendencies. The withdrawal symptoms are a nightmare, but the drug companies are always quick to capitalize on opportunities to sell a new drug.

Before the development of the new drug, which all the advertisements herald as the "feel better while you're depressed" drug, which can conveniently be taken along with the older drugs that aren't working, the drug companies recognized another opportunity. Along with the lack of effectiveness of the anti-depressants, we saw a wave of drugs to aid in sleep. If we can't effectively mask their pain with anti-depressants, by golly, let's just knock them out with a new round of sleep aids. Hey, what a concept! They will do anything to keep folks from seeking to learn to take control of their lives by their own understanding and skills and try instead to capitalize on their need for relief.

Similarly, well-intentioned doctors are under pressure to see more patients in the same time period in order to survive the high cost of doing business in their environment. The reduction of and difficulty in receiving payment from insurance companies and Medicare is taking its toll. The average doctor spends only seven minutes with a patient. Proper attention to a patient's needs and other extenuating details are ignored, and thus affected adversely.

We chase after dreams that make us feel good. That's all we really want. We don't really buy that shiny new car because we need it. In most cases the old car would serve us just fine. We just want to experience the way the new car makes us *feel*. Then what happens in a few weeks? Forget about it—the car is already old by then, so we begin to take the new/old car for granted because the newness has worn off. We want to buy something new to make us feel better, and we *do* feel better— for a while. But here's a wild thought: What if you could learn how to get and keep that good feeling without having to buy anything, and you could keep that same feeling going from now on?

There is some good news. Things can change and things *will* change if you are ready. The tools for change are here. The answer is simple: Release the pain and *Release* the Real You and a new life begins.

Very few of us actually ever tap into the treasure buried inside us—our original intent and our purpose. In fact, our treasure gets buried so deep beneath this storm of chaos that

we call life, we don't know what to do *make* things change.
The pressure builds up slowly over time and suddenly we have a
hard time carrying it. That's when it takes a toll on our minds,
emotions, relationships, and, of course, our bodies. Many times
when we search for answers in our hurry–up thinking lifestyles,
we race right past the solution.

Tapping the brakes of life and slowing down to find some
source of peace and happiness is not easy in our world of
instant gratification. It takes determination and it also takes
courage. But more than anything else, you have to realize that
a price has to be paid one way or the other. One price comes
through suffering pain and misery. The other option is to put
out the effort to make change. What is your choice now?

Chapter 21
The Sacred Wish

Just don't give up trying to do what you really want to do.
Where there is love and inspiration, I don't think you can go wrong.

Ella Fitzgerald

Deep at the center of your heart is a secret and sacred wish—your heart's desire. It is a Divine promise that yearns to realize its full potential. As the source of infinite energy, it is always seeking a creative outlet.

We are all intended to be a point of expression for God, just as a lamp is a focal point of expression for electricity. Just as God uses a rose as His expression for beauty and fragrance, we are the focal point for our spirit-centered soul. As human beings we are the conduit for God's continuous flow of good, guiding truth and unfailing wisdom. We are designed to experience that flow, or we suffer.

Psychology shows us that an unfulfilled life, depression, and physical illness can be linked to mental suppression. Most of us are walking around with a soul that is dammed up with positive and negative energy aching for release. This produces something I call "quiet sickness." If it remains stopped up undesirable results are inevitable. As long as this situation exists there will be pressure associated with the emotions of sickness, stress, anger, and frustration.

It is possible to spend our entire lives ardently seeking full expression, good health, joy, and prosperity and have little progress. Why? We grasp all these things outside ourselves for a relief, for a solution, when in truth we simply need to go inside and *Release*. In reality, what we need and what we actually do is ironically the reverse of what it appears. We must *Release* from within in order to manifest without. First we *Release* and then we are ready to allow God to express through us.

In the Middle East there are two seas, the Dead Sea and the Sea of Galilee. The Dead Sea is a salty, bitter, and stagnant body of water with no outlets. It has no way of *Release*, no outward flow. There is no plant or animal life in or around the Dead Sea.

Approximately fifty miles north is the Sea of Galilee. This sea is a fresh, flowing, and vibrant body of water with abundant aquatic, vegetative, and wildlife in and around it. It is the repository for many rivers and tributaries and has many outlets. Our spiritual souls need the flow like the Sea of Galilee, or they become like the Dead Sea.

Our calling in life is the voice of God telling us to come to Him and realize the plans He has for us. The Scripture tells us, *"For I know the plans I have for you,"* says the Lord. *"They are plans for good and not disaster, to give you a future and the hope."*

To accomplish the *Release* of our spirit, our authentic self, let's get past our self-created gatekeeper—our individual egoic minds. It is easy to question ourselves and wonder if we are on the right track—most of us do that a lot. The hard part is listening to the heart (our authentic self), where the answer lies.

Suffering can be a habit. Sometimes we get so used to suffering and so identified with it that it becomes a big part of our stories. We identify so well with our stories that we can actually become our story, which is in reality a total lie. Most psychiatrists will admit that their patients only want relief from their symptoms so they can go back to their poor health habits (which help make up their story). Few want to change. A car needs maintenance for trouble-free service, and so does the heart and soul. Just like your body needs nourishment and illumination to be healthy and whole, your soul needs nurturing and the *Release* of toxic thoughts, beliefs, and emotions to be healthy and whole. Having a healthy soul allows you to tap into God as your source instead of trying to solve your challenges on your own with your five-sensory powers, which is just accessing a re-source—not the real thing. Stop thinking of God as though He exists in some faraway place and realize that His presence is always right with you in the present moment.

A good way to find the motivation to seek a healthy soul is to get clear on the benefits. So what are the benefits of a healthy soul? How about the Fountain of Youth with newfound energy, vitality, prosperity, joy, peace, and wisdom? Sound good? Well, it is all there just waiting to get out. A healthy soul is the core of a healthy life, yet sadly so many people never have the experience. We just have to believe it is there. Have faith and dig in a little deeper and uncover the prize!

The Ocean of God

Let's imagine God as a vast, endless ocean of unlimited energy, power, and never-ending love. Since we are all a part of God, where do we fit in this image? Let's use a cup as an illustration and dip it into this Ocean of God and fill the cup. This cup represents you, an individual person and part of God, only smaller and with less power. This is how God expresses through each of us, as an individual outlet.

Now, if you float the cup in the Ocean of God, you remain an individual identity yet you are still connected to the whole. If the cup floats away from God, its source, and winds up alone on the shore of humanness, it loses its Divine connection. Then it becomes like the Dead Sea—stagnant, dried up, and suffering. If the cup stays in the Ocean of God it continues to float and experience the natural ebb and flow and goes along with God's original purpose and intention. It will have some ups and downs, but it will always be connected. When the soul's journey is complete it moves on by sinking back home to its original source where it began with God. What a beautiful reality!

The problem we have as individuals is that we fight the flow. The illusionary ego keeps rowing us toward shore. The unaware and the unconscious buy into the ego's promise of fulfillment on the shore. The shore represents happiness in humanness as a five-sensory being, neglecting our soul. It represents surviving with our own individual egos and the other stagnant egos stranded on the shore with us. These results give us only temporary successes at best and a life of fading hopes, limited promise, and devoid of dreams.

Jump ahead again and envision yourself as an older person. Consider the following questions and imagine how you will answer them in your twilight years:

- Did I discover my purpose?
- Did I make a difference?
- Did I give and receive love?
- Did I *Release* the power that was seeking to manifest itself through this outlet called *"My Life?"*

Who's Your Buddy, Who's Your Pal?

Do you remember the cartoon images from childhood with a devil on one shoulder and an angel on the other? One character is giving you good advice and the other is trying to get you in trouble. That image is actually not too far from reality.

This book and the Valeo Method are about learning how to re-interpret your life experiences. It's about applying new skills and techniques to make an immediate and lasting change.

One thing you have to get clear on is the role of the ego in our lives and how powerful it is. The ego is actually an illusion; however, to the unaware, it is very real. The ego is a master at making us trust and believe it. In fact, it wants you to believe it is your buddy and has your best interests at heart. That is so far from the truth. The ego starts out to help us adapt as children, such as when we first go to school and meet new people. We need our ego at that time. But as we become older children and adolescents the ego strives to help us fit in (no matter what kind of pain it may cause). As our individual personalities develop the ego leaps at the opportunity to establish its identity and dominance.

The ego is the devil in the cartoon and the Real You is the angel. One represents emotions of fear and the other the emotions of love. So if you remember just one thing, always know that your ego is not your friend!

Understanding Negative Self-talk

The ego is very serious about its number-one job, and that is maintaining its identity in your life and keeping you from the truth about your authentic self. The ego is behind all the negative self-talk going on in your head. The ego says awful things to keep your attention and control you. You might think, "Oh, come on—this is crazy! Why would I create something to cause myself pain?" You must always remember that the ego thinks it is helping you. You used your gift from God, free will, and you created this monster. We all do it. But depending on how much control we give it determines our individual quality of life.

This may seem intense or even harsh but how else can
I describe the number–one source of pain and suffering in
your life? This is a serious threat that you must understand in
order to live a happy and fulfilling life. Free will is an awesome
blessing when we understand it is part of our original gift and
authentic power. We can take away the ego's power and create
the life we deserve. The challenge occurs if we don't use our
free will wisely; then we are in for a constant struggle of ups
and downs. Not knowing about the power of the free will and
how to use it is like having a gold mine in your back yard. But
instead of digging for gold and getting rich, you plant carrots.

Chapter 22
Is Your Faith Trapped?

Now faith is being sure of what we hope for and certain of what we do not see.

Hebrews 11:1

The ego also traps your faith. Why? Because faith gives the authentic self power over the ego. The ego strives to keep momentum in its control over your life. Faith is an enemy of the ego that scares it (literally to death). The ego is cunning and manipulative like a dirty politician, a con artist, or a tricky circus barker. It will try anything to keep you from tapping into your authentic self, which is your source of faith. The average person lives their lives so dominated by the ego and their ego-created story with all of its limitations and distractions that they totally miss the message their authentic self is sending them.

We give our egos the tools to work with by buying into all the limiting beliefs that fill up our rule books. Too many limiting beliefs and the toxic emotions they throw off leave little room in our lives for faith. To have great faith is to have great power. When we master our faith, we conquer the ego; we master our destiny.

The illusions of the ego can be so powerful that they create something called blind faith. Blind faith is scary. It involves living life by adopting someone else's negative illusions created by their ego. Co-dependency can be like blind faith and can wreck lives. Co-dependency occurs when someone is so desperate for relief that they depend on the egos of others to survive. Usually a spouse or significant other's ego becomes so powerful that it controls the thoughts and emotions of the other person. Then these people become dependent on the other person's egoic control to function and survive.

An extreme example of blind faith is at the core of gangs and cults and is accelerated with substance abuse. The collective egoic power of group blind faith is very dangerous. This is seen in history through the horrors influenced by the sick egoic minds of people like Adolf Hitler and Jim Jones and his Guyana incident.

People don't start out looking for someone to put negative influences into their lives; it just begins to happen when they give up and surrender to a life of suffering and pain instead of trying to get control. This is called living in an "egoic trance," and it creates a life that is stuck in an endless loop of misery.

Do you know someone who is living a life of misery, stuck in a miserable ego-created story? They complain about how lousy their lives are to everyone who will listen. You hate to even ask them how they are doing because you know they are going to dump a pile of negativity and their problems on you. Yet they keep doing the same thing over and over expecting a different result. Guess who's in charge of that person's life? They will never change until they release themselves from their ego's hold. It has them right where it wants them.

No Wonder We Can't See the Light! Your Precious Diamond

Let's pretend there is a diamond in your chest the size of a grapefruit and this is your source of life. This diamond represents your essence, your soul, and your authentic self. This is your source of life energy and authentic power. This diamond gets its download of energy from the Divine Creator of the universe, which is the source of all light.

How does a jeweler get a beautiful diamond with thousands of facets to show its brilliance? He brings it to the light. But what happens if the diamond is dirty? Our Creator wants to shine His light on us. The problem is that most of us have let our diamonds get so cloudy and dirty they are covered in muck. The light our eternal source of energy and power is trying to give us so we may prosper just can't get through. God is literally trying to show us the light. (What a concept!)

What is blocking the light from your diamond and keeping it from shining? If you never polish the diamond you are guaranteed to live life as a slave to the ego.

To quote Henry David Thoreau, "Most men lead lives of quiet desperation." This means we just accept our circumstances and say, "This is my life, this is just the way it is going to be, this is who I am, and I accept it." However, deep down, we know we don't mean it, but that doesn't matter—the ego has been given the go-ahead and dances its drunken dance of victory. It's no wonder so many people are discouraged and depressed. They are shackled to the ego, they have lost their connection to God, and they are out of the flow.

So it is by our thoughts and beliefs that we dirty our diamonds. We let what I call the grind of life wear us out. We dirty our diamonds when we listen to the negative beliefs of others and when we make judgments and hold them against other people. Most of the time we make these mistakes without even thinking about them or the power these actions give through the egoic mind.

Lester Tenny

This is a story about a brave man who had lots of reasons to have a dirty diamond. I am sharing his story to show you how the power of faith can take control of your thoughts and not yield to the ego.

A prisoner of war, Lester was captured with twelve thousand other Americans in the Philippines during the Korean War. As prisoners of war, they were herded like cattle sixty-eight miles on what became known as the Bataan Death March. More than 90 percent of the soldiers died. Lester was forced to work in a coal mine only three feet high. He was caught trying to escape and was hung by his thumbs for days. Matches were jammed under his fingernails and lit. He watched his comrades trade their one small daily serving of rice for a cigarette. He knew they had given up. His ego kept telling him to give up, to succumb to the pain, and accept death. The only thing that kept him going was a worn, tattered photo of his wife. He had made a promise to her that he would make it home. It had been three years and eight months and he was presumed dead.

He was finally rescued and sent home, but he was in for a big surprise. His wife, since she had not heard from him in so long, had given up on him and married another man. He was devastated at first. Then he was grateful because he realized that the little photo hidden in his boot had given him hope and strength. He was able to fight off his ego and the negative thoughts that came with it. That photo had kept him from giving up; he believed he was going home.

That's not the end of the story. Lester remarried. He went back to school and got his Ph.D. He wrote a book about his experience, and his story has been a testimony of strength and encouragement to many ever since.

The ego can be defeated and conquered, but first you must have an awareness of what the ego is doing. We need a compelling reason to never give in or give up!

Here Comes the Judge

Judgments create the DT's (otherwise known as "drama and trauma") in your life. The ego uses this tool to keep a non-stop flow of judgments going though your mind. Judgments work well for the ego in creating continuing pain and suffering. The ego bases its judgments on the beliefs and opinions stored in our rule books. We are so accustomed to the ego's constant judging that we don't even notice the damage it causes in our lives. Judgment is a habit, and a bad one at that. We judge ourselves and others all day long. Everyone else is judging, too, but they have a different rule book. Can you see where these clashing egos and their judgments provide constant friction, fueling drama and trauma?

Every thought we have and action we take is subject to the judgmental tyranny of the ego. Judgment is the ego's friend; it is its favorite tool to keep us off guard, off balance and on the defense. Judgment keeps us from peace and robs our joy. Judgment affects your perception, which, as we discussed earlier, becomes your reality.

Through judgment, the ego lives and rules by fear. The ego always identifies with and judges external things. For example, appearance and possessions are very important to the ego, whereas peace of mind means nothing.

Jesus said, *"With the same measure that you judge others so shall you be judged."* Judgment causes us to feel bad. Judgment drains away your power. Studies show that people are in a negative state of mind two-thirds of the time. Look at the people around you. Chances are very likely that only one has positive thoughts. Because we tend to assume that others are experiencing similar feelings, we tend to attract their pain into our lives, adding to our own drama and trauma. So how do we avoid and correct this situation?

Chapter 23
The Thinking Process

Did you ever stop to think and forget to start again?

Winnie the Pooh

One way to take the destructive power of our judgments away from the ego is to understand the thinking process. All day long we are constantly evaluating what is happening in our reality. We ask these questions over and over: "What does this mean?" and "What should I do?" The next action is usually a judgment from the ego, and that is how we move forward. To break the momentum of judgment and take control away from the ego, we need to pay attention to our thinking. It takes a little practice but the results are quick and amazing.

When you have a thought like, "I am not ever going to be successful," the first thing you ask yourself is, "Is this thought based on fact or judgment?" If you don't have any facts to back up the thought, it is a judgment, so immediately you'll know that the ego is trying to interfere. Tell yourself, "This thought is not justified and I don't accept it." This may seem like a lot to think about at first, but it gets easier. It is a powerful way to take control away from the ego.

Removing Disempowering Thoughts

We do have a choice: we can live with the constant push, pull, and bullying of our egos or we can direct our attention where we can live the lives we desire. We do this by learning to recognize the ego's methods of operation, like we just did by asking ourselves if our thoughts were based on judgment or fact. Most people just try to deal with what their ego throws at them. That can be like trying to hold on while riding a runaway roller coaster, which creates constant challenges. These challenges don't just affect you, but they spill over on to the other people in your intimate circle. Oh, yes, the ego doesn't just affect you—it throws negativity on everyone around you and everyone with whom you communicate and share your life.

Are You Trapped in Your Frame of Mind?

In the *Discovery* step, we used an illustration (Page 93) that shows the spirit as a star in the sky with billions of other stars and the soul as an aura that surrounds it. In addition, we used a frame as an illustration as to how the ego sets up residence and traps our toxic, negative thoughts and energy. This imaginary frame surrounds and traps your spirit and your soul, and it is where all of your problems, unrest, drama and the seeming trauma live.

The ego tries to keep us in the egoic frame and living in an unfulfilling life. Inside the frame is the ego's haven. This is how the ego keeps you away from your power, your source of light, which is outside the frame. Every time you try to release yourself from the clutches of the false self and connect to your true source of power, the ego stands ready to leap into action. The ego just wants to make us focus on how great, safe, and beautiful the frame is (temporary success), and the more we play along the bigger and thicker the frame gets. The ego puts beautiful, ornate, but imaginary jewels on it (promises of fulfillment by listening to the ego) and makes it look tempting. These jewels are all the material things and temporary fixes the ego makes us believe can make us happy, but never do. The ego wants us to ignore our inner self and our true purpose, our calling. Why? Because if the truth is out, the ego's control and existence is threatened.

You must always remember that the ego is your adversary to peace and happiness. The ego is cunning and will constantly tease and confuse you with temporary success and fleeting happiness. Then, as soon as you reach a goal or a certain level, the ego reacts and challenges you with thoughts like, "Is this all there is? Is this the best you can do? I'm not impressed." Then it gives you thoughts like, "So what, now what are you going to do next?" No matter how great the achievement, the ego never gets enough. This is contrary to the authentic self which rejoices in every step of the journey, not just the victories.

It may be hard to accept a part of you that you actually created, an illusion of who you are, that can make you a puppet in your own life. The ego strives to keep you focused on the ghosts of your past, like your failures, disappointments, and missed and wasted opportunities. At the same time, it keeps us in fear of the future. The ego is never happy in the present moment.

The ego also uses states of selfishness and self-centeredness as crutches to keep us distracted and as a substitute for an unfulfilled life. The ego loves to use crutches that create temporary relief, like alcohol, drugs, food, and sex, and there is never enough to satisfy the ego. Some people literally break down and become mentally ill and even commit suicide while trying to release the ego's hold on their lives.

Be an Observer

Studies show the average person has around 60,000 thoughts per day. Ninety percent are repeated from the day before and are trivial and insignificant. This is the ego's playground, and it is full of confusion with few boundaries. Can you see how the ego can keep us busy and distracted, trying to figure out so many thoughts?

We can compare our minds to our computer. What happens when we pull up too many programs and leave them running in the background? It slows down the processes in the computer, right? This in turn causes the main program we are trying to use to slow down and even lock up, or worse, the whole computer could crash. Our mind works the same way. The ego tries to keep as many programs running as it can to keep our minds distracted. When we shut down the programs running in the background on our computer, it runs more efficiently and we get our tasks done more efficiently and quickly. That is what the Release step and the next step, Embrace, will do for us. We will learn not only why we have these challenges with our thoughts, beliefs, and emotions but also how to shut down those that are unnecessary and cause pain in our lives.

One of the key things you must do to get a hold on the ego is learn to observe what it is doing. We have to watch the ego like a cat watches a mouse hole. We must become and practice being an observer, always looking for the real person behind our thoughts. We have to be like a referee in a game. What would happen in an NBA game if the referee was there but never called a foul or penalty? That is what happens when we lose control of the ego. When we don't pay attention and let the ego run wild, we only partially experience life. We miss out on the good parts.

We have to learn to call time-out on the ego. We have to get to the point where we say, "Hold on a minute here!" When you start to become an observer and stop accepting things that don't feel right, you begin to understand why things are happening the way they are. The egoic frame begins to shrink. The ego loses power. The truth comes out.

The Wizard of Oz

Most everyone has seen the movie *The Wizard of Oz*, the story of a little girl named Dorothy's dream. In the dream she becomes lost and tries to find her way back home to Kansas. She discovers she must go to a place called Oz to get help getting home. She makes some friends along her way who need help themselves, and they join up with her to go see the mighty Wizard of Oz, who they believe can help them all. After an exhausting and dangerous journey, Dorothy and her friends make it to the Wizard's palace only to find a not-so-friendly (in fact, scary and intimidating) wizard. Then Dorothy is shocked to discover that the wizard is a fraud. He's just a shy, nervous old man hiding behind a curtain using smoke and mirrors to create an illusion. He was not even going to help her until she found out the truth. So when she challenged him, he gave her what she wanted.

Sound familiar? The ego distracts us the same way. It can seem so real; it controls and intimidates us the same way. In reality it's all smoke and mirrors, it is just like the illusion of the Wizard of Oz.

The ego is a master at sucking us in with tastes of temporary happiness to keep us off guard. Things like new clothes, jewelry, vacations, and cars are great, but you have to pay attention to how the ego uses things as a way to control our thoughts and keep us out of present moment thinking. Prolonged happiness is not easy to come by with an active egoic mind. We just have to be aware of the ego's handiwork and don't confuse it with true happiness. The ego also causes us to look over the little things in life and take them for granted. This is dangerous because one day we can wake up and realize that what is really important is different than we originally thought.

Chapter 24
The Real You Loves You

Make the most of yourself because that is all there is of you.

Ralph Waldo Emerson

The Real You, your authentic self, your Divine source, is the opposite of the ego—it loves you! This authentic self doesn't operate like the ego. It handles life with ease, patience, and grace. The highs and lows are replaced with the more even flow of life. Instead of feeling like a salmon swimming up-stream, you learn to accept the flow and roll with the good the authentic self brings you.

The authentic self sends us signals when something doesn't feel right. It tugs at the heart. This is our Divine connection communicating with us. Unfortunately, many times these calls of the heart are ignored. The ego uses its control to ruin our plans, interfere with us, and stop our progress toward good. As you become more familiar with the Valeo Method and how to recognize these intuitive promptings, they will become harder to ignore. In fact, you will even be able to remember past intuitive feelings that you did not act upon, which will help you avoid future mistakes.

Sometimes it takes a lot of suffering caused by the ego before we find the motivation to change. Sometimes the ego just flat-out wins. It's really sad when a person spends an entire life in an egoic trance and never sees the light. They die wondering. This is why we have to take control of the ego now and begin to put an end to unnecessary suffering and pain. It's never too late to stake your claim and gain control over the ego and the unnecessary pain it creates.

Why Am I Being so Hard on Myself?

The ego can be ruthless and cruel. Can you remember a time when you used nasty, negative self-talk? That was the ego in full force. The ego can talk to you like an angry, scolding parent or worse, a full-on enemy. It loves to grab control when you are beaten up and confused and seem to be running out of options. The ego thrives during times of trouble and uncertainty.

The ego uses criticism as one of its favorite tools of control. In fact, it can be brutally unkind. By belittling you, the ego keeps you away from your authentic self. The ego leaves you humbled, humiliated, and trying to justify to yourself as to why you are worthy of good in your life. Does this sound kind of sick and crazy? Guess what? It is. It is also the truth about how the ego works and how, if we allow it to, it will affect our lives.

The ego uses "I" thoughts and self-talk to stay in control. Pay attention to all your thoughts and internal dialogues that start with "I" for the next few days. Most people are surprised how much time they stay on auto-pilot with the ego in control. This is another way to practice awareness and loosen the ego's hold. Watch the "I" thoughts.

Learn to Talk to Your Ego

Another way to stifle the ego is to talk to it. I know it may seem a little weird at first, but so is all the craziness the ego puts us through, right? There comes a time when you have to take control of negative internal dialogue or you are going to make little or no progress. In fact, it is good to get to the point where you can carry on a real conversation with your ego. When you catch yourself feeling frustrated and confused or stressed out and worried, your ego is on a rampage, beating you up and judging every thought you have and every person in sight. This gives you an option. You can keep letting it go on, or you can confront your egoic mind head-on. That's right; just stop your thoughts and say, "I know what you're doing. I am calling you out!" Tell your ego, "I'm not getting sucked in any more. Just go away; I'm not listening. You aren't real!" I know it may feel weird at first, but just give it a try and you will be amazed how this works. I get aggressive with my ego and the egos of my clients and seminar attendees when they ask for help. I tell the ego, "I arrest you! You are unauthorized here and you have to leave now. Go sit in your corner! Your antics are not acceptable anymore!" Don't judge this process (that's your ego again!) until you try it. Haven't you heard that all super-intelligent people talk to themselves?

We have to be willing to step aside from what is going on right in front of us and become that observer. This way, you'll begin to see where all the drama and trauma is coming from. The ego keeps us in such a hurry and confused state through-out our lives, we don't see its trickery and sleight of hand.

Sometimes we have to slow down to go fast. Sometimes we have to be less so we can become more. We have to get our-selves to the point where we are sick of suffering and missing out. Isn't it time to say, "Enough is enough, this is not working for me. I'm ready to be set free." When you release the ego's hold on you, then you will realize your authentic power, which comes from your connection to God, your original source of life. It's really not that hard to overcome the ego. It's just a matter of clearly understanding what it is trying to do and being prepared to constantly confront it until it no longer has power over you.

The Part of You That Can't Love

Because the ego is totally based in fear, all its power comes from its manipulation of fear and fear's partners, doubt and worry. The ego can never give you what you want. It doesn't know how, and it never will. Your joy, future hope, peace, and fulfillment are based in love. The ego has nothing to do with love.

Even what you think you want or need can be the work of the ego. Just remember, when your life is out of control, when it is a constant battle or things appear to be hopeless, the ego is in full force. When you are using crutches like drugs, alcohol, food, sex, television, or even exercise to take your mind off your reality, rest assured that your ego has a hold on you.

Then, when you get overwhelmed enough, you just take whatever the ego dishes out. You become a victim of your own circumstances. When you begin to recognize and observe what the ego is doing, you can slow down its momentum.

Just as a speeding train is hard to stop, a stationary, multi-ton train can be kept immovable by a block of wood the size of a cracker box. The cracker box represents a little bit of faith in the authentic self and its ability to control a massive ego. The more you observe and get to know the ego, the more you can learn how to make it loosen its grip. Even a little bit of faith is too much for the ego to handle.

In Sanskrit, the word "Maya" means "cosmic delusion." The delusion is the ego's voice, tirelessly working to dominate the mind. The person we are born to be and our peace and joy are somewhere hidden behind those thoughts. The more we quiet the maya, the more the authentic self shines through.

Chapter 25
Catch and Release

Stand up to your obstacles and do something about them.
You will find they haven't half the strength you think they nave.

Dr. Norman Vincent Peale

One of the most powerful parts of the teachings we use in the Valeo Method is called Catch and Release. After you become an observer of the ego and understand the truth of its identity and how its motives are exposed, this is how you can dissolve its power.

Have you ever caught a fish and then released it? That is the concept here; to stop the voices of the ego and negative internal dialogue we all have. This is a very simple yet profoundly effective process. From now on, anytime you are having negative, worrisome and distracting thoughts, just use Catch and Release.

First, in order for the process to work, you have to know what you want to get rid of and believe that it is *possible* to let go of it. Then, you must be *willing* to let it go, and finally, you have to be *ready* to let it go. You might say, "Why wouldn't someone want to let go of feelings, emotions, and beliefs that are causing them pain?" It does seem logical that they would, but many times these are the very things they identify with and that make up their story, so without them they can actually feel uncomfortable. Think about it: Don't you know people who love to talk about their problems all the time? These people many times receive compassion and attention (comfort) from others this way, and they are so caught up in their story they don't know who they are without it. I know it sounds crazy, and it is, but that is just how powerful this force is working inside us and how effective it is at using our stories to control us.

Consider these questions: Does your current financial situation have an effect on how you feel? Do relationships have an effect on how you feel? Does your job or career have an effect on how you feel? Do your friends have an effect on how you feel? Yes, of course, you say. All of them effect the way I feel. But the real answer is no—none of these things have an effect on how you feel. *You* have an effect on how you feel. In other words, your false self, which is driven by your egoic mind, or your authentic self, driven by truth, controls how you feel—it is your choice. None of these things can *make* you feel any certain way unless you give them permission!

To set ourselves up to *Release*, first we ask these three questions:

1.   Is it *possible* for me to release these feelings of worry, stress, doubt, or fear of any kind? (It could be jealousy, lack of forgiveness, envy, or even hate. The key here is that we can release any feeling, thought, or emotion that is not desired or is limiting our lives. Ask yourself and be congruent in your answer.)
       Is it possible to Release?

2.   Am I *willing* to release these feelings, emotions, or beliefs that are binding me? (Remember, some people don't want to let go, even though they may say they do.)

3.   Am I *ready* to release them now and not wait any longer? (The longer we wait, the harder it gets.)

Let's say your internal dialogue is, "I am so stupid I will never get it together," or "What is wrong with me? Why do I always blow it and miss out?" When a thought like this pops up we should immediately realize it is the ego in action. Next we accept the feeling, acknowledge it, experience it, and notice where it is coming from and then get ready to let it go. Now, we will use our imagination and visualize ourselves throwing these negative thoughts and feelings into a garbage can and slamming the lid on them. This garbage can is attached with strings to a big, yellow helium balloon. Then we will watch these words and thoughts float away into the clouds and out of our sight forever. By catching these thoughts, throwing them in the garbage can, and then floating them away, we are creating a mental anchor of *Release*. We literally watch the pain of the words and thoughts disappear. Does it sound too simple? I challenge you to not underestimate his process; the results are astounding. Try it for just one day and you will be amazed with the results (that is, the Real You will be happy). But be prepared because the ego is persistent and relentless—it may keep bringing up the same thoughts again and again, especially if they have been conditioned in your mind for a long time. Release again and again until the disempowering thought is gone. Finally, the ego will give up and a new, conditioned response (from your playbook) can be installed.

So let's practice again. Every time a negative thought pops into your mind, just repeat the process. Ask the three questions: "Is it possible to let this thought, feeling, belief, or emotion go? Am I willing to let it go? Am I ready to let it go now?" If the answer to all three questions is "Without a doubt, yes!" then move on to the next step.

Pick up a pen, pencil or any small object and hold it tightly in the palm of your hand. Is this object a part of you? Can you let it go if you want to? Of course you can. Now, after holding the object for a few minutes, turn your palm upside down and release the object and let it fall. We hold on to our emotions in the same way. We can let them go any time we want—we just don't allow ourselves to do it.

Here is a simple exercise that proves it. Have you ever noticed how a small child trying to walk falls down and then looks around to see if anyone was watching so he will know whether to cry or not? If someone is looking, then the baby cries; if not, it is no big deal. But if someone is looking, a simple kiss will make it all better, and immediately the emotions are released. This illustrates that we all know how to release thoughts and emotions that are disempowering to us. The fact is, we just don't do it, and by now you should know why—the ego keeps us from it. We get conditioned to hold on to and savor lots of emotions; some are good for us, but many are not. There have been countless incredible success stories from our seminar attendees and my coaching clients who have used the Catch and Release strategy to literally change their lives.

The process is just one part of the Valeo Method, but it is very effective at diffusing and eliminating what keeps many of us stuck and confused. Using this process can also head off potential problems or misunderstandings before they get out of hand. It's also a great strategy to use with and teach to children.

Chapter 26
Ego and Emotion

To approach the stranger is to invite the unexpected,
release a new force, let the genie out of the bottle.
It is to start a new train of events that is beyond your control.

T. S. Elliot

If we take a small coin and hold it up to the sun at just the right angle it can block the sun. But in reality the size of the coin is nothing compared to the sun. This is an example of how small the ego is when compared to the authentic self and the connection we have to God, our Creator.

How could the ego, something so small in perspective, trick us into thinking it has so much power? One of the tricks it uses is playing with our emotions.

Emotions are the body's response to thought. Emotions are the language of the soul. In fact, the sum of the emotions equals the reality of the soul. This reality is our personality, dominated by the ego or the spirit—whichever has the most control in the soul. Emotions are the responses within your body that affect your nervous system, which affects your physical well being, and they are all very real. So think about it for a moment: something unreal (the ego) and the beliefs it operates with creates a real response in each of our lives.

It is important we understand our emotions and how they work because otherwise we cannot distinguish what is real and what is illusionary. If we don't clearly recognize our emotional responses we cannot listen to them or perceive the lie or truth behind them. In addition, we can't fully share in the joy of others or show compassion for them until we know how to experience our own.

Emotions are energy in motion. The goal is to learn to recognize where our emotions are coming from and what triggers them. This will lead us to an awareness of why we have certain feelings and responses, which is key to controlling them.

The first law of motion says, "A body in uniform motion will remain in motion until acted on by force." Our emotions, especially the negative ones, are a powerful force in our lives. The ego uses emotions to create confusion and uncertainty, which gives it a perfect working environment. Out of control emotions can put us on a collision course for trouble in our lives. The solution is simple—control the ego, control the emotions, and control our lives. This means living with awareness and clarity of our emotions and living consciously instead of unconsciously.

Positive and Negative Emotional Charges

If we go to the illustration we can understand positive and negative emotions more clearly. We see the spirit surrounded by the soul, represented by a container shaped like a dough-nut, which holds our emotions. Then we see a thick frame that surrounds the soul. This represents the ego's control and the container for our individual stories. This is where emotions of fear, triggered by the ego, are mixed with the emotions of love, which come from the spirit. This energy dynamic and interaction of emotions is what fuels our individual stories. The more negative emotions we have, the more toxic our emotional charge becomes inside the frame (of mind). At the same time, a positive emotional charge is built from our positive thoughts and experiences. We can think of the negative charge as that which inhibits the soul's natural evolvement and the positive charge as that which pushes and encourages it.

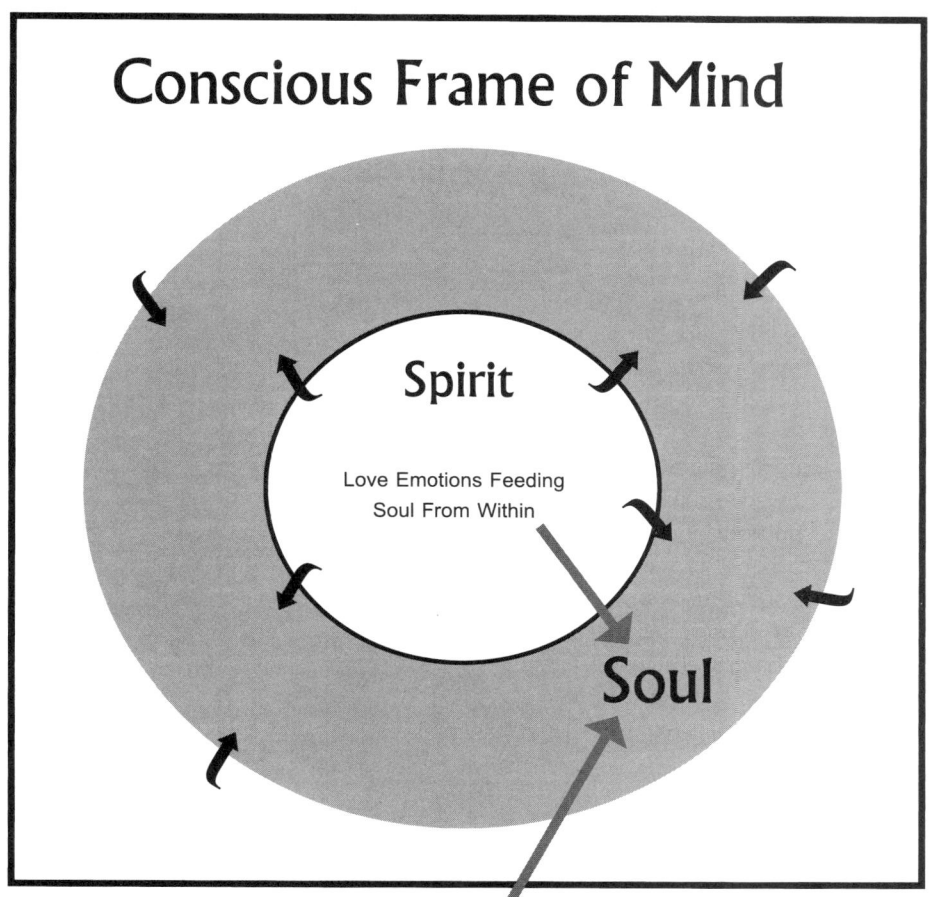

Conscious Frame of Mind

Spirit

Love Emotions Feeding
Soul From Within

Soul

Fear Emotions Feeding
Soul From Outside

Love Emotions Are Within The Spirit.

Fear Emotions Are Trapped In Your Conscious.

Most people have stronger negative emotional charges than positive emotional charges. If not released, the negative emotional charge can become like a loose, high-voltage electrical wire ready to spew at any moment at anyone who comes near or at any situation that occurs. The charge can be so strong that it smothers the love emotions, such as inspiration and the creative urges and desires associated with our positive emotional charges. In other words, it inhibits the positive momentum in our lives.

Think of negative and positive charges in relation to a computer. When you use your computer to connect to the Internet you get access to a world of unlimited information. Some is good and helpful, and some can be harmful. Many times we pick up viruses and problems in our computers sent out purposely by other people. Our computers get infected, plugged up, and can lose performance or even crash.

Our souls work the same way. If we don't clean up, defrag, clear our cookies, and empty our old files, our computers break down, and the soul is no different.

The negative and positive emotions in our souls carry frequencies. Every thought we have is charged with energy. Negative thoughts carry a slower vibrating frequency, and positive thoughts carry faster frequencies. The Law of Attraction states that like attracts like. Because the ego thrives on negative energy, it attracts those frequencies to fuel its power. This is the reason the ego is attracted to other people's misery and negative emotions. In fact, it even stirs up misery in others and feeds off of it! So goes the old saying, "misery loves company."

This is why some people love their misery and live in a pity-party life. They try to invite all the other miserable souls they can find to the party because they feed off each other's negative charges. The negative emotional charge absorbs the energy from the thoughts of others. A negative attitude is somewhat self-perpetuating and serves the ego well. Every negative thought charges the ego and creates more negative thoughts. This process has a debilitating and exhausting effect on the body, as well. It breaks it down, weakening its resistance, which makes it easy prey for disease, emotional distress, and total breakdown.

When a person uses drugs or alcohol they are only numbing and masking their pain and suffering, which can eventually implode or explode. Some people can do a great job of hiding their pain for a while; sometimes for a long time. But sooner or later, if this negative emotional charge is not neutralized, discharged, and released intentionally, by the person's own volition, it will come out on its own.

Starve the Negative Charge

So far in the *Release* step we have learned that the ego is the false self and the enemy of your happiness. We learned that by changing our negative limiting beliefs and rules we can take away some of the ego's power. We have learned to be an observer—a watcher of the ego, and catch it in the act of creating pain. We have learned how to use Catch and Release to get rid of disempowering negative thoughts and emotions.

Now let's look at the environment and conditions that support the ego. The ego obviously thrives on misery, mishaps, and suffering—ours and others.

The media is a powerful source of destructive energy directed at a society of egos and the collective consciousness of those egos which seek that energy. The ego is on the prowl like a hungry lion looking for another animal to devour. The constant flow of violence, pain, and bad news in the media feeds and fuels its appetite. The most popular shows are loaded with negative energy, which feeds the insatiable appetite of the ego.   The most popular shows are about crime, pain, and murder. The average child witnesses more than twelve thousand murders on television by age thirteen. The average child sees a million commercials to influence his or her habits before age eighteen.

The tabloids, soap operas, and weekly drama shows are packed with one story after another of bad luck, misery, cheating, and misfortune. Broken relationships, betrayal, health problems, and murder are always in the newspaper headlines.

How much *good* news do we actually ever see or hear from the media?

So what can we do about it? We can change our daily routine and stay away from it. The late J. Paul Meyer, one of the top motivation experts in the past fifty years, tells a story about an experience he had in the early sixties, during tough recessionary times when sales were way down in his eight-hundred-person insurance sales organization.

Paul brought his sales team together and they agreed to avoid television, radio, and newspapers for thirty days. They also agreed to avoid talking about anything negative concerning current times to anyone. After thirty days something amazing happened—the organization's sales went up more than 50 percent!

We create much of our own misery by the environment we are in and what we read, listen to, and watch. For things to change, we have to be willing to make some changes, and this is not always easy. If you stop feeding the ego it has to loosen its hold, allowing you to get stronger so you can break free.

Who is Influencing Whom?

The ego also gets energy from feeding off the negative charges of others. Remember, like attracts like. The ego seeks out other people's misery and causes us to feel comfort in being around those types of energy frequencies, which are slower-moving, dark energies.

For example, when people try to conquer addictions and destructive habits they are recommended to avoid people and places that create a potential atmosphere for relapse. Anytime you are seeking to move up in your life's journey, you should heed the same advice.

Earlier, we used the example of rating ourselves on a scale of one to ten, with one being the least and ten being the best. We can use this same idea to rank the people we spend time with. It works like this: Let's say you spend most of your time among five other people. Then, let's assume you rank yourself as a seven, but you rank all your colleagues a six. Five times six is thirty; then, divide by five, and you get six. That means you think you are a seven on a scale of one to ten, when in reality you are a six. In other words, the five people closest to you are dragging you down.

The same works in reverse. If you replace those five people with others who you would rank a nine, you raise yourself to a higher frequency and higher energies, and you will receive positive results.

It's not easy to change your circle of friends, the places you frequent, or your environment. Change does not occur when you continue your bad habits, which act like a magnet, pulling you back. Guess who is behind the power of the magnet? The ego is constantly working to keep you in your darker, low-energy thoughts; this way, it keeps control. It wants you to hang out around misery.

After going through the Valeo Method training, one of my clients said he couldn't even stand to wear his old clothes because he associated them with his old partying and self-destructive lifestyle. This is common as people break free of the heavy, negative gravity of the ego. They recognize the weight of the pain and they want to avoid anything, any place, or anyone associated with it. Once again, it goes back to awareness, clarity, and living consciously instead of unconsciously. You learn to not just be an observer of the ego, but a *conqueror* of the ego because you know where it gets its power and how to disarm it.

Chapter 27
Transitional Language

Words without thoughts never to heaven go.

William Shakespeare

So far, you have learned how toxic thoughts, beliefs, and emotions hold us hostage and keep us away from our purpose and original intent. Now let's look at the most powerful tools of the ego: words, communication, and self-talk. It boils down to this: The quality of your life is equal to the quality of your communication—not just with others, but with yourself, as well.

I developed the concept of Transitional Language to teach others to learn how to gradually and consistently shift away from disempowering words and negative self-talk. In other words, we need to learn to transition to a language and vocabulary that is in alignment with our dreams and goals in life. The words you use have a profound effect on how you conduct yourself, and your words also affects others' lives around you. Nothing we have addressed so far can be put into practice without getting a handle on your language and self-talk. This is a huge step in making lasting change.

The ego emerges early in your life and uses your growing vocabulary as a tool to shape your life. The ego uses your
language like chess pieces to put you right where it wants you,
in check, away from your authentic self and the truth about
your potential.

The ego uses words and self-talk to generate thoughts
which keep our attention, and this continues until we become so conditioned to our language that we operate like the
proverbial gerbil on a wheel. In fact, unconsciously, we repeat
the same words and self-talk over and over so often that we
make the ego's job easy. In the Bible it tells us, *"With your
tongue you can bless or curse your life."* Most of us know God
can bless or curse our lives, but wait a minute—it says you can
either bless or curse. This is how powerful words can be! This
is why you must pay constant attention to any words or self-
talk you use that cause you pain or hold you back from your
purpose.

When God told Jeremiah he had chosen him to be a
prophet to nations, he was young and lacked self-confidence.
Jeremiah told God, *"I can't speak for you, I'm too young."*
God told him not to use those words. So Jeremiah changed
the words he was using and became a courageous spokesper-
son. Your words can and will create or destroy your individual
experience.

Through our gift of free will we get to choose the words we
use. We can be limited by the negative words of the ego, or we
can be empowered by words of strength and courage associated with the authentic self. Words of faith, love, positive belief,
and humility carry Divine power.

Chapter 28
The Power of Words

Every spoken word arouses our self-will.
Johann Wolfgang von Goethe

Our words are meant to guide and support us—that is, if you use the right words. The ego chooses words based in and linked to fear, doubt, and worry. These types of words easily create confusion and uncertainty, and the ego loves it because it gains control.

How much can one word affect your life? Studies show that by the age of eighteen you have been told "no" more than 150,000 times. Needless to say, that's one word we're all quite familiar with and due to this it has a major influence on our lives. It's good to be told no in many situations. However, too many no's can have an adverse effect, such as feelings of rejection, timidity, or lack of self-confidence. How many times in your life have you been told yes and felt encouraged compared to how many times you have been told no? Your environment can beat you down and create negative thoughts and energies. This is fertile ground for the development of negative beliefs. If a child is told he is bad ("bad boy!") enough times in his first few years, he will start to believe it, and he will develop feelings of unworthiness and inferiority that will become programmed deep in his subconscious mind. We need to understand and pay attention to these things, particularly around children, because words like those, using this example, will manifest in his adult life as shame, poor self-esteem, and worst of all, guilt.

Isn't it ironic that we spend the first few years of our lives being told to stand up and speak, and then we spend the next eighteen or so years being told to sit down and shut up? It is funny when we look at it this way, but the sad part is this is exactly how we lose our youthful exuberance and spontaneity as we go through adult life. We lose that very nature that could keep the ego out of control and steer us toward our dreams.

One recent study reveals that 77 percent of what the average person thinks is negative. These negative thoughts get trapped in the frame of our stories and create pressure in our minds and bodies. Then they affect our language and how we communicate our intentions. Additional studies show that three-fourths of all illnesses are self-induced. The language we use to describe our situation either supports us or corrupts the outcomes of our mental, emotional, and physical reality. We can literally talk ourselves into being sick.

Habits of Self-Talk

Habits are simple repetitions of your own thoughts. Your thoughts themselves can become painful habits, supported with negative self-talk and vocabulary. Usually these habits did not get there overnight, so it can take some time and effort to undo them and reverse their effects.

When you hear something over and over in your mind (internal dialogue), you get conditioned to it; you tend to accept it, even if it is a lie. This is just another way the ego gains dominance—through repetition, it wears you down.

We become what we believe, think, and talk to ourselves about. As long as we never change these three things, we never change our lives. Just think of one of those old vinyl record recordings. If there was even a tiny scratch on it that sound just kept on repeating itself and we could not get rid of it. Our minds get deeply etched with self-talk and vocabulary exactly the same way. We use our conditional language to communicate with others and project an image of who we are as individuals. This is an obvious statement, but what is not so obvious to many is how their words affect others around them and the powerful impression they leave behind. Size and elo-quence of vocabulary means little in this context. The energies behind the words are what matter.

We must be very careful with labeling, as in labeling our-selves based on our circumstances or how we feel. Saying things like, "I am such a loser" or "I am so stupid when it comes to fill in the blank." We actually drag ourselves deeper into these places and situations when we label ourselves with these words. The ego does not have a sense of humor, and neither does the subconscious mind, where your thoughts are stored. What we think about, focus on, and how we label our-selves will come about, and many times it is not what we would hope for.

We also want to be careful how we label other people. Labeling others can backfire on us. Even joking around with a child and calling them a "goofball" or "silly" or a "nutcase" in jest can get buried in the subconscious of that individual and used by the ego later in negative ways.

Words: The Long-Term Effect

Here are some examples of the long-term effects that carelessly used words and language have had on people's lives: A busy working single mother came home from a hard day's work with a headache. She was tired and stressed, and all she wanted was peace and quiet. Her eight-year-old daughter was running through the house, bursting with energy and sing-ing her heart out. After a while the mother lost patience. As the daughter was bouncing about, her mother snapped at her and screamed, "Stop that dreaded singing. You have an awful voice!"

The mother's reaction, fueled with emotion-packed words, burned an indelible impression in the young girl's developing mind. She believed her mother's words. From that moment on, she never sang again—not even when she was by herself. She believed she had an awful voice and was embarrassed by it. She thought she would annoy anyone who heard her sing. She was afraid of being insulted by others and embarrassed or humiliated.

The story is bad enough if it stopped here, but there is more. The girl grew up shy and introverted. She was horrified when she was asked to answer questions in class or speak in front of a group of even a few people. She avoided being involved in groups, meetings, and organizations. One experience with harsh words from her mother dramatically affected her entire life. The little girl believed her voice was something bad, and it kept her from feeling and receiving emotions of love.

This situation not only happens to children—it happens to adults, as well. This is the true story of my thirty-four year old client, Larry. Larry had a hobby of singing karaoke. He played the guitar and would practice songs at home so he could meet his friends at a local pub and sing on Thursday evenings. One particular night Larry got up and sang a song he had been practicing. He sang his heart out. After he finished, an acquaintance of his came over to Larry who smiled at him, anticipating a compliment. Instead, the friend said, "That was an awful job of singing. You ought to be embarrassed. You should never try karaoke again. In fact, the last time you were here with a date, I looked at her while you were singing and she just rolled her eyes at me."

Larry was devastated. He had received many compliments on his singing before but none of that mattered then. He loved to sing, and it made him feel good about himself. But soon he stopped going to sing on Thursday nights. He rarely even picked up his guitar and sang at home. The pain of those harsh words had torn him apart. Would that "friend" have done the same thing if he knew the pain he had caused Larry? Would the mother of the little girl have changed her words if she knew the pain she would inflict on her child? Most people would change what they said, but many times they never realize they hurt someone's feelings and the damage they caused.

One six-year-old boy named Michael loved to visit his elderly neighbor. They enjoyed interesting afternoon chats together. The neighbor stopped by Michael's house one day to visit. He did not know that Michael was listening in a nearby room. The neighbor told Michael's mother that he felt that Michael was a gifted and creative child and would someday do great things. Michael grew up remembering those words. Years later, Michael Vance became the Dean of Walt Disney University and was considered one of the most creative people of his time. Oh, what a difference a word makes, and how damaging a careless remark or inconsiderate opinion can be!

These are common stories. Can you remember similar occurrences in your life that profoundly affected you? How have your thoughtless or thoughtful words affected others?

Shhh... The Children Are Listening

Parents are always shocked when their child first speaks a bad word. Usually it is well-spoken, with correct pronunciation and voice inflection. We have all been deeply affected by the language we heard growing up. If you had a parent or parents who used bad language toward you, you were affected by it. If you had a parent who tended to look at a glass of water as half-empty instead of half-full, you might take up a pessimistic choice of words to describe your experiences. If you had a parent who used a half-full glass attitude in the same example, you would probably use words that would affect you in a different and more positive way. The words our parents used to describe things have a huge influence on the vocabulary we use as adults.

Consider the consequences when people use negative language. A parent says to a child, "What is wrong with you? Can't you get anything right? How could you be so stupid?" When an unaware or poor-thinking parent makes these types of comments, they are etching their words deep into the psyche of their child. Were you affected by the harsh words of others, even many years later?

In the early development of the mind, the child is not prepared to distinguish between a verbal jab and an intentional statement. The person receiving the verbal abuse, which could even be influenced by alcohol or drugs, just logs them away to be potentially converted to beliefs that can seem very real in the future. This is one of the ways painful childhood wounding occurs, a subject we will cover in more depth in the next section.

An important part of *Release* is letting go of words and language that hold us back. We must become acutely sensitive to how our language affects our daily lives.

Clean It Up

We discussed the powerful concept of pain and pleasure as a motivating factor in making change. If your language is holding you back, draining your power, and keeping you from unleashing your full potential, isn't it time to release the words that don't serve you well and use Transitional Language to replace them with empowering words?

We have also discussed the concept of modeling the success of others in order to duplicate their results. How do successful people talk? Honestly, do they curse and use foul and negative language as a general rule? How does it feel when someone you respect goes off on a tirade of negative talk? Does it energize you or take energy away from you? Do you feel uplifted by that person or let down?

Our language is our verbal signature. If we spew bad language, negative statements, and judgments, we are giving up our personal power and losing our ability to get what we want and influence people.

When you God D_ _ N something, you are asking God to damn this person, event, or circumstance. Do you really want to go that far, going around damning and cursing people, events, and situations? Can anything positive come from it? Does it ever cause a person to feel better? Does it create credibility or give you authentic power over anything? Does it really serve any good at all?

What is even worse is the habit of using these words uncon-sciously and not even thinking about what you are doing. That is akin to a drunken sailor on a battleship, just launching missiles with no regard to who is getting hit. Using profanity just doesn't work for a person who is trying to tap into their true, authentic power.

When I was younger (not that I'm old now) I cursed quite a bit of the time, especially when I was around my male friends. It seemed like the cool thing to do. Then one day I met a man who became a dear friend to me. He was someone I looked up to and wanted to be like in many ways. He was different; he had more success than I or any of my other friends did at the time. What stuck in my mind the most, though, was that he never used bad or negative language, ever, no matter what the circumstances. I found myself dropping my bad language around him. One day I told him how I noticed he never said anything bad or negative. He said, "I always strive to get ahead and set a good example. There is a lot of competition in the world. I need every edge and advantage I can get." This man didn't even know it, but he caused me to clean up my language. I noticed over the next few months how much bad language my friends were using around me, and it made me feel uncomfortable. I didn't get all self-righteous, but I told them I was striving to model successful people and that the people I looked up to used positive language. When I told them why I changed, I felt like my decision gained their respect and made a difference in their thinking about their own language.

Dr. Don Miguel Ruiz, in his book, *The Four Agreements,* writes, "Just imagine what you can create with the impeccabil-ity of the word. With the impeccability of the word, you *can* transcend the dream of fear and live a different life. You can live in Heaven in the middle of hell." You can live your dreams in heaven on earth, fulfilling your purpose with the power of your words.

So be encouraged, and the next time you start to God D _ _ N someone, how about trying something for me—"God Bless" them instead. When Jesus sent out his disciples, He told them to give out blessings to the houses they entered. He also told them if the people in the house didn't except the blessing, to let it return to them. So I look at it this way: If I give my blessing to someone and they don't accept it, I can't lose, because if they don't want it, it just bounces back on me for trying. Remember, your thoughts and words carry a frequency, a vibration, and like attracts like. When you send out damning thoughts and words, you attract the same back to you. If you send out love, good energy, and blessings, look out—they are coming right back at you.

Walls or Bridges?

Words can build bridges or put up walls. They can injure egos or ignite hearts. Beliefs are molded with words, and with words they can be changed. With the right words you can heighten or deepen any experience. At the same time, the wrong choice of words can devastate.

Look at the powerful effects properly chosen words have had on history. Patrick Henry said, "Give me liberty or give me death." His words sparked an explosion of emotion and united a nation of people dedicated to freedom and the end of tyranny. The right words can change a mundane experience into one that is empowering and full of passion.

Anthony Robbins says, "People with an impoverished vocabulary live impoverished lives; people with rich vocabularies have a multi-palate of colors with which to paint their experience, not only for others but for themselves as well."

The Transitional Power of Words

Within the word lies the power to attract and manifest in your life. The emotions you feel, the dreams you realize or miss, and everything in between are woven together with the words you choose. The average dictionary contains more than 500,000 words. The English language has twice as many words as any other. Surprisingly, with such a large pool to choose from, linguists tell us the average person still only uses about 2,500 to 5,000 words.

Further observation shows that there are approximately 3,000 words that describe emotions. Out of 3,000 words, about 2,000 describe negative emotions and 1,000 describe positive emotions. It is no wonder there are so many depressed people in our society. You have twice as many negative words as positive words to describe your experience? The words we choose create the recipes for our experiences. Well-chosen words create a pleasant result. The wrong words cause pain.

Here is a question to ponder: Is the language you use in alignment with the people you admire, respect, and want to model? This isn't referring to just foul language; it means, are you using more negative words than positive ones? Are you using them consciously or unconsciously? Do you use different language around certain people? Does your language give an accurate representation of the image you want to project to others? Good language attracts good results, bad language attracts bad results, and confusing language attracts uncertainty, and so forth. Proper language can give you joy and peace, but bad language can enslave you.

Just think how the power of words has been used to destroy. Hitler caused seemingly normal people to commit atrocities beyond belief on their fellow man with the power of his words. Messianic madman and religious cult leader Jim Jones used his manipulative words to coax hundreds of people to commit suicide by drinking poisoned Kool-Aid and then giving it to their own children in Guyana.

The way we use words actually alters our feelings and perceptions. We actually represent our experience through our words. Science has proven we use our words as a primary tool to translate our experience into reality through our nervous system. Our words actually have a biochemical effect on us. To illustrate this, just think how insults, negative commands, and racial slurs affect our emotional states. How do these occurrences make you feel? Do they change your state of mind? Do they give you a positive feeling of love, encouragement, praise, and gratitude, or do they relate the opposite feelings? The words we use trigger neurological responses that flip switches in our brain that cause us to feel good or bad.

Being Impeccable With Your Word

The word "impeccable" is derived from a Greek word "pecatus," which means "sin." The "im" means "without." So, being impeccable with your words means being without sin, and what is the definition of sin? It means to "miss the mark." When we use negative self-talk about ourselves we are committing a sin, or missing the mark to have success because the Spirit of God that rests within us is being attacked.

Science continues to discover how much the brain is like a computer. Even though the brain is only three pounds of grey matter, it has amazing capacity and power. What we store there is deep-seated and slow to change. What we store in the files in our brain becomes our resources for future reaction and response. The old computer phrase "garbage in, garbage out" (GIGO) applies here for sure. Just imagine sitting down at the computer and programming in negative information like, "I'm a loser, I never get a break, I'm too old, I'm too young, I'm never going to be successful, God has forgotten about me." Sounds kind of silly, right? You would have computers full of worthless garbage. That is exactly what we do with our own minds. Then, when we need a response, the brain searches our files and out comes the garbage!

From a strictly scientific approach, the brain responds to our self-talk automatically through a network of neurons, which are electrical impulse switches called neurotransmitters. They send a message to the right place in the brain to turn on and off switches, which create your responses and control the body and everything we feel and do. The brain provides information to help us make good choices, just like the computer; we just have to put in good information for it to draw from.

The brain also responds to electrical chemical impulses, which are our "thoughts." We tend to act and project how we see ourselves. If our thoughts cause us to see ourselves as a failure, a loser, or powerless, that is what we project. If our thoughts cause us to see ourselves as kind, loving, and compassionate to others, that is what we project. Empowering thoughts create an empowering image.

Just think about the ability negative language has to trigger hate, anger, and pain. Negative words not only drag us down, they hook others and take them down, too. Do you know someone who drags others down when they talk because of their negative language? When we use foul language and anger in communicating, we are creating a toxic aura around ourselves.

When we live with and surround ourselves with people who use negative language we are enabling them if we just listen to them and receive their pain. We don't have to get self-righteous and become the language police or admonish people publicly. That kind of reaction could create problems itself. But we can share our feelings about their negative language. At least we don't have to listen to it; we can get away from it. Don't allow yourself to listen to disempowering talk and get sucked down by it. Change the environment, hang up the phone, leave the room, and change your own thoughts immediately. Sometimes we unconsciously use negative self-talk and language and don't perceive the damage it is causing. But by allowing it, we are hurting our souls. What we think about and speak about, we bring about.

I was conducting a seminar in a hotel and a lady in the front row came back from the break with a large cup of coffee she had bought at the lobby coffee shop. As she sat the cup on the floor, I heard her say, "Now watch me spill this." Five minutes after I started the seminar she knocked over the drink on the floor and made a big mess. Our thoughts and words become our reality!

What is Your Opinion?

Another way you can work on your transitional language skills is by paying attention to and being careful about your opinions. Remember the old saying, "Opinions are like noses; everybody has one"? The ego obviously loves opinions and revels in diving into the rule book to start giving opinions and making judgments.

There is nothing wrong with good objective and supportive opinions. The problem arises when the opinions allow the ego to come storming in. Do you know someone who allows their ego to whip them into a frenzy with their opinions about politics, sports, or religion? Some people are addicted to the adrenaline rush they get from aggressive responses.

Here is the key issue with opinions: Take a moment, just a brief pause, before you give your opinion and ask yourself a question, "Is this opinion from my ego, and does it disempower me?" Remember the opinions given to the little girl by her mother about her singing? Opinions can do long-term damage to others.

Can you remember a time when someone asked you, "Are you feeling okay? You don't look so good." What happens immediately? The mind takes in those words and begins to react—unconsciously, we start to think that something might be wrong. One person's opinion can affect your entire day! So be careful about the opinions and negative comments you make. You don't want to carelessly hurt others, and at the same time, what you put out comes back. When you find something good to say when you would have normally made a negative comment, you are on the way to mastering Transitional Language.

The World's Fastest Growing Plant...or Not?

It took me a lot of work and patience to learn to use Transitional Language. I had to clean up my communication with myself before I could help others do the same. This is something we must always be working on; it takes practice and commitment. In the beginning, I was constantly catching myself using disempowering words, self-talk, and opinions. Then, after a while, my habits changed and it felt comfortable to use the right language and uncomfortable to use the wrong language. I learned to do the uncomfortable until it was comfortable.

Using this process can change your life. As simple as it seems, it will make a difference. You will notice a change in the way people react to you. You will increase your attraction, power, and influence.

The key is to just keep working at it every day. It's like the Chinese bamboo tree. This tree is the fastest growing tree in the world. But it doesn't start out that way. When the seed is planted it requires a lot of water and it doesn't come out of the ground for five years. That's right, five years! Then, after the fifth year, it grows around seventy-five feet in six months. The consistent care and feeding pays big dividends. But here is the question: Did it take over five years or six months for the tree to grow seventy-five feet?   It is the same way with mastering your empowering language. It won't take anywhere near five years; in fact, you may not even realize you are making much progress—you will likely just wake up one day and realize you made a major shift in your reality.

Be Acutely Sensitive

A big key to becoming a master of Transitional Language skills is to simply pay attention and become acutely sensitive to the words you use to communicate with yourselves and others. There is no way to reach your full potential without getting a handle on your language and communication. Without it, you're like a beautiful sailing vessel headed around the world with three anchors down.

The first step is to just become sensitive to the pain you are inflicting on your own spirit and soul when you say bad things. Since our words turn on the neurotransmitters in our brains and trigger emotional responses, doesn't it make sense that when we tone down the words, we tone down the feelings associated with the words? Instead of saying, "I'm pissed off," why not transition to "I'm really peeved," instead? Notice a difference? Instead of saying, "How could I be so stupid?" why not say, "How could I be so unique?" I know it may sound weird at first, but just keep it up. For example, someone who normally hears you say, "I'm really pissed," like a spouse or your children, might feel tension and stress in their bodies because of your choice of words. Is that the reaction you want? Is making other people feel your negative fear-based emotional responses going to serve all concerned in the best way possible? All this bad habit does is throw out a screen of negative low-energy thoughts and vibrations. Then these energies attract more of the same into the person projecting them, which in turn poisons and restricts life for all concerned.

Another way to soften up emotional responses and take control away from the ego is to diffuse your responses with the word "little." Instead of saying "I'm really upset," try saying "I'm a little upset," or even better, "I'm a little bit concerned." Instead of saying, "I'm worried" try "I'm a little worried," or even better, "I'm a little perplexed." Instead of saying, "I'm overwhelmed," which triggers all kinds of up and down emotional responses, try saying, "I'm a little amazed," or, one I love to use, "I find that fascinating." It may sound overly simplistic and even silly to do this at first. Just be prepared—the results will be surprising.

When I began to work on and master my own Transitional Language, two things began to happen. First I noticed myself being calmer and even laughing at myself and some of the new language I was transitioning to. Instead of being "confused" I became "bum-fuzzled," and instead of being "frustrated," I became "fascinated." Soon, "overwhelming problems" became "a little challenge."

The second thing that happened to me was that people I often communicated with started to notice the difference. They commented on my funny and in control way of dealing with life's problems and challenges. In other words, my changes in language were rubbing off on them. Most of us don't realize how negative our words are and how unconsciously we throw them around. When we use Transitional Language to Release the language that is holding us back, it opens us up to living our lives in the flow.

Chapter 29

Acting on Purpose and With the Flow

A good intention clothes itself with sudden power.
Ralph Waldo Emerson

The best way you can support the universe and your individual role in God's cosmic plan is to do what you were created to do. Holding back your God-given talents creates resistance to the natural flow of the universe. We must open up and surrender to the universe and let it flow through us. Geese were meant to fly south, apple trees were meant to apple, and we as human beings each have an individual purpose we are meant to experience. The one way we do this is by doing what we love to do more than anything else. If you are struggling with what you are the supposed to do, there are some tools and strategies later in the book that are going to be a great help to you.

As the old saying goes, when you can "let go and let God" be the coach in your life, you will learn that He never sends in the wrong play. When you are in the flow, life is a joy, it takes less effort. There is a basic rhythm to the universe, and the rhythm carries the flow.

Hidden deep within the Real You is a spark that instigates an awakening process when it knows you are ready. It patiently waits to take over your consciousness to guide and direct you. When that time comes, the Authentic Self chooses itself over the ego and incarnates. But the ego must be weakened or the Authentic Self may never escape. When the Authentic Self emerges, you will still have the same mind, the same talents and gifts, and all your good personality traits—the only difference is the Authentic Self will be in control and not the ego.

Being in the flow means sensing the moment instead of just thinking about it. It is about experiencing the stillness and peace and fullness of being alive in the present moment. What else do you have besides your desires, thoughts, and feelings? What happens when you stop thinking, evaluating, and wondering for a moment? It's not that hard.

The Real You is easy to take for granted. It is like the air we breathe; it is always available—it's just there, and we forget about it. You can actually learn to be aware of the Real You and be in the flow most all the time. It is such a wonderful, natural state once it is achieved on a consistent basis, no one ever wants to be out of the flow again.

Getting in the flow is accepting "what is." When we can accept that God "Is" and God is in the business of "ising," then we can realize the majesty of the constant and never-ending flow. We must keep reminding ourselves that everything happens for a reason and a purpose and that it serves us. God doesn't repeat Himself, and He doesn't make mistakes. His universe is on purpose. The Scripture tells us, *"And you know that God causes everything to work together for the good of those who love God and are called according to His purpose for them."* So we need to get busy living on purpose (dream of the soul) and live in the flow so God can do His business and pour out His blessings and prosperity in our lives.

Words such as happy and unhappy, good and bad, comfortable and uncomfortable are just evaluations of the mind. If you take away the evaluations, all you have left is "what is." This is where you find the Real You. Because our default position is to not be in the flow, and since we are conditioned to not know any better, we naturally live in ego identification. The ego fights "what is," and that opens the door to suffering. The result is we block ourselves from our true essence and divorce ourselves from the real moment. You always have a choice of being in the moment (in the flow) or at the ego's will. Unfortunately, our programming and conditioning causes us to surrender easily to the ego's will and not question its value. This is the part where we discover newfound skills—we learn to be observers and recognize ourselves as the one aware of the thoughts and not the one (ego) that is thinking them.

Being in the flow is our natural state of being. We are not trying to change to something new, just to be normal. Remember the bundle of joy we were as babies? It's still there! That feeling we had then is the flow! Have you been looking at that childhood photo as suggested in the earlier action plan? We just have to be ready to experience and nurture our true nature.

Arrest the Ego!

When we get in the flow we are taking back what we started out with from the ego. Being in the flow is about putting the ego out of a job. When we go with the ego's direction we are actually at variance and uncertainty with the universe. We are on our own and opposing the flow.

We do have a choice; that is what free will is about. We can surrender to the flow and experience its ease and grace. The alternative is to suffer and to continue our journey by learning lessons and suffering the consequences of the ego's control. I am not trying to convince you to become a monk and go bliss out in a cave. It's about allowing perfection to express itself through you. It is allowing "what is" to flow through you. Your reward for allowing this to happen is to experience a beautiful feeling of freedom of expression instead of thought and effort.

When you are in the flow, you learn to allow God and His constantly unfolding plan to handle the details. Another benefit of being in the flow is that you pick up more natural, intuitive guidance. You must remember that you are not just connected to the source of God; you are an extension, or an expression point of God. There is no getting ahead when you fight the flow. Fighting the flow will bring you guaranteed pain, tension, confusion, and dis-ease of the mind and body.

You have to get ready and be willing to wake up to and experience the moment. This may seem like a difficult concept to grasp at first. Are you tired of running from the ghosts of your past or fearing the illusions of the future? That is where the ego likes to keep you. When you jump into the moment and feel it, you learn to welcome all experiences—even those that are not so great. Try this: The next time things seem like they are not going well and there are challenges mounting, ask yourself, "What is great about this?" It may seem like nothing is great; it may even seem bleak. Dig deeper and ask another question: "What *could* be great about this?" Be a good-finder; there are always great things we can find about every challenge if we look hard enough. The sooner we learn to recognize it, the sooner we can live in the flow. This is called letting go of ego-identification. It is called taking control of our story instead of being a victim of it.

Just Say Yes

Because suffering is the antithesis of "what is," the ego is at war with the present moment. If the ego keeps you distracted, you are divorced from the present moment, under its control, and out of the flow. When you "just say yes" to the moment, you are taking the wind out of the ego's sails.

Suffering is a gift if you understand it. You develop strengths, you learn, grow, and discover through suffering. You are serving your purpose and fulfilling your destiny when you receive the gifts of suffering, like patience, kindness, compassion, wisdom, freedom from the ego, faith, grace, and, most importantly, love.

Your Natural Flow

There are those wonderful moments when you just step into the natural flow. A beautiful scene of nature like a sunset, a waterfall, a mother duck and her babies, a new mother gazing into the eyes of her newborn, the feeling of looking into your beloved's eyes—all these are about being in the flow.

A baseball fielder is in the flow when he is racing to catch a fly ball but not knowing where it is going to land, yet in perfect stride and grace he catches the ball. A musician knows the flow as he effortlessly finds the notes of his instrument and senses the rhythm of the music as he plays without even looking at the notes or his instrument. An artist or painter knows the flow as his hands are guided by unseen forces toward beautiful images and vistas. Writers know the flow as words flow magically from their pen with ease and grace. Speakers, preachers, and actors know the flow when their speeches, presentations, and performances happen with amazing eloquence, piercing effect, and perfect timing. Many times they say, "I don't even know how I did it." Heroes, after an act of courage, gallantry, or bravery, often say, "I don't even remember how I did it." How about the mother who lifts the overturned car off her child and rescues her child seconds before the car bursts into flames and later remembers nothing?

These are examples of the power and grace of being in the flow. These amazing things aren't hard to do; it doesn't feel like work. This energy that makes these things happen is in all of us. How close are you to living in the flow?

Are you ready for some great news? The flow is waiting on you! This powerful source is available to access 24/7, anytime you need it. Sadly, most of us don't even know it is there nor have a clue how to access it. So it just waits patiently until there is enough suffering to cause the Real You to wake up.

Finding the Flow

The ego's job is to keep you out of the present moment. Just notice how little interest the ego has in the present moment. It loves to dwell on the past and worry about the future—anything to avoid the present moment. This does not suggest that we ignore the future. Future success and happiness acquired through lasting change is the goal of the Valeo Method. The way we take control of our future is by taking control of our present moments—away from the ego. We do that by creating our future moment in the now. What is now but a past thought manifested, right? By tapping into the present moment awareness, we access the flow where you find motivation, insight, creativity, inspiration, energy, and passion.

What if you just relax and put your attention on the present moment? If you just stop, take a few deep breaths, and drink it in? What would happen if you followed your thoughts to see where they would take you? You might say, "That is what I do now, what is the difference?" The difference is that in most cases we are not paying attention to the moment; instead we are riding along with the force of the egoic mind.

Remember, the ego is charged with negative emotions like pride, envy, and jealousy, and it is ruthless. When we focus on the moment we drain the ego's power. This opens the door for the flow. Think about joyous moments from your past. Christmas and birthday surprises as a child, winning a trophy or achieving a hard-earned goal, overcoming big obstacles—those are feelings of flow.

Being in the flow is contagious. People are attracted to you. It is a true natural magnetism. And do you know why? Because your flow awakens the flow inside others, which is also seeking release. Another benefit of being in the flow is to help rescue others who are stuck and suffering.

Love is the purest form of being in the flow. Love is the core and the foundation of the flow. If you were asked to describe the feeling of being in love, how would you describe it? How do you describe the feelings from the happiest, most fulfilling moments in your life? That is the flow!

Flow Creates Curiosity

Getting in the flow is such an awesome feeling that you will want to do whatever is necessary to cause more and more of it. Once we start to connect to the flow, we tend to develop a curiosity and thirst for more ways to experience this Divine connection. We seek to be naturally inspired and informed. When this happens we can celebrate because we are on the way and there is no going back. Now we really begin to accept that everything happens for a reason and there are no accidents or coincidences. We understand without a doubt that everything in the universe is on purpose. We know all our life situations are a result of our prior thoughts, words, and deeds. We accept that a prior present moment caused us to arrive at this present moment. We realize the flow is part of our role in God's cosmic play, His creation, His plan. We realize the good in life we are seeking is also seeking us!

When we seek our authentic self, when we are fed up with things being out of control or things not pleasing to us, the authentic self has a way of breaking through. It pierces the veil of the ego and that's where hope is hidden. Glimpses of the flow show up in moments when we are really focused on something, when we are totally absorbed with the task at hand and we feel the joy of the moment. Then the ego quickly snatches us away, back to what it calls reality. This is why recognizing the flow is just half the battle. Most of us get so beaten up and bruised, plus we are so tired, we just let the ego win. But at the same time, curiosity created by the flow keeps us searching for more.

Taking Back the Mind

Getting in the flow is about taking back the mind from the ego. The ego makes life more complicated and difficult than is necessary. Think of the ego as the enemy of the flow. The ego creates and spins stories. The stories are almost always negative and they focus on what is missing from the moment, not what possibilities it brings. The ego is not going to accept things the way they are; if you are in any way happy, it is going to manipulate you. It is committed to take you where it wants you to go, and that is always away from the flow.

You were created by God to experience the wonders He provides. You are meant to interact with all creation and co-create a life of joy, prosperity, and abundance. But you can't even experience these gifts until you take back the control you started out with and get into the flow. Then you get to be the mouth, hands, feet, and eyes to the world. You get to have the awesome experience of recognizing flow and helping others wake up to it. Each of us gets to evolve, experience, grow, and learn from the flow in our own unique way. No one can tell us how to find our own specific flow. By following the concepts of the *Release* step of the Valeo Method, it puts us on the right track. Then we can just step on the gas and go.

Timing and the Flow

Any time you are rushing, feel impatient, or forcing a decision, you are not in the flow. This means paying attention to where the flow wants to go and acting on it. It's a feeling of certainty and confidence; it just feels right. It brings feelings of relief, satisfaction, and peace. It goes back to just saying yes and letting the natural process flow. When that feeling of knowing comes with the flow, there is no need for resistance, hesitation, or confusion. The knowing brings with it an unshakeable feeling of certainty. You can learn to trust, to wait for, and anticipate this feeling. This is when you are in the flow and living by the power of the God-inspired Real You.

Listening to the Flow

When you get in the flow, you get out of God's way and let His plans be done in your life. As the Scripture tells us, *"The Lord will work out his plans for my life for His faithful love endures forever."*

Be aware of feelings that belong to the egoic mind like self-centeredness and selfishness. The ego loves these traits because they make it hard to be satisfied. When these feelings arise, listen to the flow. Otherwise, you will get locked into the ego again. We all have these feelings; the key is to recognize them and move away from them.

Are you curious about what the Real You has in store for you in any particularly moment? Get into a state of listening. Cultivate a habit of being receptive. It takes a little practice but the benefits are huge. Breaking the hold of the ego means making little choices over and over to not identify with the "I" of the ego and be the observer instead. Just get out of the drama of the story. There's no flow inside the ego.

Then one day, and it doesn't have to take long, the Real You just moves into control and the ego is left sitting in the corner pouting while a bold, fresh, and happy Real You steps in its place. You'll discover in the *Manifest and Maintain* section how to reach a stillness (which the ego hates) through mediation to support the flow.

The ego doesn't give up easily. It will pull out all kinds of weapons when you start spending more time in the flow. The ego is lightning-quick to respond with criticism and create stumbling blocks. It can be brutally unkind and persistent. Just be prepared.

Roll with the Flow

"Roll with the flow!" How powerful that statement is! It's like floating in the middle of a fast-moving river instead of banging off the sides. You are in the flow, you are "allowing" the flow to carry you where you need to go and direct you along the way. The flow is constantly refining you to advance to the next level of life. Its subtly teaches you how to reach your destiny. The flow adjusts the energies around you. It adjusts your desire for activities to fit harmoniously into the present moment.

Example of a Person with an Ego Dominated Soul

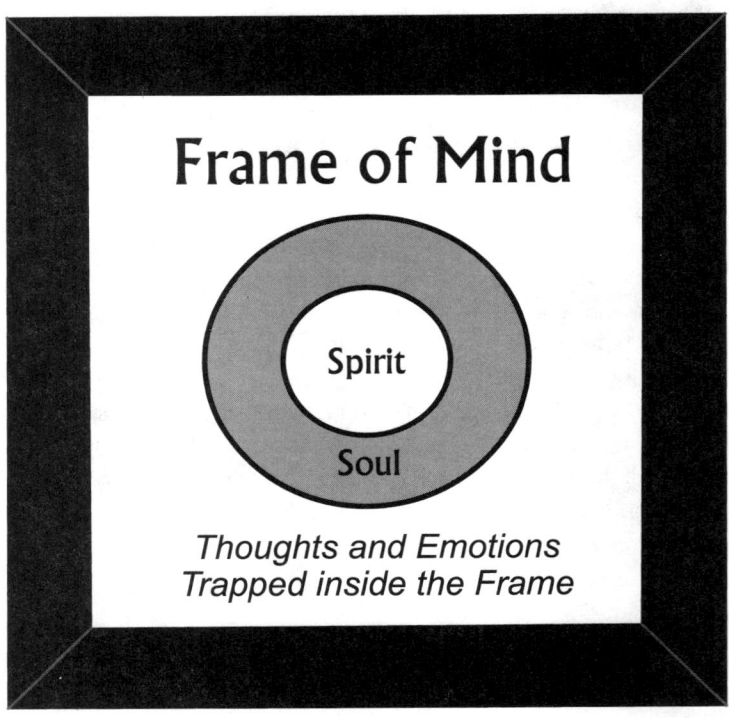

Frame of Mind

Spirit

Soul

Thoughts and Emotions Trapped inside the Frame

The Thick Frame Blocks the Light, Giving Power to Dark Thoughts and Negative Emotions

The Frame Keeps Us from Connecting with the Light of Others who are Enlightened

In contrast, the ego does not adhere to this kind of life. It operates by schedule, bosses you, scolds and makes you feel guilty if you do not comply. Of course what follows is stress, upset, and drama (back to your individual stories).

The ego's favorite way to interfere with the flow is forcing choices on you that cause stress. The flow presents positive feelings that draw you where it is best for you to go. Examples would be confidence in making decisions instead of the pressure to decide, urges to take positive action or to get answers, powerful intuitive realizations, and feelings of gratitude, appreciation, and love that come from being in the flow.

The Real You is not happy when there is suffering going on in your life; it is always working to rescue you. A crisis is a tool the Real You uses to stir you, to awaken you to a potential collision course of consequences. It can happen through illness, loss of job or money, or taking something away. A crisis has a way of stopping the ego dead in its tracks. This is an opportunity for the Real You to step in and offer new directions in life. This is another reason to be sensitive to messages coming from the flow, which may be disguised as crisis events.

In the next illustration, you see the picture of the spirit, the soul, and the egoic frame around it. The Real You is trapped inside the ego's hold and cannot receive the energy of the flow.

It's important to note that we all have the frame; we all have our egos and our own individual stories. The stronger the ego, the stronger and thicker the frame, and the less chance of light coming in (en-lightenment), and the less we are in the flow. This example shows a person dominated by their ego. This person is smothered in pain and suffering and probably lacks hope and motivation. The fragments and overpowering fear-based emotions dominate his life. This is the way many people live and die, and sadly they don't know why things are the way they are in their lives; they just die wondering why life was so hard.

The next illustration is of a person who has been through the *Discovery* process of the Valeo Method. This person knows the truth, the real deal about life. This person has discovered how and why we have our egoic identities, our individual stories and our individual circumstances. This person has learned how to Release. The person has already begun to release toxic negative and limiting beliefs because she knows what is and is not real. When she released the negative beliefs, she released the toxic emotions associated with them.

This person released negative words and self-talk that poisoned her environment and stopped her flow. She used Transitional Language to create new empowering words and self-talk to attract good and repel negative energies in her environment.

Now because of releasing all this pressure and stress, she feels better physically and is energized. She realizes the most important part of all life is finding and living the dream of the soul. No longer trapped, her flow seeks to connect with its source and all the energies, people, and unseen forces that were pre-chosen to help her realize the dream of the soul.

As you also notice in the illustration, the frame of the ego has shrunk substantially. The ego has lost its power; the truth put it in its rightful place. Remember, the ego never totally goes away during our mortal life, and it also never gives up. Even though it is weakened and beaten down, it always looks for a chance, an opportunity to take back control. We have to always be sensitive to this fact.

In addition, we notice the frame is not only thinner, it has spaces where it is broken and is allowing light in. When this happens we are becoming enlightened. Here is another special and powerful benefit of releasing and getting in the flow. We activate a God-given gift. You are able to see your spirit outside the frame, and like X-ray vision you can see through other people's frames, no matter how thick they are, and connect with the Authentic Self in each of them. Now we are able to connect with their essence, the Real You in others, and help them "see the light" and find their purpose.

Since we all are connected to the Infinite Oneness of God, when we help others we are helping a part of ourselves. This opens up more flow and joy in our own lives.

Example of a Spirit Dominated Soul.

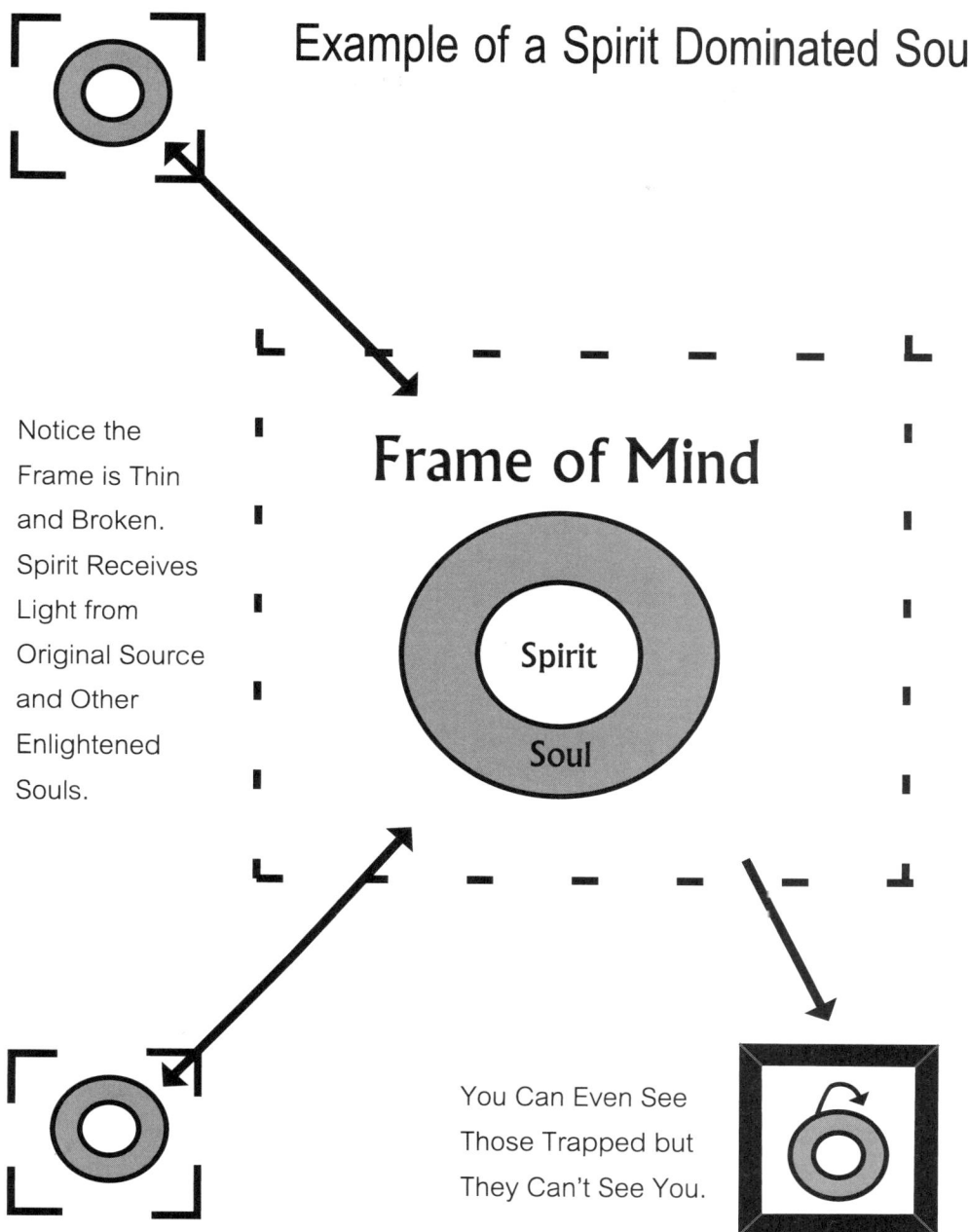

Notice the Frame is Thin and Broken. Spirit Receives Light from Original Source and Other Enlightened Souls.

Frame of Mind

Spirit

Soul

You Can Even See Those Trapped but They Can't See You.

Note: Even though we can see their Authentic Selves, they are trapped by their egos in their stories, inside that thick "frame of mind," and they can't see our True Essence. That is why we need to help them learn what we now know and help them release and be free!

Feeling Free

When we finally are released from the ego's dominance something awesome happens. We feel lighter, free, happy, and relaxed. We feel elated to be where we belong. It's the release of a longing that has been waiting deep in the soul. It is a feeling we learn to love, honor, and trust.

Now it becomes easy to understand and accept why we had to endure suffering and why we can even feel grateful for it.

When we learn why there is suffering it is much easier to accept it and overcome it. That's right—no more pity party here. No more feeling like a victim, that life is just picking on us, or feeling like we missed out. We know our authentic selves make room for us to shine; it knows our place and guides us there. Now we will know the timeline and the specifics of what we are supposed to do, be, and have. It will be released based on our faith at the perfect moment. We are glad to wait, be sensitive, and pay attention to "what is" while living in the joy and anticipation of knowing something wonderful is coming to us.

Eventually, with practice you will experience more and more of the Real You. Then you will start to experience constant "Aha" moments. Good ideas will pop up. The light just comes on and solutions to problems come easily. Since these thoughts come from the Real You they have a feeling of being right, and a feeling of total certainty about them. That, my friend, is called using your authentic power.

Before going to the next step of the Valeo Method called Embrace, go through the checklist at the end of this section and review it thoroughly. You are one step closer to finding and realizing the wonderful, amazing, unstoppable Real You! Get ready for the Embrace step, which will allow you to turn up your inner source of strength and discover some amazing gifts and surprises that are waiting on you!

Progress and Strategies

1. We are addicted, as individuals and a society, to "instant gratification," and it keeps our attention away from the pain that is building up inside our spirit/souls.

2. The soul needs maintenance and nurturing just like our bodies do in order to be healthy and pain-free. A neglected soul is a suffering soul.

3. We need to have a "Release," a mental and emotional cleansing plan to keep us moving toward our true purpose and total fulfillment.

4. It takes faith to release toxic thoughts, feelings, and beliefs because they are deeply ingrained.

5. My ego traps my faith because it is a threat to the ego's hold.

6. Judgments that I make give the ego leverage and validation of my lack, failure, and loss of courage.

7. A diamond shows its brilliance the closer it gets to the light. My soul is the same way. I can release the cover over my spirit/soul, my diamond.

8. Catch and Release is a powerful and easy-to-use strategy that I can use to Release all day long, no matter where I am.

9. My spoken words are powerful. They are spirit and life. I must pay attention to what comes out of my mouth and avoid negative words that draw negative energy toward me.

10. When I Release, I allow the natural flow of good and pow erful energies to manifest through me.

Summary and Action Plan

1. I will be an observer of my ego. I will step back and watch what it is doing. I will be like a referee watching a game, my game of life.

2. I will watch my "I" thoughts for the next few days. I will pay attention to how much I am using "I" statements. Then I will know when the ego is in control.

3. I will recognize my ego and talk to it. I will let it know that things have changed. A new sheriff is in town. I am taking a stand. I know what it is up to, and I am not going to be manipulated any more. (Get ready for this. You will be surprised what happens, so pay close attention!)

4. I will practice Catch and Release when undesired, negative thoughts, worry, or doubt creep into my mind. I will get rid of them before they have time to do any damage. Negative thoughts are like termites; if I get rid of them quickly and don't wait too long, they can't cause major damage.

5. I will rank myself on a scale of 1-10 on my self-confidence. I will determine the average rank of the five people I spend the most time with. Is their average higher or lower than my rank? I will ask myself do I need some new folks to hang around?

6. I will make a list of positive words and self-talk that I use most. I will also make a list of negative self-talk I use the most.

7. I will make a list all the words I now use that need to go and make it a practice to avoid them.

8. For the next thirty days when I run into a challenge (notice I did not say problem), I will ask myself, "What is great about this? What is the lesson I am meant to learn from this?"

9. I will keep a journal or notebook of my Release experiences. (This is extremely important because some profound things are about to happen that need to be recorded to give you confidence to keep it up. This process is ongoing. It is not a one-time fix but a permanent solution for those who are committed to learning these skills.)

PART V
~
EMBRACE

We must embrace pain and burn it as fuel for our journey.

Kenji Miyazawa

This part of the Valeo Method is about taking the time to examine another part of who we are as a person and exposing the places where we are stuck, hurt, or incomplete. Most of us don't realize we are harboring deeply suppressed emotional issues from our past that unconsciously distract us from living a fulfilled life. It is not about going back but "going in" to find answers.

This part of the Valeo Method may be at bit of a stretch for some people. It is definitely an important part—in fact, it is the very part that is left out of most books about self-improvement and personal growth. It is not for the lighthearted, and it is usually the part of getting our lives together that most of us miss. It is ironic that in order to find our true selves, we must look into the darkest and most dreaded places of our psyche. In fact, meeting and facing this deeper part of ourselves often robs us of our innocence, but it is so worth it. If we don't connect with this part of ourselves and address it, it will never stop haunting us.

This step involves more releasing, but what it really involves is diving deep into our true identity and uncovering things that may not be comfortable to face. It is about getting in touch with the most delicate, sensitive, yet powerful part of our nature. It is about getting to know intimately the sensitive self inside each of us that knows the most about what it takes to make us happy.

Here is some good news: Follow through with this step and some very special gifts await you from your very own sensitive self—you will be happy to receive them.

Are you thinking you don't have any deep emotional issues from your early years to deal with? Are you thinking this only applies to people who are screwed up? Just wait, you are in for a surprise. I want to challenge you to play full-out here. Take this seriously, and it is worth saying again: casualness breeds casualties. It could not be truer with the *Embrace* step.

I knew as I developed the Valeo Method that this step had to be here, and it was the hardest part to put together. It is also the part that offers some of the biggest breakthroughs for my coaching clients and those who attend my events.

Chapter 30

The Sources of Wounding

All learning has an emotional base.

Plato

It could be another careless remark by a frustrated parent or jealous insult by a fellow student in elementary school. It
could be an uncomplimentary nickname from some silly mistake
you made, or it could be a teasing about appearance or lack
of athletic ability. It could be a teasing from a bully as a child.
Possibly there was an embarrassing event or mishap that was
painful emotionally. Maybe it was a poor performance in a
sporting event or being chosen last for a team.

All these things may seem trivial, yet the future potential for
emotional pain and wounding as a result of these seemingly in-
nocuous events can be great. We touched on the power of our
words and language in the *Release* step; this is a continuation
of that process at a deeper and very necessary level.

It could be the verbal or physical abuse of a parent, sib-
ling, or relative that needs to be addressed. Then there is
the worst—it could be the humiliation and disgrace of sexual
abuse. These are just a few examples of events that can have
a dramatic to traumatic effect on our emotional health, peace
of mind, and who we become as adults. They can leave deep

emotional scars that follow us throughout adulthood and even to the grave. They may even appear to have died out or ceased to matter. But you are about to discover, depending on the event or circumstance, that they rarely just fade away.

These events are most impacting and create the biggest hurdles to overcome when they occur in the formative years up until school age. However, they can also create damage when they occur during adolescence and even in adulthood. These experiences can create lifelong emotional wounds that can even be passed on to future generations. Left unchecked, the suppressed pain from these experiences gets locked away. At some point, after years of suppression, it can erupt when the right trigger is activated. In the meantime, while the pain is waiting to get relief it wreaks havoc on our physical, mental, and emotional states.

Unfortunately, none of us is exempt from this damage. No matter who we are or how we were raised, whether we have had lack or abundance, we all have issues related to childhood wounds that we must address in this Embrace step of the Valeo Method. Our goal here is to learn how to stop running from the past as a way to avoid the pain. Instead, we are going to turn around and address it head-on.

Hidden within our pain lies big rewards and surprises. We are going to learn how to free our impacted emotional pain once and for all. This will at the same time allow us to discover our unique gifts and traits that have been locked away—sometimes for long periods of time—as a result of our pain. As we open up this part of ourselves we will find that the way to ultimate freedom is to express and experience wholeness. If we don't address and do the work to heal this part of ourselves by nurturing it, we will face dire consequences. One way or another, this suffering part of each and every one of us will find a way to express itself. It is a form of pressure that builds up inside. Relief can come through painful drama or through an empowering release. If relief comes from a desired and controlled intention to release it, we will be able to experience a beautiful Embrace of a special part of our unique, sensitive, and precious selves.

Many people experience a middle-age crisis, or even the middle-age crazies, depending on the severity of the individual situation. It is common among people who have reached midlife yet still seek their purpose. They go through radical life changes in their lifestyles trying to find themselves. They experience uncharacteristic changes in attitude and outlook. Some make major changes in their appearance, some change jobs and careers; some get divorces, and some buy sports cars. They take out-of-character risks to try to define themselves. Actor Kevin Spacey won an Academy Award for his role in a movie called *American Beauty*, the story of a man who turns his life upside down trying to release his deep inner suffering caused by an emptiness inside. Although he appeared to be happy and successful on the outside, he was suffering from an identity crisis and was dying on the inside.

The movie was a commercial success because so many people related to this man's suffering. They knew what he was going through while trying to find his purpose and get rid of his inner torment before he thought he would run out of time.

Up to this point we have discovered how we create our egos and how it dominates and controls your life. We have addressed why we take some of the actions we do, which give us undesirable results, because we let our egos control our thoughts and emotions. When we learned to recognize the ego's actions we found we could catch ourselves and heed off unnecessary challenges.

The most sensitive part of our makeup is not a part of the ego. Even though we are learning to improve our quality of life and how to get control of the ego, this other dynamic is totally different. This is why we have to address our sensitive self; otherwise, this lingering part of us would always beg for our attention. Our mission with the Valeo Method is not to patch things up and limp along in a life that could be much better. It's about creating wholeness of body, mind, and spirit, and learning the skills and developing the confidence to use them so we can create lasting change and never give up until we are truly "living our calling."

The Elephant in the Living Room

To conquer this next hurdle in making lasting change, we have to take a deep, relaxing breath and get ready to dive deeper. Learning how to put a leash on the ego was a big step, but there is still an elephant in the living room. This challenge can only be overcome by dealing with unaddressed, unexpressed emotional wounds from past events and experiences. This is the pain that has been imprinted on your soul and locked away—usually even forgotten. Yet it is always there, taking a part in your life in the present and in your future—that is, until we deal with it.

Many people tend to think, myself included, that this would not apply to them. My childhood was great. I was never mistreated or abused by my parents, but there are always issues that affect our developing personalities that do relate back to our parents. This is where many of our problems reside. Some of us have turned suppressing our unwanted memories into a fine art form. We don't even know a problem (that elephant) is there. Sometimes emotions all the way from childhood just linger along and leak into our adult experience.

My fascination with this subject and my desire to understand it has driven me to study it with a passion and near-obsession. I have studied more than seventy experts in this field, not only for my own understanding and because I found it fascinating, but because I also wanted to be able to help others. I have worked with large numbers of people in my seminars and individual coaching sessions, and my experience is that we *all* have issues related to what I call childhood "wounding"—and yet not necessarily with our parents. In fact, the very people who deny they have any issues are usually the ones who suffer the most because they cannot bear to face the truth of what happened.

Chapter 31
The Sensitive Self

The deepest feeling always shows itself in silence. Not in silence, but restraint.

Marianne Moore

Now, we will focus on what we will refer to as the "wounded inner child," or the "shadow." In the Valeo Method, I like to refer to this part of ourselves as the Sensitive Self. The Sensitive Self holds our most sensitive feelings created from locked-away beliefs and emotions we usually don't even realize we have because we keep them deeply suppressed. This part of who we are is loaded up with positive and negative emotional charges. By practicing what we learned in the Release step, we will let go of the needs, roles, and symbols of the ego, which will allow us to enter this new realm and discover what appears as new parts of ourselves. We'll tap into your positive gifts and powers hidden away in your psyche and aching to get out.

As the saying goes, "What you resist, persists." Whatever you have repressed holds a tremendous amount of energy with great, positive potential. The shadow is the mirror image of the ego. It is the part of the personality where the ego hides, waiting. It is almost like siblings who are very opposite in nature, yet when they come together they create a whole of sorts by virtue of blood and DNA. We accumulate these unacceptable qualities, and they take form as our inferior self, the shadow.

When we focus on getting ahead in our lives, normally we want to leave the past alone. However, there comes a point in which we have to go back and *Release* even more so we can continue to move ahead, where we deserve and desire to be. This backwards journey may seem like a waste of time and energy. Going back and working on things from the past is *not* easy. We tend to have a "what is done is done" mentality, and in most situations this is good. Because we live moment-by-moment we always seem to be moving forward in time, and that concept holds our attention. However, until we integrate our past and expose the places that cause us to be stuck and incomplete, we can never be whole in the present. We are constantly experiencing some element of our past. Our past haunts us because it is closer than we think; it is just under the surface of our daily consciousness and seems to watch our every move, just waiting to pounce on an opportunity to point out our weaknesses, failures, and lack.

It may begin with a circumstance like the mother who yelled at her daughter. It may be something as small as an insult from a person you love and admire. It could be a comment about your appearance from another kid at school like, "You are a fatty," or "You have big ears," or "You have bird legs." Something happens in literally an instant that can cause a lifetime of pain. These careless comments carry toxic energies that burrow deep into the mind. From these experiences, memories and associations are created, emotional tattoos and psychological anchors that link us to a lifetime of reoccurring pain. These energies remain locked away—the negative ones seeking Release, and the positive ones seeking *Embrace*.

Daniel's Story

A man named Daniel came to one of my seminars. Daniel was a successful government employee in a trusted and respected position. On the outside he appeared to be happy and in total control of his life. But on the inside he was suffering with turmoil and was miserable. He was using alcohol to anesthetize his pain.

Daniel had spent his adult life in a relentless passion for success, constantly seeking to earn respect from his peers. His inner drive to be accepted, appreciated, and loved stemmed from a childhood incident. But Daniel never realized the cause of his inner battle until he learned to look back and discover its origin, which he had hidden away and forgotten many years before.

His first step was to realize and accept that something in his past could be triggering and prolonging his pain. Then, we were able to trace the source of his pain to an incident with his father.

Daniel's parents divorced when he was six, and his father moved to another state. Daniel's father was his hero, and he longed for his attention and savored every moment of it, although he rarely got it. After he left his father didn't see Daniel for more than three months. Finally, his father arranged to come pick him up and spend a weekend with him at a hotel and do things together. Daniel was elated that his hero was coming to spend a whole weekend with him. As Daniel struggled to share his story, I watched a thirty-eight-year-old man sob, with huge tears literally pouring down his face. The obvious pain had resurfaced in full force. He wept uncontrollably.

Daniel went home after school on the Friday his father was supposed to pick him up, and his mom helped him get ready with a nice outfit, combed his hair perfectly, and packed a small bag neatly to carry with him on his highly anticipated visit. Daniel was so excited that he started waiting on the porch at 5 p.m., even though his father wasn't supposed to arrive until 6 p.m. Daniel waited till 6 p.m., then 7 p.m., then 8 p.m. His dad never came. Daniel cried himself to sleep that night. He did not hear from his dad again for months. When he did talk to his dad, he never mentioned not showing up, he never apologized to Daniel, and at the age of thirty-eight, Daniel had never spoken of that weekend to anyone besides his mom.

Daniel was deeply wounded from this event; the seven-year-old boy felt his father, his hero, did not love him. He felt something must be wrong with him. He couldn't bear to be around other children with their dads. Even though Daniel and his dad did spend some occasions together as he grew up, the damage was done, the pain was deeply imprinted, affecting Daniel's entire life and the lives of those around him.

This is a perfect example of how a wounded, sensitive self is created and spends a lifetime suffering. Daniel tried to convince himself he had gotten over the incident, and he really believed he did. From the day of that incident forward, however, Daniel's life changed. His feelings of not being good enough to receive his father's love haunted him. Daniel, a father of two himself, now found himself even repeating some of the traits he hated in his father. He had allowed his obsession to prove that he was a worthy person cause him to neglect his own children and his family responsibility. He believed that if he acquired enough success, he would be worthy of love.

Daniel went to a psychologist for many sessions but felt no progress. His pain was so great he began to drink every night to attempt to mask it; to cover it up. He gained weight, woke up with hangovers, and fought with his wife. Daniel was desperate. A friend told him about the Valeo Method and he attended a seminar. When Daniel discovered what was going on inside with his ego and how it was still causing him pain, he dug deeper and realized he still had a hurt, sensitive, seven-year-old boy still trapped deep inside who needed love and attention. He also realized he was never going to get well until he dealt with these challenges. The part of Daniel that got hurt the day his Dad stood him up stopped growing that day. Daniel learned that by addressing his deep, sensitive self he could re-lease himself from torment and change his life.

Exposing Blind Spots

This story is just one example of how your childhood wounding affects the sensitive self and how it can continue to contribute to a lifetime of pain.

We all have blind spots and blemishes from the past that we don't want to face. This is a source of traits and tendencies that we may simply refuse to admit are ours. In order to heal, we have to be willing to take the time, even if it means going back chapter by chapter in our lives, to expose, express, and experience the sources of our pain.

This also means we must make a decision. When you consciously decide to go back and revisit the parts of your past that continue to affect your future, it can lead to a Divine event. Healing these wounds of the soul is a sacred process. It means deciding to step away from the drama and trauma and the smallness of ourselves. From this experience comes many rewards—one of them being wisdom. This means that when you find the courage to break free of your past you can then embrace something truly amazing about yourself. Our emotional wounding carries positive gifts with it. For example, one of Daniel's gifts was that he developed a determination to do well in his life. He felt he could earn love by performance and accomplishment. He was a star gymnast and athlete. He received high marks in school and college. He raced to the top in his career and was admired by many. Daniel's pain caused him to suffer, but it also taught him about perseverance and determination!

We all have our wounded emotional issues. A great thing that can come of these issues is that we can be healed from them—and that pain holds gifts for you, just like Daniel received. A big step is realizing (seeing with "real eyes") that what happened in our past has an effect on our adult lives, so we have to be ready to Embrace our gifts.

When Daniel realized that what happened to him was not his fault he was able to move on. He accepted that the events had occurred as part of his journey, his intended path. He accepted that these events were necessary to his growth as a person. He accepted that everything happens for a reason, and he was finally happy about his life. He was grateful for the gifts his determination had brought him. He was also excited about his new dedication to being a caring father and husband. He found and embraced healing because he found and embraced his sensitive self.

Chapter 32
Role Models

As you get older it is hard to have heroes, but it is sort of necessary.

Ernest Hemingway

As children, it is our natural instinct to observe our parents. We see the choices they make and the pleasures they allow themselves. We see the talents and skills they develop, the possibilities they ignore and the ones they embrace, and we see the rules they follow. What children accept or reject from their parents has a significant impact on their lives. This can become a guide, right or wrong, for navigating their lives. Did you sincerely seek to model your parents, or did you just evolve into it?

The personal shadow, or sensitive self, is composed of thoughts the ego rejected during the ego-building process. The sensitive self is a mirror image, or the opposite, of the ego. In other words, your outer world is a reflection of your inner world. Undesirable and unacceptable qualities accumulate in your unconscious psyche and take form as inferior personality traits. The sensitive self is in reality a natural byproduct of the parts of the personality the ego rejects. These parts are real and hold energy—they never go away. They lie dormant, waiting to erupt and explode with the right trigger from a life experience.

Breaking the Yoke

The sensitive self keeps us warring against ourselves as the ego seeks to maintain control. The sensitive self is just seeking to be exposed, heard, and experienced. This dark side of the psyche, which we suppress, contains negative forces, negative programming, and impacted pain. If these traits are left unchecked and unattended, they can lead to imbalance, confusion, bad decisions, and general unrest.

However, the yoke of this burden can be broken, and when it is wonderful things happen. When you gain connection to and control of the sensitive self, you take a big step. Now you can end chaos in your life and find peace. You go from carrying a negative charge to being *in charge*. This allows you to make use of the highest application of the positive resources of your sensitive self. Then you will be ready to fuel the momentum of your soul's intentions (the dream of your soul, your purpose).

The tools of this step expose the ego's needs and its roles in righteous behavior. Here we discover parts of ourselves that are not new, but that have been rejected. These parts also hold our unique talents, strengths, and gifts. This opens the door to the "Real You" and not the person many of us think we are, hiding behind our ego-created stories. With this experience comes a feeling of being more alive. The more we connect with the sensitive self, the more vibrant we become. We also become more attractive to other people. We appear to have what others are seeking, even though they don't consciously realize they are seeking it! What a bonus!

But think about it: When we see people who appear to have magnetism, who seem to be bigger than life, it is because they have conquered the ego and embraced the sensitive self. The power of the sensitive self with its unseen force of good connects subconsciously with the same force shared by all other people.

Chapter 33

Fear, Anger, and Grief

Fear is the path to the dark side. Fear leads to anger.
Anger leads to hate. Hate leads to suffering.

Yoda

We addressed earlier the fact we only experience two foundational kinds of emotion: love and fear. All of our challenges related to childhood wounding are based in fear and linked to experiences with fear, anger, and grief. It is our intention here to get these feelings to the surface so we can address and *Embrace* them and then move forward, free of their prior hold on us. Traditional thinking would seek to re-cover from the suppressed feelings, which is actually just masking the pain. Our approach here is to un-cover these feelings and deal with them once and for all—not re-cover them so they stay hidden and keep popping up, causing more pain and suffering.

What we're dealing with here are early life experiences which carry emotional imprints. Emotions from early childhood tend to re-emerge and leak into our current experiences. Left unintegrated, the cycle constantly repeats itself, causing us to experience mental and physical fatigue and imbalance. It is safe to say that our current uncomfortable life situations are a result of our emotional ghosts of the past.

Our most impacting emotional wounding is created in our early developmental stages, before age seven. There is no escaping this part of growing into our emotional maturity or lack thereof. The challenge comes when our wounded inner child gets stuck at the emotional age at which the pain occurred. Some obviously have more traumatic issues to deal with than others. The point is, we all have them, and they aren't going away on their own.

There is no running from the past. Some people change jobs, mates, and even move to another city to escape and change their circumstances. Then they find out they can't run from their past because what is *inside* you goes *with* you, and the dissatisfaction returns.

So let's dive deep into the emotional abyss and find out what gifts await us in the dark. The master teacher Jesus Christ faced constant tension but demonstrated to us that by faith, the darkness could never conquer us. He taught us that beneath our sins and demons of the past lies the pure light of the Way to peace. It is time to go from letting our stories use us and abuse us to embracing the sensitive self and using our stories to *serve* us. Then we can benefit from our special gifts, and so can the rest of the world.

Locked-Away Beliefs

While the ego is busy building our stories it creates many beliefs about how we must think and live. Some of these beliefs are *easy* to accept and fit into our lives and our interactions with others. We addressed current and core beliefs in the *Release* step of the Valeo Method. Here, we will address locked-away beliefs. There are beliefs that we associate with painful experiences in our past. We lock them away to avoid facing them. The more painful the belief, the deeper we lock it away until we forget about it.

It may seem like locking away a painful belief is a good thing to do. There is one problem, however; the locked-away beliefs cause our negative emotional charges, which are never locked away.

God's gift to all of us, free will, comes with the ability to create situations that give us emotional responses. We get to feel the joy of love-based emotions. Within our individual stories we have a dark side and a light side. Depending on how much pain we have locked away, our fear-based emotions can create a Dr. Jekyll/ Mr. Hyde scenario inside of us as we move back and forth from love- to fear-based emotions.

Clinging to Your Story

Without help and awareness, managing the sensitive self can be a life-absorbing process. We get really wrapped up in our stories because we can always retreat to them and feel safe. Remember, our story is our comfort zone; it is who we think we are, and it has always been there when we confront pain.

We cling to our stories as a way to find meaning in our lives. In reality, though, we are just playing into the drama created by the ego's domination while the sensitive self is trying to be heard. This is how we get sandwiched into being a victim of our stories. Have you ever found yourself in the "someday when," "if only," and the "as soon as" syndromes? This is a great example of a hurting soul using the individual story as an excuse to be a victim.

When most people understand the dynamic of the individual story, they just want to get rid of it to prove they are worthy, important to others, and loveable. This can be dangerous. We have to remember that we have *become* our stories, and we proudly present them. We didn't get our stories overnight and it takes some commitment and attention to eliminate or change them in a healthy way. I mean, come on, if we are not our stories, then who are we going to be?

Here is the challenge: Because of the pain in the sensitive self your story can turn on you and sabotage the very thing you desire the most and the things you are trying so hard to change. This means you must be careful to not allow your locked-away beliefs to overwhelm you.

I Just Want To Be Happy!

Sound a little complicated? It really isn't—the biggest hurdle is exposing what is going on and we have done that. We all have a natural yearning for peace, for finding our intended path, and living our purpose. American psychologist Abraham Maslow was noted for conceptualizing a theory he called "the hierarchy of human needs." It states that man's highest value stems from an inherent need for self-actualization or search for meaning and purpose. He said the lower needs of man motivate us until they are satisfied, and then we must move on up. We fulfill our highest need when we achieve wholeness.

Hidden in the dark side of the psyche is the answer to life's puzzle of individual meaning. Carl Jung said, "The gold is in the dark." The key to finding the Real You is aligning and embracing the sensitive self, which is usually in the darkest part of the mind. Then we get to have that "Aha" experience, the light comes on, and suddenly we understand our true, intrinsic value. Then we feel good about who we are, which reflects in our self-esteem, self-confidence, and life decisions. Finally we have the one thing that gives us self-esteem—control of our thoughts. In reality, we are simply saying hello to our authentic power—our original source of life.

It Takes Courage

As we get older it is natural to lose bone density and muscle tone. Something else we lose just as quickly if we don't pay attention is courage. This is the very reason we need to get busy and act now.

The word "courage" is derived from the Latin word "cor," meaning "heart." It takes heart to do this work in the Valeo Method. This part could be the most challenging part of the process. At this critical point you are being asked to have courage. Be determined to open your heart and connect with the Real You and claim the prize that awaits you.

When Moses was forty years old he left Egypt because he had murdered a man whom he saw beating another Hebrew. He feared for his life and went east to a place called Mid-iron, where he got married and became a sheepherder for his father-in-law for the next forty years. When Moses left Egypt he was a powerful and prideful man. After forty years as a sheepherder he became humble. In fact, the Scripture tells us that Moses was the most humble man of all time.

This was also when God told Moses he had chosen him to lead six million of his fellow Israelites out of slavery in Egypt. Moses was not jumping-up-and-down excited at eighty years old to take this job. But God knew he was ready because God knew what Moses had deep inside.

We all know the story of the successful exodus of the Israel-ites from Egypt and the Pharaoh's oppression under the lead-ership of Moses. But here is the message: God has to empty us of our prideful selves so He can fill us up with a higher power, which will give us the courage to fulfill our purpose. A person is never too old and it is never too late—all that is lacking is courage.

When I teach folks how to embrace the sensitive self, some participants are skeptical and hesitant to open up at first. Skepticism is soon replaced with confidence as they start to see the rewards from finding answers, healing, and experiencing personal breakthroughs. This work allows us to see how we are our own inner jailers, trapping ourselves in an invisible prison of a distracted mind. The only way out of this prison is through the ego and to the sensitive self.

It takes making up the mind and meaning it to make this kind of change. Just knowing you need to change is not enough. How many people know they need to eat better, drink less, lose weight, or stop smoking, but they keep putting it off? The ego and the story it created for you doesn't change or give up easily.

Our stories have good and bad parts; they are not all bad. Remember, our stories, each and every one of them, have a purpose. Without pain and suffering we never get to experience growth, joy, and purpose. Our story can force us to see the big picture and discover our unique contribution to the whole. We are not ever going to get rid of the ego; it will never totally go away. What we can do is learn to recognize and control it by getting rid of our limiting stories and setting the sensitive self free.

It's Not My Fault

It's easy to get caught up in blaming others for our sad stories, bad breaks, and shortcomings. Remember what you are doing when you b-lame others? You are being lame, taking the easy way out, and avoiding responsibility for your circumstances.

Yes, many people affect your life, including parents, spouses, ex-spouses, friends, abusers, employers, and co-workers, just to name a few. We allow these people's actions to influence and fuel our stories. Another option is to just blame ourselves. This is how we martyr ourselves and become self-righteous and justified in our shortcomings.

When we blame ourselves and others, it sucks the life out of us and takes away our personal power. Blame drives us deeper into our stories, making life harder instead of better. In other words, when we blame, we lose because we are prolonging our own drama.

In reality, we use blame to hold on to our stories, which keep us in suffering and victim mode. With blame comes lack of forgiveness, which finds us in the very situations that we don't want. As long as we harbor blame, we can never rest. We will always be striving to justify and keep alive the blame so we can make ourselves right. Therefore, we are victims, controlled by someone or something that we let sabotage our lives to validate our resentments. In essence, we are savoring our misery.

Chapter 34

Forgiving Your Parents

Everyone says forgiveness is a lovely idea until he has something to forgive.

C. S. Lewis

Your parents, being your first nurturers and teachers, had the biggest influence on your future beliefs through their examples. But we have to remember our parents are human too, and none of us has ever had a perfect situation. Parents have their own stories and dramas to deal with. Where did their beliefs come from anyway? If their parents were abusive, neurotic, alcoholic, or unloving, how does their history affect their own children?

The parent could create feelings of fear in their children through acts of anger and intimidation. The parent could be critical and always find fault. These remnants of pain make it hard to forgive people we love the most. Blame is a habit; it's easier to keep doing it than it is to change it.

Here is the challenge: Until you stop using blame as an excuse, you cannot embrace your sensitive self and move forward. When you learn to accept that what happened to you has a lesson and begin to search for that lesson, you can open your heart to healing.

This does not mean saying, "My parents did the best they could with their situation," and not meaning it. This is just covering up and making excuses. If that attitude is acceptable as an accurate reality to you, move on, that is great. Otherwise, it only puts a Band-aid on a big gash.

The solution is to *Embrace* your history with your parents as part of your evolutionary journey. Remember, there is a Divine plan behind who your parents are and only God knows why.

If you had an angry father it could be that his rage was meant to teach you to be a kind and attentive parent. This way, you change the cycle of your father's bad tendencies to your future generations.

It could be that an alcoholic, spendthrift mother who kept the family finances in shambles teaches a child to be good at handling money in the future. Every bad situation caused by a parent has a positive side to it with a lesson, if we just seek it. In fact, it is usually staring us right in the face and we can't see the forest for the trees.

Any time the temptation to blame parents comes along, it is time to use "Catch and Release." Stop the thought, slam it in your big garbage can, and let the yellow helium balloon float it out of sight into the sky. Repeat the process every time until it stops coming to mind. The ego will give up sooner or later.

Juan's Story

Here is an example of how the sensitive self is created. Juan was a nineteen-year-old man who attended my course. His friends persuaded him to participate, though he was reluctant at first. Juan was one of the loudest, most obnoxious hell-raisers I had ever seen. He was always screaming and poking at someone and trying to aggravate people. He was constantly in trouble for menial screw-ups.

I knew he was going to be a challenge right from the start. For him to be acting out the way he was, I knew he had some emotional wounding that needed attention. He was literally screaming for help.

Even though Juan only finished the tenth grade, it become obvious to me that he was very intelligent. He started out be-ing the class clown, trying to be cute and not taking the class seriously. He realized quickly his antics weren't going to work in this environment because the people in the class had been on a waiting list to get in, and they were serious about getting results and making changes. He also realized I was committed to helping him. Something clicked inside him, and the authentic self and the sensitive self in Juan awakened. He found a life line and grabbed it.

Juan had an interesting background. He was raised in the projects in Puerto Rico by crack addict parents. They were dealing drugs, taking drugs, and stealing as far back as Juan could remember. From as early an age as six, he was taught to steal in stores while his parents pretended to shop. If he refused he was beaten with a belt. By age ten he was delivering drugs for his parents. When his father abandoned him and his mother went to jail, he landed in state custody, followed by many foster homes. From the foster homes he went to juvenile detention. He finally landed in federal prison at age eighteen for drug dealing.

Juan became a dedicated participant in the class. His transformation was amazing, and it inspired others as well. His heart was literally crying out for love. He believed there was something wrong with him because he never felt loved by his parents. They were so busy with their own demons that he was neglected and lost.

Juan had some breakthroughs in the class. Other inmates took an interest in encouraging him. He started reading self-help books and attending church service. He was beginning to develop a relationship with his sensitive self. His wounds were beginning to heal.

Juan used all the steps in the Valeo Method to heal and prepare for his future. He returned to future classes to share his story and encourage others.

This is what Juan shared with the class. "I hated my parents for making me do bad things. When I told them no, they would whip me and punish me. My father had an awful temper and he would threaten me and call me names. My only relief was to hide somewhere and call them names and dream of running away someday. I hated my parents and I didn't care what happened to them. As I got older, I would drink alcohol and smoke marijuana to escape the pain. I felt like something was wrong with me and I deserved the pain. I believed I was a loser and had no future and would wind up with a miserable life like my parents.

"Now I've learned I have a choice. I have accepted that my pain was there for a reason and I have learned from it. I have a future, I have a plan, and I like who I am now. I am determined to make something of my life."

Juan's story may seem an extreme example, and it is hard to imagine his pain as a child. Yet what happened to Juan happens to all of us in varying degrees. Our wounds from childhood pain are buried deep inside and we struggle hard to hold them down. It's like trying to hold down a giant ball in the ocean. It is impossible because it keeps finding a way to pop out.

I do not watch a lot of television. I find there is too much negativity, drama, crime, and bad news. I have enjoyed watching a show in recent years called *The Biggest Loser*. After losing eighty pounds myself and keeping it off for years, I can relate to these folks, their weight problems, and the effect it is having on their lives. Anyone who watches the show gets a great opportunity to see the pain of internal conflict in these poor, suffering individuals. Many times the show focuses on their "stories" of why they became obese, and there are always issues arising out of these stories. To deal with their pain and wounding, these people anesthetize themselves with food. They need the Valeo Method; I would give every one of them this book!

This is a clear, public example we can all witness of the power and potential for destroying lives both psychologically and physically and the power the egoic mind and childhood wounding have in our lives.

As we seek to recognize and *Embrace* our sensitive self and the emotions it holds, we are moving closer to wholeness. Carl Jung said, "It is better to be whole than to be good."

Chapter 35
Tired of Self-Sabotage?

*Self-sabotage is when we say we want something
then go about making sure it doesn't happen.*

Alyce P. Cornyn-Selby

If we don't do this work and tend to our wounded, sensitive self, it can get our attention by causing repeated self-sabotage. It can become like a nasty, infected wound that just won't heal no matter what we do. So the mistakes we have made in the past just keep showing up and repeating themselves. Our lives can seem stuck in a rut, with the pain and suffering continuing, and we can't figure out why.

When Juan looked inside he saw that he could *Embrace* a bright and creative person trying to get out. He discovered he wasn't a loser. He found out it was okay to express his feelings and pursue his dreams of getting married, raising a family, and having his own business.

Handle With Care

When you take the journey into unhealed anger, grief, and fear, it is a journey from head to heart. The potential for opening up emotions and physical discomfort is great. Many times the sources of pain have been locked away in painful memories and frustration for years. Don't think you are too old to do this work. I have seen clients in their seventies experience major breakthroughs. One particular seventy-four-year-old highly successful man wept like a child as he finally confronted his long-buried childhood issues. His neurotic alcoholic mother's treatment still haunted him, decades after the experience. The relief of finally embracing his sensitive self for the first time was an experience of overwhelming joy.

Remember, the emotional child doesn't grow older with the physical body. This part of you stays the same age as when the pain or trauma occurred. The hurting child is still alive inside.

Fruit or Root?

For many years I was on a relentless search to understand why some people were successful and happy and others were not. I studied many concepts and strategies related to traditional and esoteric psychotherapy, hypnosis, Neurolinguistic Programming, metaphysics, and spiritual psychology. The one thing that stood out in my mind was that most strategies for change worked for a while but failed in the long run because they focused on the fruit, not the root. They were addressing the effects and not the cause of the problem.

For example, in the '90s, as mentioned earlier, mood-altering drugs and anti-depressants like Prozac, Zoloft, and Paxil became popular. These drugs increase the production of natural mood-elevating chemicals in the brain that cause people to feel good. A similar concept is used for hyperactive children by giving them Ritalin.

Here is the point: The doctor, not always but in many cases, addressed the fruit of the problem, the effect, and ignored the root of the problem. Most of the time, though not every time, the sensitive self is the root of the problem. The Valeo Method deals with the root—not the fruit.

Chapter 36
Understanding Suppressed Feelings

All, everything I understand, I understand only because of love.

Leo Tolstoy

As a normal, healthy child we are naturally exuberant and spontaneous; we are pure energy in motion. We were created to be in joy (to enjoy ourselves). Unfortunately, our environment and our parents tone down much of our joyful behavior. Remember when your parents would remind you to settle down and not to be so playful and wound up. Sometimes our behavior as a child definitely needs to be tempered. But what happens when a child is called down too much? Positive emotional experiences can get locked away just like negative emotional experiences, causing people to feel uncomfortable about expressing themselves. The feelings locked away in the sensitive self are not just painful emotions like anger and embarrassment. There can also be positive feelings of expression that seek *Release and Embrace.* In other words, the sensitive self needs to feel it's okay to release positive emotions.

When children cry or pitch a tantrum, it is not just to get what they want. The sensitive self wants to be accepted. That crying emotional child inside of us never grows up—and it shouldn't. It just wants to be recognized, accepted, and embraced. The longer these combined negative and positive feelings are ignored and suppressed, the less authentic you are as a person.

This ongoing dynamic creates an inner conflict that will show up as acting out, acting in, or projecting feelings and pain on another. As time goes by, the stress of this piles up and real internal pressure arises. This leads to a life spent seeking a solution "out there" like business success, relationships, and even bad habits to get relief.

We are also influenced by where we grow up, who we spend the most time with and their beliefs and circumstances, as well as the negative drama that society and the news media pound into our minds.

Pleasing Your Parents

As a child, there is no feeling like the joy of knowing you pleased your parents. This desire to please them is an innate part of our make-up. We seek to prove ourselves or to get approved to justify who we are and our reason for being.

Even if we seek fame, fortune, and recognition, the underlying, dominant need we all have is to fulfill this missing part of any unconditional love we did not receive as a child. Does that statement seem hard to accept? How could something missing in my childhood be making me unfulfilled as an adult? Does it seem too long ago, too small an issue?

Robert was a thirty-eight-year-old man in a nowhere job, boring relationships, and tired of being stuck. He spent days fighting depression and considered suicide. He could never seem to get any success going in his business or personal life, even though he felt like he had tried. After attending my seminar I worked with him one on one and we started diving into his past. He shared a story with me from when he was in the sixth grade. He said, "My father was always riding me to do better in school. My older sister was a straight-A student and at the top of her class. My dad was always throwing it up to me and making me feel bad about my grades. I made mostly C's, a few B's, and an occasional D. He told me he believed I could do much better. My dad was a strict disciplinarian and stingy with encouraging words.

"He made a deal with me that if I got all A's on my next report card, he would pay me ten dollars for every A. I got excited because that seemed like a lot of money to an eighth-grader. I worked hard and studied every night and on weekends. I even stopped playing basketball after school with my friends, which I loved to do. When the report card came I was elated to see all A's and I could hardly wait to show my dad. I'll never forget what happened when he came home that evening. I glowed with pride as I anticipated the moment Dad would gaze on my accomplishments. When he opened my report card at first he had a huge smile, and I swelled up with pride. Then the smile turned to a disapproving frown. He said, "You have two A minuses, and A minuses are not A's, so the deal is off, no money for you, young man."

Robert told me, "I was crushed. I knew right then that all my work and discipline wasn't worth it. I felt like I wasn't good enough, and in the future no matter how hard I tried, I would never be good enough, and something like this would just happen to me again. So I haven't tried that hard to do anything since."

As a result of this experience, Robert's life became a trail of incompletion and half-hearted efforts. The Valeo Method helped him realize how this one event and the pain it caused had robbed him of a better life by planting an unconscious belief that determined effort meant pain and disappointment and it wasn't worth it.

He then understood what he had to do to change his future. Robert realized that while avoiding a repeat of pain from this childhood memory, he also had avoided embracing his sensitive self and delayed finding his purpose for more than twenty years. He realized it wasn't too late to find his purpose and change his life. Robert's life is totally changed today, and he is searching for new mountains to conquer.

It is disturbing but true that a large number of parents actually lead their lives vicariously through their children. Some parents secretly or even subconsciously decide their child will be what they longed to be and are not. As a result, they push the child beyond his or her capacity. This is done at the expense of the child, which was the case with Robert and his father. What parents fail to recognize as they push their children too far is that he or she may not be developed mentally, emotionally, or physically enough to reach these levels. They could be wrecking the child's life and creating shadows to follow him or her as an adult.

Another effect that many of us carry into adulthood develops through the common problem of belittling by comparison, which also was an issue in Robert's life. His dad was always comparing his academic performance to his older sister's. This situation creates a compounding sense of inferiority. In addition to his own sense of lack in his makeup, now the child compares himself with others he looks up to. This can be a devastating blow to his self-confidence, which he will carry forward as an adult.

When our parents ask us what we want to do when we grow up, we log this away in our minds as a way to earn unconditional love. So we set out to "earn a loving" from our parents by pleasing them with how we earn a living. This desire follows us throughout life, and from age eight to eighty we never forget it. It is the same for those of us who were raised by caretakers or someone other than parents—the same dynamic applies.

We spend our lives, usually subconsciously, chasing these illusions, thinking they will complete us. We secretly believe if we could just be or do this certain thing we would arrive at happiness and a sense of completion. The reality is, we never find wholeness being what someone else wants us to be; we only find wholeness when we find the answer to our own individual, imprinted destiny, the dream of the soul.

Many of the pitfalls and mistakes we see in life's struggles could have been avoided if parents understood and applied the principles in the Valeo Method. Then they could have done a better job at cultivating their children's self-confidence and self-esteem, and so much pain and suffering could have been avoided. Thank God you are here now. I pray this message is received well because there is no doubt about the positive effect it will have on your life.

The margin of difference in ability, skill, and intelligence between those who are great achievers and those who fail is tiny. My experience has been that we are always closer than we think to our individual breakthroughs. It is the little adjustments in thinking, awareness, and understanding in a few key areas that close the gap between just surviving and thriving in our lives.

Chapter 37
The Fragmented Personalities Dilemma

A perfection of means, and a confusion of aims, seems to be our main problem.

Albert Einstein

The ego manipulates its collection of fear-based emotions to hide anger, greed, jealousy, and envy in us to manipulate our lives and control how we interact and deal with others. These emotions feed into the soul from the outside-in, and at the same time love-based emotions feed into the soul from the spirit inside-out (see illustration on following page).

The illustration shows how the personality is created. From this doughnut-shaped soul surrounding the spirit, we express who we are as a person. Here is the key point to understand: The stronger and bigger fragments of these emotions dominate who we become as a person and how we communicate with others. This is important because a person could have a strong sense of compassion and the desire to help and serve others, yet the fear-based emotion of jealousy could overpower this compassion. Fear has the capacity and energy to dominate compassion in our souls, if we let it.

The dynamic that takes place here in the formation of our individual personalities is interesting. There exists the contribution of opposing emotions, which battle to create who we become as an individual personality.

The stronger fragments dominate; the stronger emotions win. An example would be if a person had a large fragment of kindness, but in opposition there was an even larger fragment of greed. This would cause the person to have compassion for another person who was struggling financially, but not enough kindness to keep from taking advantage of them to make money.

This is how the ego takes control of an unaware person's life. Clashing, fragmented emotions can create extreme pain and suffering in our lives. We tend to respond to the love fragments and react to the fear fragments. This is the point where, many times, fear is able to conquer our love-based emotions.

As children, life can be going along smoothly and we can feel loved and supported. Then the inevitable happens; circumstances beyond our control show up. Maybe a parent is lost through an untimely death. A divorce splits a family. A parent deserts a family and provides no support. Maybe the parents lose a job or suffer a financial hardship. A family could move to a neighborhood that presents a negative environment. Something awful could happen like physical or sexual abuse by a family member or relative. All these situations can shape the fragments of the personality. As a child, our tendency is to hide behind the painful fragments of our history because we aren't capable of surviving and coping in any other way with what appears as a scary, uncertain world.

What Voices?

Within the fragments of the soul lie the sources of the voices of the ego and the voices of the sensitive self. In the Valeo Method, we refer to them as voices of self and voices of the ego. We could compare this to the earlier example of the cartoon with the devil on one shoulder and the angel on the other, a metaphor that becomes closer to reality as we go forward.

The voices stay at war within, fighting to control your every thought, move, and decision. It is this simple; if you are unhappy, the voice of the ego dominates; if you are happy, the voice of the Authentic Self dominates. Where the voice of the ego is condescending, insulting, and painful, the voice of the Authentic Self is soothing, encouraging, and strengthening. The voices of the ego are loud, abrupt, and upsetting. The voices of the self are soft as a whisper, peaceful, and they instill you with a reminder of your innate goodness. This is the part we want to embrace, and this is the foundation of a healthy, happy, and rewarding life.

FRAGMENTED PERSONALITY

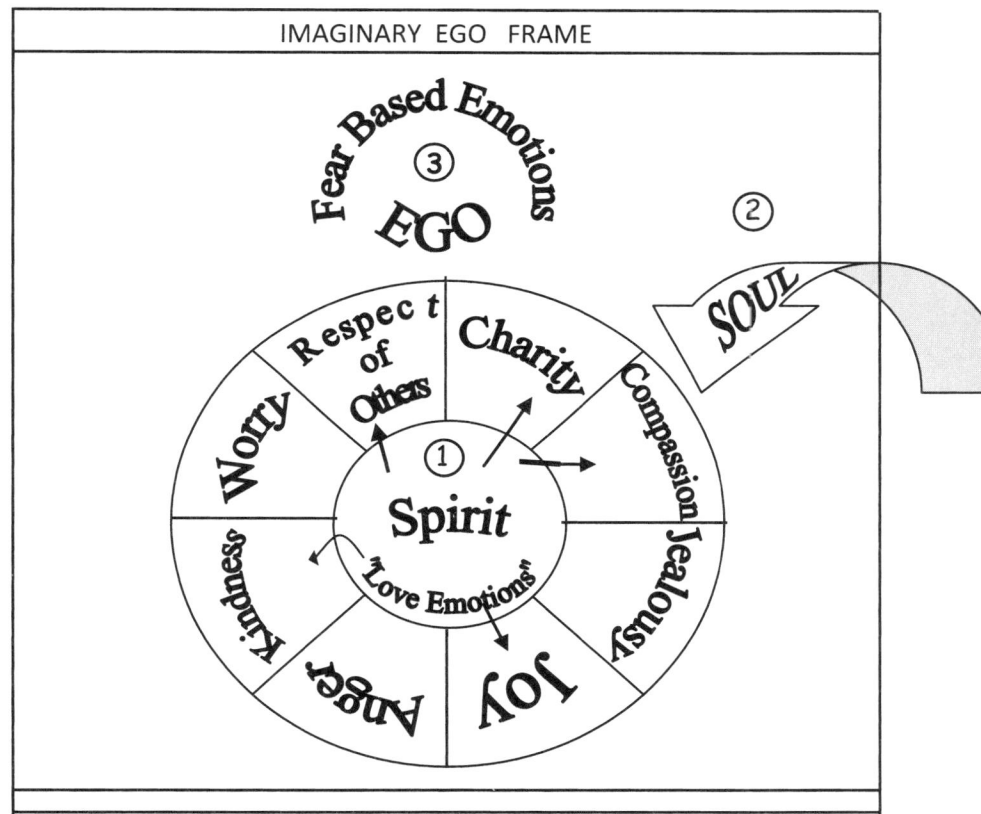

(1) THE SPIRIT IS THE CENTER OF YOUR BEING.
IT IS YOUR CONNECTION TO GOD AND YOUR SOURCE
OF THE   EMOTIONS ASSOCIATED WITH LOVE.

(2) SOUL (The Mind) SURROUNDS THE SPIRIT LIKE A DOUGHNUT.

(3) EGO LIVES IN ITS IMAGINARY FRAME AND HOLDS YOUR
FEAR-BASED EMOTIONS.

ARROWS SHOW LOVE AND FEAR-BASED EMOTIONS
PUSHING INTO THE SOUL. THIS RESULTS IN A FRAGMENTED
COMBINATION OF EMOTIONS AFFECTING LIFE.

Your goal should be to recognize every negative voice and remember that hiding beneath that negative and ugly voice is a treasure for you. It's as if your ego is protecting something valuable for itself. In reality, it is protecting its own identity because if you get past the ugly voice, you realize the ego has no power; then, you can gain control over that fragment of your personality.

In essence, you are peeling the onion of your persona in order to expose that which serves you and that which does not. It is a fascinating process to watch as a Life Coach, the effect this part of the process has on people, especially people who did not think they needed this type of inner work. The result can be quick and progressive. The more you *Release*, the faster things tend to change, and you then begin to attract the life you desire.

There is so much under the surface in our lives waiting to be exposed. Compare it to the ocean; the waves on the surface toss, turn, and thrash about, while underneath it is calm and eternally peaceful. The inner spirit, where the sensitive self resides, is the same way. It is that layer covering it up where the trouble resides. A person who never does this type of work and doesn't tap into the core of who they are may never know anything but life's turbulence and instability.

Chapter 38
Child Abuse and Adult Consequences

Child abuse casts a shadow the length of a lifetime.

Herbert Ward

Just as beliefs are passed down from generation to generation, in many cases abuse is also passed down. This can cause a cascading generational effect on families. It can be in many ways like a curse. The wounded sensitive self of the person dishing out the pain never heals by itself without help or serious trauma to force change. It is never going to just fade away or exhaust itself and get better on its own.

The child of an addict often finds himself an addict as a way to cope with the pain of the hate he felt toward the parent's abuse or neglect. Until something is done to change this and the pain stops, the process just repeats itself again and again.

A child who is abandoned by a parent finds herself as an adult unable to commit to a long-term relationship with another because of the fear of potential abandonment. A woman whose father beat her mother and is suffering from the painful memories of these witnessed events will be attracted to abusive men. She perceives this type of behavior as part of the way to receive love and nurture the wounded, sensitive self. This inner child is crying out for help and relief. These people are victims of their unconscious belief that they were at fault and that their abuse will allow them to feel love. This result is sadly very common; growing up with guilt and pain.

If you are affected by these words because you can relate, the Valeo Method will help you. I urge you to stay with the steps. You deserve to be free, and you are closer than you think.

Sarah's Story

Here is an extreme story of a lady I worked with to illustrate how a person can overcome her circumstances. Sarah grew up in an isolated rural area on a small farm with her parents and four sisters. Her father was a dominating and abusive alcoholic. He was also a control freak who loved to use fear and intimidation on his wife and five daughters.

Once when Sarah was eight years old, she stayed outside playing in the yard after her curfew, when it was dark. Their home was in a secluded area with the forest surrounding them. Sarah was scared to venture past the yard and avoided the wooded areas after dark.

Her father, drunk that night, was furious that she was outside past her curfew. To punish her, he loaded her in his truck and took her two miles down a lonesome road and put her out on railroad track that passed near their house. He left her crying and screaming in fear in the dark as he drove away. He told her to find her way home.

Horrified with each step, crying and cold, Sarah made it home. Her ordeal wasn't over. When she arrived home her father had locked her out of the house. She climbed in the back seat of the family car, horrified and shivering cold. Sarah's Mom, who wanted to help her, wasn't allowed to assist or else she would have been abused, too. This event had a traumatic effect on Sarah's future.

On another occasion, Sarah's father punished her for talking back by holding her fingers under scalding-hot water. Another time he punished her by having her stand a few feet away as he shot her in her shins with a BB gun. Once, he pulled out one of her fingernails with a pair of wire pliers.

When I first started working with Sarah, I saw she was attractive, intelligent, and outgoing. But on the inside she was a wreck. She had been from relationship to relationship. She had gone through several different jobs, all in sales, and she had owned two semi-successful small businesses. She had been through four psychologists, one psychiatrist, and two group therapies. She had been on a chemical gauntlet of every anti-depressant drug known to man, plus Ritalin, Librium, and even anti-seizure drugs (she had never had a seizure), with all these in fascinating and even dangerous contraindications. I could not believe she appeared as functional as she did.

Sarah never opened up and told the whole truth of her story to any of her therapists. Her father also abused her sexually. She had forced herself to deny it and blot it out, but the memories would not stay down. They kept rising to the surface of her thoughts. None of her therapies or counseling ever got her to a level where she could reach her sensitive self. All the attempts were directed like many therapies toward treating a confused personality—a result, or effect, of the problem, not the cause, which was much deeper. She needed healing for her wounded and aching soul.

After all her attempts to get help were only temporary at best, she was ready to give up. She had all but lost hope of ever being normal, and she attempted suicide. She had masked her pain as much as she could. Sarah was getting help fixing the fruit, not the root of her problem.

Sarah had her breakthrough with the Valeo Method and by using the exercises in this section. She discovered her driving force in her life was to be worthy. She had a burning desire to prove to her father, even though she rarely if ever spoke to him, that she was a winner. She excelled and overachieved at everything she did as an adult. In relationships she got the man she wanted (even though she couldn't make it work). In business she found the best people to model and succeeded. In her sales jobs she was always a leader. But nothing made her happy because her accomplishments were never enough to impress her father. All she really needed was to feel the love, approval, and praise she never got as a child.

It is sad to see a person with all this talent, drive, and personal power to be in so much pain that they want to take their own life and die. This is how devastating the power of a wounded sensitive self (child) can be.

The Valeo Method helped Sarah to have an epiphany. She was able to finally recognize what was causing her pain; she released her limiting beliefs, and by doing so let go of the painful and toxic emotions that were accompanying them. She learned to embrace her gifts. She realized that the gift behind her pain was an incredible drive and passion for accomplishment that most would love to have.

She accepted that as hurt-filled as her childhood was, it served a purpose. It was part of her journey to find her gifts and embrace them. Years later, Sarah is a happily married woman, an incredible mother and grandmother who is changing the abusive trend in her family. She is living a very successful and happy life.

No More Secrets

Doing this type of coaching work with clients like Sarah, I have been shocked at the backgrounds and histories of many adults. It has given me a deep compassion for the pain of others and compelled me to help them find solutions. Opening the heart and nurturing the sensitive self is not easy. This precious part of every one of us longs to communicate with us and be assured that any abuse or perceived shortcoming was not its fault. This encouragement needs to happen over and over again until it is accepted. We have to let all shame and guilt hear the voice of love and feel the compassion and relief the sensitive self offers. We have to be able to accept, know, and feel that childhood abuse was not our fault, but that we were the victim.

Eddie let his pain go too far. "Somebody was always drunk at my home growing up. My life was always in an uproar, never peaceful. I first started to drink at thirteen. I felt booze was the answer. It eased my pain. I just wanted somebody to love me. I knew something was wrong with me because I felt less than inadequate. I lacked guidance and was smothered in prejudice, poverty, and abuse. I learned violence from my father and landed in the streets because of my anger. I turned my back on lessons in living. I never enjoyed being me. I just repeated what I learned at home and on the street. My lifestyle was addictive, and it destroyed me."

This story is extreme, yet it shows how powerful and destructive our impacted emotional pain is and how it will tear apart and destroy life until it gets attention. Childhood abuse makes a person vulnerable, helpless, and weak. It seems ironic and unlikely that a victim of child abuse would become a victimizer; however, it is very common. The abuse is their response to their own weakness. The abuse got them attention as a child, which they associated with receiving love.

In order to find the strength of your sensitive self, you must seek its voice and hear it out. It has something to say to you. By letting the pain speak out to you, the door opens to the love it is covering up. If it is difficult or seems awkward to listen, find someone to talk to—a trusted friend, relative, minister, clergy, or best of all, talk to God. Share the feelings that are causing pain. Many times just talking loosens the hold of the voices of the ego, and it loses intensity. This effort takes away the need to beat ourselves up mentally and subject our-selves to continued pain.

It Is All About Love

We all have basic, intrinsic needs. We need to be loved, to feel cared for and safe. If these needs are not met, the voices of the ego haunt us with fear and all its related emotions, which include anxiety, grief, shame, and anger.

All addictions and abusive and compulsive behaviors are a signal that the wounded, sensitive self needs attention. The authentic part of us is always seeking the voices of love it missed as a child. All the love in the entire universe is in our basic nature. The *Embrace* step emphasizes that our happiness equates to our ability and capacity to give unconditional love. At the same time, all our misery and emotional upset equates to our need to receive unconditional love. Our soul must give and receive love to grow and evolve. When we indulge ourselves in self-centered behavior and ignore the needs of the soul, it is like telling a needy child, "You must suffer now because I have to do something for myself that is more important than you are at this moment in my life."

The ego is so manipulative and controlling that it actually makes us fear giving love to our sensitive self. Why? Because the ego fears being discovered and losing control and its identity. One trap many fall into is co-dependence.

Chapter 39
Co-dependence Kills the Dream of the Soul

Your vision will become clear when you look inside your heart...
Who looks outside, dreams. Who looks inside, awakens.

Carl Jung

When a person is dependent on someone or something outside themselves, they are co-dependent. Co-dependence is a serious problem and a disease of the mind. Co-dependence thrives in a dysfunctional family environment, affecting developing children as well as adults. It doesn't have to be a person; the co-dependency could be a Mercedes, clothes, jewelry, a particular job, a social standing, or an organization. Most commonly, however, it is a person and a relationship.

Some people get so dependent on other people and things that when they lose them they are so lost it drives them to misery, horrendous acts, and even suicide. They would literally rather die than lose these things that mask their pain.

Alcoholic parents often create co-dependency in the whole family. The fear and uncertainty of the situation they bring about causes everyone in the family to develop insecurity and adjust their life around it. They find themselves always on guard to protect, defend, or assist the addicted family member. This is at the expense of their own quality of life.

Co-dependency issues are always rooted in the insecurities and emotional pain connected to the sensitive self and its lack of unconditional love. The individual substitutes their lack of unconditional love with another person, thing, or habit. For example, they make themselves believe that all they need is a particular person or relationship, and the pain is bearable and they can deal with it. Otherwise, their alternative is to face the pain, and they just cannot bring themselves to do it.

Parental Addictions and Compulsive Behavior

The worst pain a child can experience is abandonment. Addictions and compulsive behavior by parents create feelings of abandonment in their children, even if the parent is not physically gone. It leaves the child feeling wounded and empty. The child's quest to fill this emptiness drives them, as developing children and then as adults, straight to the very behavior they hated in their parents or caretakers.

Alcohol and drug abuse lead as the most damaging addictions due to the behavior they cause. Although there are many other addictions that take attention away from being a responsible parent, like work, sex, food and overeating, gambling, sports, shopping, and money, alcohol and drug abuse is the worst.

Anything to distract, mask, or cover up feelings is just that—a mask. Addictions provide the source of distraction for the parent while the child receives the wounds. Many times it begins as an occasional escape from pain and moves to taking on a life of its own. Then it drains the energy and quality of life. The addiction can be so powerful and dominating that what remains of life is boring and low priority, which sadly could be the children of the addicted person.

Pain/Pleasure and the Sensitive Self

As I have emphasized earlier in the book, people will do more to avoid pain than to gain pleasure. By healing our wounds and making contact with the sensitive self, we are on the way to removing the pain we have been avoiding. Now the tendency toward compulsive/addictive behavior loses power.

The love-based emotions that have been with all of us from birth are always there to empower and direct us. Let's use a metaphor of a grand mansion with many rooms; each room represents an emotion as an illustration. As we interact with other people and situations, we are sharing our mansion full of rooms (emotions) with others. When our emotions are injured or our feelings are hurt, we close the door on the emotion that is causing us pain. Eventually this big mansion has so many closed-off rooms we might as well be living in the equivalent of a small apartment. Facing life without these resources rocks the quality of life.

Also, there are many rooms in the basement of the mansion. These rooms are the homes of all fear-based emotions. The ego prowls the hallways of the basement of our mind to make sure all the doors are open to the fear-based emotions.

With the Valeo Method, we will reverse this process and open the doors to the love-based emotions and close the doors to the fear-based emotions. (The ego hates this process, by the way.)

Chapter 40
Reaching the Innermost Self

*What lies behind us and what lies before us are tiny matters,
compared to what lies within us.*

Oliver Wendell Holmes

Our goal is to touch and embrace the sensitive self.
The more we open the doors of love emotions, the more we
cancel out the negative emotional charges that carry our pain.
By healing our dark nature, we can reclaim unlimited amounts
of personal power and ability. Most of us are hideously crippled
by our personal dark side. As we reduce our negative emotional
charges, we become present enough, mentally clear enough,
and emotionally mature enough to enjoy who we are so we can
express the authentic self.

To accomplish this valuable task of connecting with our
innermost, sensitive self, we must have an open mind. It may
seem a little awkward, or even weird at first. This is a normal
reaction. Remember, the ego does not want you to heal anything. The more it stays in control, the more you stay in pain.
Just be aware of this so you will know where any reluctance
you feel is coming from.

Contacting the sensitive self is not a complicated or difficult process. It just takes some discipline and patience. The good news is the rewards can be life-altering and happen quickly. Resist the temptation to feel silly or get discouraged. Many people have found their way to new joy and happiness through this process. Why not you?

Get Ready, Get Set

Making contact with your sensitive self and its negative emotional charge is an experience you need to be ready to have. Any discomfort you feel can actually be viewed as a measure of success. Moving in and out of these experiences allows you to gain control over your ongoing reality.

What can you expect after the discomfort? Increased harmony, joy, better health, better relationships, and natural abundance are a few examples. When you become more aware of your imbalance, you are actually creating balance. What do we do when life causes us to have questions like, "What is wrong with me? Will I ever be happy?" This is the beginning of "rising from the emotionally dead" by facing what is causing this kind of suffering and then dissolving it by embracing it.

Don't Look Back

The ego is brave and bold, so initially it may not get in the way of your commitment to change. The ego may even act like it wants to change, but don't be fooled!

This is why habits die hard. Let's say someone decides to quit smoking. This is a tough habit to break. If a person makes a commitment to quit, the ego might respond, "That's a great idea, go for it." So a person quits for a while, but then they start again. It doesn't even matter that it is a habit that kills. Death is the ego's most powerful tool of intimidation and fear.

Every time you attempt to stop a bad habit the ego gets a stronger hold on you. The ego gains more ability to keep you from penetrating the veil of fear-based emotions that are blocking your way to the sensitive self.

Take a Breath

In order to embrace the sensitive self we have to engage our free will. This is a process of doing something for ourselves instead of what we are expected to do for others. This may not be as easy as it sounds for some of you because you are so conditioned to spending your lives pleasing others. Some people have a hard time making time for themselves. In fact, some people do this so much they become unconscious of their own needs. I mention this here because to Embrace the sensitive self, we have to make time for self-analysis. For some this is a stretch, but you have to get over that feeling if you want to heal. There is no other way. This is no time to be a martyr.

As a child, our biggest gratification comes from doing what we need to do to please our parents. Sometimes we hate all these things we do. We don't see any other option, so we just live with our lives the way they are. We accept our lives as the way the cards were dealt to us. It is no wonder so many people are unhappy.

Now we are going to do something just for ourselves. We are going to activate and use our willpower to breathe. This may sound overly simplistic; however, for some people this is a challenging exercise. Why? Because you aren't used to doing many things for yourselves and using your free will. Think about how many times you said yes to something when you really meant no or vice versa because you felt like you had no choice, or were expected to do it. How many moms live every minute of their lives this way? Every time this happens you are feeding power to the ego and burying the sensitive self a little deeper.

This simple breathing exercise is designed to build the habit of using free will. This will give you power and resolve to overcome the obstacles to make lasting change. This opens up your inner world and enhances your outer world at the same time.

It is time to be alert. When the ego sees that you are really serious about making changes in your habits or stories, it will get busy and start trying to do anything it can to get in your way. Doubt and negative self-talk will start rushing in. This is where you get to hear your ego screaming, "Change is wrong!"

Awareness of Breathing

Breathing is so natural that we take it for granted. Hidden within our breathing is the connection of the soul and the authentic self, where the sensitive self is hidden. Here, within, lies your link to your essence, the source of life, our Creator.

Human beings are different from other living creatures because we pause when we breathe. We also have the ability to control the pause in our breathing. This is significant when we are seeking to connect with our source of life. Notice how a dog or cat breathes; you see no pause. They have a constant, rhythmic pace. If they are scared or threatened, they speed up their breathing, but they still don't pause.

Having the ability to control your breathing gives you the choice to use this tool to bring yourselves into present-moment awareness. When you concentrate on your breathing and eliminate the pause, you are bringing yourself closer to the present moment. This removes you from the illusion of time—past and future. This brings you to being in the moment, or in the flow.

This next point is a very important to understand: the ego can't survive in the present moment. Knowing this is the best way to block the voices of the ego.

When We Embrace, We Are Healing

It is time to start with our presence awareness session. You need to find a comfortable place with minimum noise. This is not always the easiest thing to do in your hectic and paced life. It is a huge step in reaching the sensitive self, however, and the more comfortable you can be while you are engaged in this process, the closer you move to intimacy with your sensitive, precious, and deepest self. We are about to begin a basic process of age regression. You are going to go back and meet with the part of you that has something to tell you and something to give you.

Sit in a comfortable position and relax. Make sure you have good posture. You can sit in a chair, on the floor (legs crossed or not), or sit up in the bed. It is best not to lie down unless you must because you want to avoid getting so comfortable that you fall asleep and lose the concentration on your breathing.

Once you are comfortable and relaxed, close your eyes and take in seven deep breaths. Breathe in peace, exhale any worries, breathe in love, exhale stress, breathe in peace, exhale fears. Relax. Breathe in gently, no pause, just steady, controlled, in–and–out, flowing breathing. You may start to feel some heaviness in your body, and this is normal.

You are inviting something very enlightening to happen to you. You are about to let your sensitive self know that someone is there to be with him/her and share in his/her feelings and innocence. You are about to open up a channel to love and nurture this precious part of yourself. There is nothing religious about this process; it is a journey to your inner spirit, and if anything, it is spiritual. It is not hypnotism either; life puts you in a similar trance several times a day, just as you are right now, so being in this state is natural and you can stop anytime you feel uncomfortable.

Continue to practice breathing in and out without pause and feel the peace and lightness. Feel more relaxation with each breath. As you breathe, feel the inner strength building within. Try to notice the gentleness and love of the spirit. Feel your body as you are breathing. Feel the air moving in the room. Listen to as many sounds as you can in the quietness surrounding you. Relax and allow yourself to absorb the moment. Breathe, relax, breathe, and relax. If you haven't closed your eyes, then close them now. Allow rising thoughts to pass by like words going across the screen of your mind, passing through, but not staying.

Now it is time to use the imagination (while continuing your steady, controlled, yet effortless breathing) and imagine yourself standing at the top of a beautiful staircase and looking down on a wide, expansive, sacred garden. You are going into your very own personal safe haven. Picture the perfectly manicured grass, magnificent flowers and blooming trees with brilliant colors, pure blue skies and endless parades of puffy clouds. There is a refreshing and pleasant breeze. Smell the aroma and fragrance and the freshness of spring. Listen to the birds sing in harmony and the leaves gently moving against one another. Just stop and take it in. Take a deep breath, now release, another deep breathe, then release, that's it.

Now, you begin to walk down the staircase into your garden and when you get there, find a place to sit—anywhere you like. You can sit on the ground or on a special white bench that is there just for you. Relax and settle into the moment while continuing to control your breathing.

Now it is time to invite your sensitive self, your wounded inner child, into the garden. Think of a time when you felt frightened, alone, or unloved. Think of a time when you felt hurt or abandoned. Bring that time forward in your mind. See yourself at that age, at that time, through your eyes as a child at that time. You can do it. How does the world look? How do you feel now? What age do you see yourself? Try to notice the age; this is important.

Now it is time to ask this part of you, the earlier you, to come forward and join you in your garden. Tell this child it is safe and that you want to show him/her love, kindness, and encouragement. Tell him/her you want to show him/her love, support, and compassion, and that you miss him/her.

Visualize your inner child self, this sensitive, younger self slowly coming into your presence. He/she might appear at age four, six, or eight years of age. Whatever age it is, that is the age that needs attention the most. As he/she comes forth, maintain your constant breathing. Look closely at the appearance of the child and into the eyes. Tell the child you love him/her. Ask what he/she needs at this time. Follow his/her lead; there may be a need for reassurance, he/she may need a hug, or he/she may need to cry out and release pain.

This sensitive part of your younger self may need to be with you and play something that was lacking during childhood. Let him/her know that things are different now and that you are here to show love and support from now on (this is very important). Promise to always love, nurture, and protect him/her.

He/she may appear angry, hyper, aggressive, or sad. As you seek to embrace him/her, feel the emotions that are present.

Hold his/her face in your hands and look into his/her eyes. Notice his/her youthful innocence and smile at him/her. Listen to whatever he/she wants to tell you. Be there and comfort him/her. All this part of you wants is to reconnect with you and to be loved unconditionally and feel protected and safe. Watch and be patient, and he/she will become relaxed, peaceful, and relieved to be with you.

Now, one last time, look at your younger, sensitive self and tell him/her that this is a new beginning of your relationship. Tell him/her that from now on you are going to spend more time with him/her and be there for all his/her needs. Tell him/her that he/she will never have to be afraid again. Promise you will make time to have regular visits, like this one. Tell him/her you will meet again in the sacred garden anytime he/she needs you. Now have one last loving embrace and say good-bye. Let him/her fade back into your heart until you meet again.

Gently follow your breathing and come out of this experience. You should feel rested, relaxed, but also energized with your new discovery. If this exercise seems bizarre or a stretch for you, don't feel bad; that can be normal. The key is to not take it for granted. Don't be surprised or startled if the child is aggressive or upset; this is actually a good sign, because you have discovered a part of you that is responding to an opportunity to heal. Part of your healing process is getting yourself to have the humility and courage to complete this exercise. Your ego is going to convince you not to do it, so be prepared.

Congratulations. You have taken a huge step toward opening up and knowing the Real You and becoming whole as a person. I know this may be a stretch for some people. I challenge you to push through it and don't give up. It is a very powerful exercise, and it is worth it. If you have a difficult time imagining, stop and try again later. It will get easier; you can do it. Be encouraged!

Be Prepared

There may be some discomfort either during or after performing this exercise. Memories that are buried deep and locked away because of the pain they caused may seem long forgotten. Be prepared to be shocked, pleasantly surprised, and potentially overwhelmed with emotion. This process can cause unusual experiences, and the more emotional sensitivity, the more potential for relief and positive results.

The process works for everyone who commits to seeing it through. If you want to get to the truth about who you really are and stop sabotaging yourself, this road has to be traveled sooner or later. You have to embrace the sensitive self, your locked-away beliefs and emotions, to be free.

I was very reluctant initially to do this process. In fact, it seemed kind of silly. The more I researched the concept, though, the more I was convinced it was real and necessary if I wanted to experience wholeness. My own experience was totally rewarding and resulted in a release and unexpected explosion of emotion. I was totally overtaken by emotions of relief and joy. Now, as I witness the people I work with on a one-on-one basis experience the same feelings, I am re-anchored to my own joyful experience, and I encourage you to see it through, as well. If you don't get results at first, that is okay— let me encourage you again—continue the exercise. You probably weren't relaxed and breathing well enough to get focused, or your ego was causing you doubt. Remember, the ego hates this process and will try to use everything it can to distract and discourage you. Be prepared!

John Bradshaw, a pioneer in inner child work, recommends writing a letter to your inner child. I have found that for some, this works well if the previous exercise is too difficult. This is especially helpful if you have a hard time visualizing things in the mind, as required by the exercise. Bradshaw even recommends writing with the non-dominant hand. Although awkward, it tends to access parts of your mind that you normally do not use.

There is a story about a young girl who was trying to learn to jump rope while playing in the front yard. Her mother was in the yard with her, working in her flower bed. The local minister from the church stopped by to visit. Upon seeing the child struggling to jump rope, the minister said, "Let us help you try again, and every time you are successful, we will clap." After just a few attempts, the girl was jumping consistently. Her mother and the minister provided a steady series of claps. Caught up in conversation, the adults stopped clapping for a few minutes. The little girl, now frustrated and struggling, stomped her feet and protested, "Now listen! I think I am going to get good at this jumping rope thing, but I am going to need lots more of that clapping!"

You can't see me, but I am clapping for you right now! We all need encouragement for sure—no matter who we are or where we are in life's journey.

Chapter 41
The AFIG Process

*The deviation of man from the state in which he was originally placed
by nature seems to have proved to him a prolific source of diseases.*

Edward Jenner (Discoverer of the Small Pox Vaccine)

We will move to another phase of the *Embrace*
process. It's time to learn some skills to move you forward in
your personal growth and give you the protective tools to avoid
slipping back into less desirable behavior and emotional states.
The Valeo Method teaches us to recognize which parts of our
personality fragments are represented by the ego and which
parts are represented by the real self. Otherwise, we just live
with the ones that are the strongest and accept that "this is
who I am." Without being conscious of this dynamic and doing
exercises like the previous one, we are serving the ego, not our
authentic selves. What you did in the last exercise was about
following the pain and addressing it.

When you decide to align yourself with your authentic self rather than the ego, you create a reality that reflects who you really are, and not who the ego wants you to be.

You have to let the voices of spirit, the language of your soul, speak and unfold in your life to become whole. In order to do that, we are going to defuse the ego every time it raises its head until it doesn't have enough power to influence you anymore.

When the ego starts bringing in negative self-talk, judgments, confusion, and language that you don't accept, the first step is remember Catch and Release. Catch the thoughts and words, slam them up in your garbage can, and immediately float them away in the yellow helium balloon. Get rid of them before they take root. It may take practicing and using Catch and Release several times, so don't get discouraged; it works, unless you give in to the ego. Make Catch and Release a part of your daily life—make it a good habit, and it will change your life. We have many success stories from our support groups from those who are committed to Catch and Release, and they teach it to those they spend the most time with.

The next tool we are going to learn and use in the Valeo Method is called AFIG. AFIG is a mnemonic we will use that represents an extremely powerful process: **A**cceptance, **F**orgive, **I** love you (yourself) and **G**ratitude. AFIG is the next level beyond Catch and Release, and they are designed to work synergistically together.

The concept of "A fig" comes from the representation of man's knowledge in the Bible. Adam and Eve chose to eat from the tree of life and gain knowledge. The serpent (Satan) convinced Eve that they needed knowledge and that God was keeping something from them. After realizing their mistake of going against God, committing sin, and losing paradise, Adam and Eve were embarrassed and used fig leaves (representing knowledge) to cover themselves and avoid shame. We do the same today, only the ego is another representation of the serpent, who supplies each of us with knowledge that keeps us in pain and suffering.

With AFIG we will cross over to the bridge of awareness. You will learn to use these simple steps to avoid going the wrong way and to escape the grip of the ego.

Crossing The Bridge Of Awareness

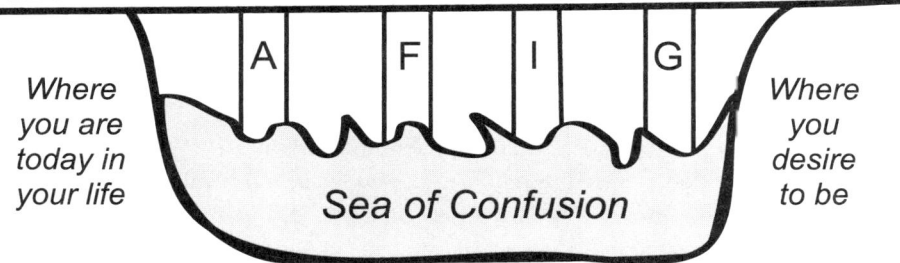

Each step of AFIG takes us away from

confusion and uncertainty and unto

self confidence and control

The illustration shows two shores, a body of water, and a bridge between the shores. One side represents an unfulfilled life dominated by the ego, and the other is a life of freedom, strength, empowerment, and peace. The bridge is supported by four pillars, labeled AFIG. Across the bridge are great rewards, but the journey is not easy. Along the way temptations call from the ego to come back. Also, in order to keep you from crossing, the ego presents dark energies along your path. These dark spirits represent all your fears. These are all spirits of doubt, worry, defeat, laziness, discouragement, envy, jealousy, and anger. They are all spirits that cause defeat and failure and for you to surrender to the ego.

There is something you need to know about these spirits. It is their job is to reach up and grab you as you cross the bridge and scare you so you will want to run back to the other side where there is true fear, lack, and disappointment. But here is a secret: Believe, use the steps in AFIG and have faith in the process so the dark spirits that grab you can't hold you for long. If you know the AFIG process, you will be able to bounce right back on the bridge and continue to cross it. But you must remember that the minute you start to doubt and the bridge starts shaking, the negative demons (your limiting thoughts from past references) will try to grab you in the darkness of the moment, but only temporarily. They cannot hold you. You have access to a power that is no match for them.

This illustration is to provide you with a mental image you can pull up when you face emotional challenges and the pain and suffering related to them. In the illustration we see that before you cross the bridge there is unconscious living, fear-based emotions dominate, and there is much uncertainty. After crossing the bridge, you will experience conscious living, confidence and courage, love-based emotions dominate, and you are living a life of certainty.

By using the AFIG illustration, we are removing the fig leaf of protection and allowing ourselves to be vulnerable, which is necessary in order to make change. That is what happened in the last exercise with the sensitive self. This way, we reveal to ourselves, like Adam and Eve did, that "man's knowledge" is a false sense of identity. We are in essence humbling ourselves to expose who we really are—spiritual beings having a human experience, not human beings having a spiritual experience.

Acceptance

As you start across the bridge of awareness, the principle of "acceptance" comes first. Throughout the Valeo Method there is constant emphasis on accepting "what is." To accept that everything happens for a reason and a purpose is a huge step toward conquering limiting beliefs, emotions, and fears. Yet most of us are a little stubborn, and we have traits, tendencies, and even blind spots that we simply refuse to admit to ourselves.

Who hasn't tried to analyze and figure out why things are the way they are? Most of the time this process is frustrating, right? Why? The Bible tells us, *"My thoughts are nothing like your thoughts,"* says the Lord. *"And my ways are far beyond anything you could imagine."* Most of us will agree that we can drive ourselves crazy trying to figure out God! As soon as we can accept that whatever is happening in our lives today is part of our journey, the sooner we discover peace of mind and wholeness

Acceptance means seeing your life as a play staged by God, with each event simply a scene in the play. This allows you to see each event as a lesson, a message to you from the Almighty. Then you learn to automatically ask: "What am I supposed to learn from this challenge?" or "What is the opportunity behind this challenge? There has to be something good here for me. What is it?"

Some things we are just not meant to know, and trying too hard to figure them out can cause us grief. I heard a story about two friends who were professional baseball players. They had an ongoing discussion about whether there was baseball in heaven. They made a pact that the first one to go would come back and tell the other if there was baseball in heaven. When the first player died he went to heaven and as he promised, came back to visit his friend and share what he found out. "I have some good news and some bad news," he told his friend. He said, "I am going to give you the good news first. Yes, there is baseball in heaven." "Wonderful!" his friend exclaimed. "But what is the bad news?" His friend answered, "You are pitching next Thursday."

Sometimes it is really better if we just don't know why things are happening. A person might say, "All this positive-thinking stuff is too much for me. My life is a wreck, and nothing is going right." We actually attract situations and people into our lives to teach where we have lack and where we need to grow. Do you have discouragement in your life? Are you ready to accept it is there to teach you to have courage? Do you have distrust in your life? Are you ready to accept it is there to teach you to have trust? Do you have anxiety and find yourself frequently rushing? Couldn't it be there to teach you patience? These are just a few examples. If you don't learn the lessons life is trying to teach you, the pain doesn't stop—in fact, it gets worse.

Nobody said it is easy to accept everything and hope for the best. This is especially true when the past is right under the surface of our consciousness, stalking our every move, reminding us of our failures and shortcomings. Healing the wounds of our past is a sacred process. It is a Divine event, a moment when we decide to step out of our dramas, the smallness of ourselves, and see the sacredness of ourselves. The only way to win this battle is to surrender. Not give up and surrender, but give in to the Divine plan that is meant to guide your life, to get you into the flow. If you are ready to go to the next level, it is time to get out of your own way and let your life unfold. Now, this doesn't mean to sit back and let life beat you to pieces. It means to stop fighting it like a drowning person fights the water. It is time to accept where we are as part of our intended path and put as much faith in our dreams as we used to put in our reasons why things wouldn't work in our lives. We must remind ourselves that our souls yearn to realize their full potential. When you accept God's plan for your life, you get to live in the flow. The angels will cheer you on, they will be singing, "Glory, Hallelujah, another one gets it!"

Before going to the next step of AFIG, resolve to live in acceptance that whatever is happening in your life at this moment is there on purpose and you will learn and grow because of it.

Forgiveness

Forgiveness is a huge step. The weight we carry from lack of forgiveness is very heavy. It takes a lot of character and love to forgive. Lack of forgiveness also carries a big price. It is like a cancer that eats away at a person. It can destroy relationships and ruin lives. It stops progress toward personal growth and spiritual enlightenment dead in its tracks. A heart that cannot forgive is bound, limited, and will never be free until it forgives, never. Jesus tells you, *"If you forgive those who sin against you, your heavenly Father will forgive you. But if you refuse to forgive others, your Father will not forgive your sins."*

You must learn to *Embrace* your past in order to forgive and change the present. Some people can't forgive their parents and blame them for their circumstances. Others blame their ex-spouses for wrecking their lives. Some blame siblings, business partners, or friends. Are you blaming someone and letting it hold you back?

Here is the problem: No matter which person you have a problem forgiving, by not forgiving them, you are not in control of your emotional pain. The person you blame is controlling you, and they don't even know it! They are going right on with their life while you continue to suffer, day after day after day.

Forgiveness is what we call an energy dynamic. Lack of forgiveness drains your energy and your ability to move ahead positively in your life.

Forgiving is not about pretending or hiding your true feelings. It's about completely meaning that you forgive. By forgiving, you are not giving in and saying what someone did is okay. You are just accepting what happened and refusing to be bound by it. Forgiving in some ways is a selfish act because it releases you from the pain of your own judgments. When you forgive, you loosen the ego's hold so the healing process can begin. Forgiveness is a kind of relief valve. Plus, when you look beyond the behavior of a person, you can learn to recognize the innocence of their souls, which makes it easier to forgive.

This doesn't mean you should take abuse or be mistreated in order to forgive. It doesn't mean being weak, either. On the contrary—it means being strong. Who do you admire the most, a person with a short temper who attacks in an instant, or someone who is calm and hard to provoke? Author Rabbi Harold Kushner once said, "When I was young I admired people who were clever; when I got older I admired people who were kind." The older we get, most of us tend to naturally soften our feelings. But then it can be too late and we sacrificed ourselves to years of unnecessary pain and suffering instead of forgiving.

Now is the time to free your spirit from the anchors of past lack of forgiveness. Forgiveness is only valuable when it is given away. We must not let our lack of forgiveness own us, control us, and sour our lives. We must not let it keep us from what we are entitled to.

How do you go about forgiveness? It's simple; you address it, state your feelings, forgive, and move on. Remember, every time you forgive, you strengthen your forgiveness muscle and move one step closer to God and His grace. When you carry past bitterness forward, it sabotages your future.

When you forgive you loosen up, you lighten up. Forgiveness is a cornerstone to freedom. It creates a humbling of the heart and spirit that brings big rewards. The beauty is, you don't have to look outside for this gift; you can give it to yourselves when you are ready to forgive.

Don't go on to the next step of AFIG until you have really focused on having a forgiving heart, and that especially means forgiving yourself of any guilt or shame you are carrying.

I Love You

The "I" in AFIG represents saying, "I love you" to yourself. Not in an egotistical sense, but in an appreciation of who God chose you to be. Each individual soul seeks to be nurtured and loved. When you don't like or even hate who you are as a person, you are going against nature, against God. No matter how out of whack and off-track your life may seem, this kind of thinking is never good. No matter how sick you are, or how many demons are taunting you, or how money mistakes you have made, or how many relationships you have screwed up, God created you for a purpose, and He loves you. He is also counting on all of us to fulfill our purpose.

Since God planted His spirit in each of us to begin life, there is something important we should know. Saint Paul tells us, *"And we have received God's spirit (not the world's spirit), so we can know the wonderful things God has freely given us."* Let's consider the light of God as an eternal flame. Let's picture God taking a small flame from Himself and placing it into each one of us at our inception as that bundle of joy, even before He gave us DNA. That puts the Light of God within each of us. If we hate or even dislike ourselves, not our egos, but our authentic selves, we are having those same feelings toward God! When we do this, we are blocking the flow of God and His favor and blessings through our lives.

Let's consider this: None of us has any talents or gifts. God has them; He just chooses to express them through us. All we have to do is get out of God's way and let Him flow through us. That means loving who we are individually and what we are, an expression point, a vessel, for God's Divine purpose. How can we not love ourselves when we have this consciousness? We have to get out of God's way so He can use us and bless us. This means loving and embracing who we are, broken vessel and all. The more we love ourselves, the less room for the ego, which is just another name for fear. And fear is no match for love. Saint Paul tells his spiritual son Timothy, *"God has not given us a spirit of fear and timidity, but of power, love, and self-discipline."*

When we make peace with ourselves, we are automatically making peace with everyone else in the world. We stop thinking who is better than whom. It doesn't matter anymore.

Don't go on to the next step of AFIG until you have contemplated how awesome and amazing you are and how God thought so much of you that He created you in His mind before you were even born. In fact, according to the Bible, He saw your whole life and recorded it in His book before you were born. Wow! That makes you some kind of special person and chosen for greatness!

Gratitude

The last step is gratitude. This brings together the AFIG healing process and allows for a transition to peace. There is an importance to the order of these steps. The first three steps set up the last. They get us ready to have gratitude.

It is impossible for depression and negative emotion to take root in a grateful heart. Have you ever noticed that the word "gratitude" has some interesting similarities to the words "great attitude"? Giving and a great attitude go together.

When you own stock in a company and it increases in value, you say it is "appreciating." And when you "appreciate" something, it increases in value. Through conscious choice we cause whatever we focus our attention on to increase in value. What you experience in your life is what you put the most attention on. Your current life experience is your proof of this truth. This would prove that whatever you love, acknowledge, and Embrace increases.

It may be hard sometimes to be grateful. When these feelings come, it is time to search your soul and just ask, "What am I grateful for right now?" You might say, "My life stinks. I'm just grateful to be alive, and that is it." If that is true, God Bless you. Do you know why? Because if you are here and alive, there is a good reason for it.

I saw a sign on the side of the road the other day that said, "Nothing to be thankful for? Check your pulse!" If you have a pulse, God is not finished with you. He has plans for you or you wouldn't be here, my friend. The past does not equal the future, and God is in the miracle business—He has one right now with your name on it! God works best in tough situations. God's delays are not God's denials.

Since you are alive, here is some more good news—you are in God's favor. Good things are waiting to be discovered by you, for you. When you put your attention on God and be grateful for what you have, as little as it may seem, something incredible happens. You are accepting God's unconditional love, and this brings forth His grace. What is grace? Grace is unmerited or undeserved favor. You are focusing your attention on and being grateful for what you have, and look out, here come the blessings. The Bible says, *"For whoever finds me finds life, and finds favor with the Lord."*

The Bible also tells us to be grateful and thank the Lord constantly for what you have. That means life, health, family, friends, talents, gifts, and every meal. When you feel grateful, you automatically open the spigot of God's unceasing grace and blessings, so get ready, hold onto your hat—heavenly help is on the way!

If you have followed the four steps of AFIG preceded by the use of Catch and Release, you will be feeling tremendous release. You will have let go of energies, thoughts, and emotions that were causing you pain. What follows will help you know how and when to use and teach AFIG to increase the quality of your life and those around you.

Using AFIG

Let's put it all together now. Remember to get in the habit of using Catch and Release to constantly clear your mental path of the ego's distracting chatter and negative thoughts. Now you are ready to use the AFIG healing process to ease and arrest the rising of recurring emotional pain and suffering. AFIG can also be used to diffuse any negative self-talk or any fear-based emotions like worry, doubt, or stress that are causing you discomfort.

The goal is to move from unconscious pain and suffering across the "bridge of awareness" to the Promised Land of conscious, controlled thoughts. It is easy to get discouraged and give up and want to go back. Dream stealers and energy suckers love to push you off the bridge or drag you to their pity parties. Then you are back where you started, only more discouraged.

Ancient Hebrew history tells us how people on a long journey would make big piles of stones along their paths. This way, when they become discouraged they could look back and be reminded of all their blessings and how far they had gone. Also, they could remember the place they did not want to go.

AFIG should be used as a response to a trigger of emotional pain or upset. Repetition is the mother of skill, so the more you practice AFIG, the better you get at using the process. Eventually the ego loses power, negative self-talk and language is replaced, and the quality of life takes off. Consider AFIG as a secret weapon to diffuse and stop your emotional pain.

Here is an example of how AFIG might work. An upset arises, so think immediately, I need to use AFIG, and start going through the steps, one by one. Let's practice now.

Step One: I *accept* everything happening to me right now as part of my journey. I accept "what is" even though I don't understand it. I accept that all events are part of my intended path, they are governed by God, and they will serve me and the greater good of all concerned. By accepting, I am allowing Divine power to flow through me.

Step Two: I *forgive* myself for losing my composure, overacting, getting angry, being worried, being scared, or lacking faith (or anything that caused an upset). I forgive any person who has caused me upset. I understand that I attract all events in my life so I can learn, grow stronger, and get better. I forgive this person because I don't know the circumstances they are facing in their lives. I believe they are doing the best they can with the resources they have at this time.

Step Three: I *love* who I am, I love who I am becoming, and I have a Divine purpose. When I am kind to myself, I will be kind to others; they will in turn be kind to me. I love myself first because it affects how I give love and how I receive love from others.

Step Four: I am *grateful* for this experience as an opportunity for me to learn and grow. I am grateful that because of this upset and the way I am handling it, I am one step closer to wholeness and peace. I am grateful that I don't allow this challenge to control me anymore because I receive the message it brings me.

Congratulations in advance for using this healing process! You will take a huge leap forward in honoring and healing your soul. You will have nurtured the part of yourself that is your essence and the connection of your soul to God.

The success stories from committing to and using AFIG have been nothing short of amazing. I highly encourage you to take this process seriously and use it, master it, and teach it to others. Just think about the difference it will make when all the people around you learn to use this powerful tool to control their painful upsets, negative emotions, and worries. Have fun with it and be encouraged!

AFIG allows you to go from reactive thinking, which the ego controls, to responsive thinking, which the authentic self controls. This offers you new confidence for taking charge of life.

Use AFIG on all types of negative and undesirable beliefs— current, core, and locked away. This is about learning to stand with courage on your own two emotional feet once and for all. Now you are driving the bus that is carrying around your emotions through life instead of riding in the back with a reckless driver (the ego) at the wheel. AFIG has another purpose you will learn about in the next section called *Activate and Attract*.

Chapter 42
Controlling Anger

Anyone who angers you conquers you.

Benny Morris

When the pain of emotional wounding is intense, the sensitive self may need more than Catch and Release and AFIG. This situation occurs when the pain gets to the point at which it causes angry responses. By understanding your imbalances, you can learn to change, control, and eliminate your anger. All anger originates from pain and discomfort and the result of impacted emotions. Anger is blocked and trapped negative emotion. Since emotion is energy in motion, in reality what you have is negative energy or a negative charge seeking an outlet. The anger happens as a reaction to a trigger, which is set off by a thought or memory of a past painful event or circumstance.

Anger causes heat and friction in your physical bodies as the upset develops. We even communicate our feelings by saying things related to the heat we feel. Examples would be, "I'm boiling mad," or I'm about to blow my top," or "In the heat of the moment I screwed up," or "I just lost my cool." When we are controlled by the ego, self-talk like these examples fans the flames of a negative emotional charge. This can keep a person poised like a cocked gun for an angry reaction.

Anger is not all bad. It can have its benefits. It is a signal to protect ourselves and stand up for what is right. It allows us to deal with unjust treatment and defend ourselves.

When an angry mother reacted to her daughter's unnecessary death caused by a drunk driver, she saved thousands of lives. The Mothers Against Drunk Drivers organization has changed the attitude of the courts, getting and keeping drunk drivers off the road.

John Walsh's anger over the kidnapping and brutal murder of his young son Adam caused him to take action. He created and launched *America's Most Wanted* television show. The show has single-handedly brought hundreds of dangerous and violent criminals to justice.

The problem with anger comes when we take it for granted and it hurts others and ourselves. Anger gets us in trouble when we keep it suppressed too long and the pain becomes unbearable. This leaves us vulnerable to potentially bad decisions from anger-fueled reactions. Most people don't know how to deal with anger in a healthy way.

In order to *Embrace* the sensitive self, we have to *Release* our anger. We accomplish this by doing the opposite of what comes naturally. Instead of avoiding our demons and running from them, we will face them and blast them with energy, and they will go away. This may seem scary and awkward at first. Just remember, on the other side of fear is where the living is found. If you are willing to do the uncomfortable until it is comfortable, get ready to find a source of great strength and power. The alternative is to do nothing and expect things to get better.

Unreleased anger will eventually release itself—one way or another, like it or not, it is going outward—through outwardly expressed emotions, hostility, resentment and aggressive behavior, or the opposite way, inward, with depression, self-abuse, self-hatred, or loss of motivation. It could get even worse, resulting in physical sickness or unbearable pain, which could even lead to suicide.

There is another option, and that is to let the pain fuel your energies to do something different and seek to conquer it. This is exactly what Eula McClaney did. She likes to refer to herself as just an ordinary person with uncommon drive caused by a life of hardship. She was born in rural Alabama to black sharecropper parents. She had three brothers and one beautiful sister. She watched on like Cinderella as her sister was favored and received pretty clothes and was not forced to work in the cotton fields.

Eula had to leave school in the sixth grade. About that time the family home burned down and they were forced to move into a shack. Every Christmas she received the same thing: two apples, two oranges, and four pieces of candy. Seeking change, she married a miserly sharecropper. She had a son and a daughter. They lived in a two-room shack with no glass windows.

Eula was working in the fields six days a week—the only female among a bunch of men. She was ambitious and saved her money. Her husband resented her dreams and blocked her every way she turned (NIOP). She was tired of working in the fields and was determined to find a way out. She took her savings and bought a large house and rented out rooms. She continued to save and buy properties. Nine years later she had thirty-two properties.

Her success continued, and she bought a mansion in Pittsburgh. Her husband was still jealous and envious of her success and refused to move in with her. She divorced him. At her death in 1987, Eula was worth over $100 million. She owned a Rolls Royce, jewelry, furs, and she gave millions to charity. She met presidents and was interviewed in magazines.

Eula let her pain fuel her drive and found peace and success. She released her frustration and did not let it destroy her. She embraced her gifts and found her purpose. As a result, she encouraged and helped many.

Eula's husband is another consideration. People who don't feel comfortable with themselves or the idea of success for others get relief from exerting dominance over others. People who feel good about themselves don't need to prove themselves by showing power over someone else. People who constantly strive to show power over others are living at the mercy of their egoic mind and will never be happy unless they realize what is happening to them. The sad part is, very few of them ever discover the truth.

Simply put, if we don't face our anger and deal with it, we are headed for undesirable behavior, health-related issues, and other consequences sooner or later. If we face it and deal with it, we can find emotional balance. Some people get stuck in the middle with passive-aggressive behavior. This results in finding ourselves in places of heat, anger, and stress one minute, and nice, cool places in another, which is also very destructive behavior. Then there are those who deal with it like Eula Mc-Claney.

Now we move to another phase of the *Embrace* process. It's time to learn skills to move us ahead in our personal growth and give us the protective tools to avoid slipping back into less-desirable behavior. It is important that we learn how to distinguish which parts of our fragmented personalities are "soul" and which parts are "ego." If we just live out the ones that are the strongest and accept them as who we are, it can create constant calamity in our lives. Without being conscious of the dynamics and doing exercises like meeting the sensitive self, we are guaranteed to serve the ego and not our authentic selves. In the last exercise we followed the pain and addressed it.

When we decide to align ourselves with our authentic self rather than the ego, we create a reality that reflects who we really are and not who the ego creates us to be. This is also what happens when we let the voices of spirit, the language of our soul, speak and unfold in our lives.

Understanding the Anger of Others

There is a huge benefit in understanding why and how we create our own anger. It helps us recognize and deal with the cause of anger in others. Why would this be valuable to us? Because we will be able to sense and see anger before it quite gets to us, and it will help us not take others' anger so personally. We don't know what suppressed negative emotional charge another person is carrying.

I used to get mad at disrespectful, noisy, and rude people. I thought there was no excuse for their behavior. Now I feel sorry for people who act out and display these traits. I have a different perspective. Since I know what causes my emotional pain, I can have empathy and realize they are experiencing un-integrated, painful emotions that are causing them to suffer. This immediately has a calming effect on me. Just as Jesus said on the cross, *"Father, forgive them, for they do not know what they do,"* I now realize that these folks don't know what they are doing to themselves and others or what is causing their behavior.

Knowledge and understanding has power, and now we are going to learn to use our power to test the authentic self and the sensitive self, the source of your compassion. Against this source of love, anger cannot survive. This is Mike's story.

"I hated my dad. He would love me and treat me well occasionally, and I would feel so happy. He was gone most of the time and would come in drunk and yell at my mom. Sometimes he would be rough with her, and me, too. I was angry at my mom for letting him keep coming back. I was so angry, I wanted to kill him or just run away and never come back. When he was killed in an auto accident, I was even madder at him for abandoning me than for the abuse.

"As an adult I found myself living my worst nightmare. I was acting just like my father towards my son. My relationship with my son was becoming like the relationship I had my father.

"When I found the Valeo Method I had an awakening. I discovered the reason I was acting like my father was a reaction to the pain of my sensitive self. When I learned to release the pain, I took control and embraced my sensitive self. My behavior changed and my relationship with my son changed and is growing every day in a very positive way."

Sadly, Mike's story is common. Anger comes with a big price. In the heat of the moment it doesn't seem to matter. Then here comes reality and the huge regrets. By understanding the source of anger in others, it is easier to avoid conflict, take a deep breath, and prevent an upset. Anger is a natural byproduct of the ego-building process. It is the neglected and rejected parts of us that cause us to feel the pain. These locked-away parts of us are usually outside of our awareness, hovering near the surface, waiting for a chance to pop out. This is what happens when we find ourselves saying, "I don't know what happened; I just lost it."

Childhood Anger Experiences

Many adults carry memories of frightful and painful childhood experiences. There are those parents who constantly yelled and screamed at each other or their children. There are parents who used fear as a way to control. Sometimes parents are neglectful or constantly critical. Parents who make unreasonable demands or unjustified accusations can cause even worse pain than physical violence. All these actions discourage their children from being spontaneous and self-assertive in a positive way. At the same time, they are contributing to the negative emotional charge of their children.

If the parents were heavy drinkers, alcoholics, or substance abusers, they may not even realize or remember their actions in order to be able to take responsibility for them.

This creates a child victim with serious potential challenges for the future. This leaves a child grasping for an understanding of what is right and what is wrong. This is how childhood victims are created and become frustrated adults who are constantly unhappy and seeking relief.

Since children don't have sufficient knowledge to understand this type of behavior, they repress their feelings. But
repression doesn't block just their painful, negative feelings.
It blocks the ability to feel *anything*—good or bad. When you
are given an anesthetic before surgery, it doesn't just block the
pain, it blocks all your feelings. When you repress your feelings,
you become numb, and it affects your ability to feel normal,
positive emotions, also.

It is estimated the average person carries a substantial
amount of undischarged and unacknowledged pain. The Valeo
Method is not a one-time fix for eliminating this pain. What it
does provide is a process for learning the skills to control and
release the pain in a consistent and healthy way. Getting relief
and keeping it is an ongoing process. The good news is it does
get easier with time. This means being acutely sensitive to when
work needs to be done and knowing which skills we need to
use. This allows us to condition ourselves to being on a constantly self-correcting course toward enlightenment and wholeness. The more we practice our skills, the better we get, and
the easier it is to stay on course. Then, since we are constantly
controlling and diffusing our current and potential drama, we
avoid getting sucked into the same in others.

Now, instead of having a knee-jerk reaction to our emotions, we are able to take a breath, step back and say, "Wait a
minute, I'm not playing into this drama. I know what is happening here. I refuse to take someone else's drama personally
and get into an egoic dual." This concept is not hard to master
with the steps ahead.

Don't Shoot the Messenger!

"Emotion" is just a word for energy-in-motion. Since we
are all carrying negative charges of energy, how do we get
them out of our systems effectively? What causes this Pan-
dora's Box to open? The answer lies in our understanding of
reactive vs. responsive behavior. We must recognize reactive
behavior never resolves pain, it merely suppresses and post-
pones it, and the pain reappears.

Most of us spend our entire lives thinking the whole world is "happening to us." In reality, we are creating and attracting our very own future circumstances every moment through our present words, thoughts, and actions. Sometimes we just keep stepping into our own mess and continuing to be a victim because that is all we know how to do. We don't realize we are on an intention-driven journey.

Because we want to avoid the pain associated with painful past experiences, we pack them away, out of our consciousness, and bury them somewhere deep inside us. We don't plan it that way; it just happens as a natural preservation process. Yet when these challenges resurface, it is not always under the best circumstances.

It is not necessary that we go on reliving every painful past experience. Many people are uncomfortable and even terrified at the thought of confronting past suppressed feelings. They fear the unknown and that what may be waiting for them could be overpowering. Those who find the courage to take this bold step forward find out just the opposite is true.

The sensitive self wants to be acknowledged. It wants you to Embrace its pain. Until you call out this aching childhood part of yourself and address its pain, it will never rest. We are constantly reminded of and triggered to re-experience pain by our reflections and suppressions. Reflections are mild; they are just memories that pop up and remind us of something. However, they bring an emotional response with them. The reflection is the first signal of a trigger.

How we react to a trigger determines whether we go from a reflection to a more intense projection, where we experience the most sensitive pain. When a person or event causes you to have an upset, it is important to realize you are relating to the past. Your reaction to tapping into this old pain, either physically or emotionally, is a projection. Projection is the sensitive self's way to get it out, to release the pain.

When a trigger is fired off and we react, most of the time we don't realize what is happening—we are just upset. We certainly don't welcome the trigger. Our new strategy is to pay attention to an upset and ask ourselves a question: "What part of me wants attention?" Because I am upset, a part of me is telling me it needs attention—it needs relief.

Our prior thoughts, words, and deeds attract people into our lives who become "messengers." These people are attracted to us through the oneness connection of all people. We are meant to learn great lessons from them. The irony is they don't even know they are messengers; their spirit just compels them to show up. This is just one of the amazing ways God works behind the scenes in our lives. These messengers actually become "mess-enders" in our lives, playing roles in the emotional drama in our individual "plays of life." Therefore, when these messengers do show up, it is not to hurt us; they have a key purpose and a role to play in your journey. Knowing this allows us to learn to always ask ourselves, "Why is this person here in my life now? What am I supposed to learn from this encounter?"

If we ignore the messenger or trigger and get angry, we are just prolonging the pain and running away from the dream of the soul. Instead, if we accept the message and believe it is there for a purpose, we get to move ahead and grow stronger. We don't take it personally, and we win. This enables us to open up a whole new world of self-discovery and possibilities. When the mailman delivers the mail you don't get mad at him and curse him when he delivers a bill, do you? He is just the messenger! The messengers who trigger your emotional responses are the same.

But in real life, what do we do most of the time? We react and shoot the messenger. We get upset and experience angry, hurt feelings. We are being asked here to step back and take a deep breath before we react. At first, some find this not so easy to accomplish We are conditioned to react, and we are good at it. Change takes effort, and now we have a reason to change because we understand why triggers are showing up. Practice pays off; once again, repetition is the mother of skill.

The sensitive self is attracting this person or event to teach us a necessary lesson. The sensitive self has a link to all other souls through spirit, and this is how it attracts and draws other people and situations to us. It actually creates a "setup" in order to create an "upset" and get our attention. It is as if it is saying, "Help me, I'm in pain."

So the next time someone cuts you off in traffic or a clerk in a store is rude to you and you begin to feel that anger rising up inside, stop and take a deep breath. Then just smile and say, "Okay, what am I supposed to learn from this?"

Maybe the angry driver is there to make you slow down and drive more carefully so you will avoid an accident ahead. Maybe a rude clerk is there to remind you to be a little kinder to people today. Maybe your friend is upset to remind you to have more compassion for others.

This process is fun when we understand it, and it pays off to make it a habit. It is just another skill to learn and teach to others as you move toward releasing the dream of the soul and finding your calling through meeting the Real You.

Chapter 43
Recognizing the Intuitive Experience

Intuition is the clear conception of the whole at once.

Johann Casper Lavater

As we come to understand what triggers are and why they happen, it opens the door to understanding our intuition. It has been said that when we pray, we are talking to God, and when we have an intuition, God is talking to us.

We have all heard the saying, "There are no such things as accidents or coincidences," but do you believe it? I like to think coincidences are God's little miracles He chooses to remain anonymous about. Did you know that in the Hebrew language there is no word for coincidence? Why? Because the ancient Hebrews believed God had a reason for everything that happened, which is a very powerful belief.

If you agree, it means you accept that you are on a totally intention-driven journey in your life. It has been my experience that the more spiritually aware and centered a person becomes, the more this concept makes sense. Here is another way to look at it: "Things don't just happen; things happen just."

Have you ever been thinking about someone and they just showed up or called you on the phone? Have you ever had a feeling that something was going to happen and it did? Have you ever started to do something and you got a feeling it was a bad decision, so you stopped and then later realized that decision saved you a lot of grief? Have ever just felt someone was watching you even though you didn't see them at first, and then discovered you were right? Those feelings are called "intuitive hits." Something outside the physical reality is working in your life.

We also call these "oneness experiences." They happen when your oneness connection, through the blueprint of humanity, reveals itself. Our individual spirits are intimately connected to our Creator; we are connected to the spirit of God by our spirit/souls. Our minds have no permanent boundaries so we are also connected as individual spirits. We receive our intuition through this God/spirit/soul connection. The Valeo Method teaches us how to unblock this connection and receive more flow and more instruction from the dream of our souls, and here is some great news—it is all sponsored by God!

These oneness experiences are happening constantly in our lives, and they never stop. Unfortunately, most people are like I was, so caught up in my ego-dominated dramas of life I didn't even notice these important signals were being sent to me. I missed the warnings of potential pain, and not only that, I missed out on some great opportunities. It happens to all of us—instead of seeing and hearing the message life is trying to send us, we just keep playing into our same old blah, blah, blah daily drama. This can happen so much that we miss out on identifying and using our gifts, encouraging feelings, direction, confidence, and peace, just to name a few. Quite a price to pay, don't you think?

Every time we are being set-up with an upset, our sensitive self is sending us a message (experience) to clear an emotional blockage. So, an upset is an aggressive form of intuition, a compassionate cry for help. This concept is a different way of thinking for most people, but consider this: a fever comes on to help fight off illness and infection. The same concept is true with triggers that bring on an upset. They are coming on to help us survive and live a healthy life with peace and wholeness. If we continue to ignore our intuitive triggers, what can we expect?

Learning and Growing Through Pain

We are all created differently, and we each have a unique spirit/soul personality. God gives each of us tender gifts, which are the strengths of our individual souls backed by love emotions. One person might be sensitive to children, another might be good at working with the poor and underprivileged, one might be driven to be a public servant, and one person might give hope to others, another person gives courage, while another ministers to others. Some use their gifts to become great leaders or business builders, scientists or artists, musicians or entertainers. We all have love-based gifts and traits. Sometimes these gifts are so covered up and shattered into such small pieces that the fragments of love get smothered, but they are still always there. God gave us these gifts unconditionally; they will never go away.

The sensitive self fights to break through the negative emotions we experience to be recognized. This is ironic because it actually causes these emotions to attract attention to the part that needs healing! A person who has an issue with anger will attract angry people and situations into their life. A person who has an issue with trust will attract situations of distrust. A person who is greedy will attract situations where there is a need to give.

Take a moment to think about it. Do you know someone who seems to attract negative things into their life? How about a person who has a problem making money or finding a job? Do they attract more and more situations that cause their finances to get worse? This person's sensitive self is attracting situations of lack for a reason. They need to address the emotions that are causing the undesired result. The sensitive self of this person will keep setting up more upset and lack situations until this person addresses his issue of poor self-esteem, lack of self-confidence, or some other related emotion that is causing the problem.

Does it sound too simple? Doesn't it make sense? It's really easy when you wake up and realize how God set up this whole thing called "life." We have to be willing to wake up and help ourselves. For things to change, we have to change. Otherwise, these situations will continue to occur and cause pain for an entire life.

Chapter 44
The Four E's "For Ease"

*There came a time when the risk to remain tight in the bud
was more painful than the risk to blossom.*

Anais Nin

The four E's is another process we use in the Valeo Method to create ease in the midst of emotional tension and pain. Then we can learn to integrate the sensitive self into our lives and live on purpose and be happy and whole. Here are the steps:

1. Expose
2. Experience
3. Express
4. Evolve

The first step is Expose. You are going to expose the impacted emotional pain caused from wounding, language, beliefs, and shadows from your past. The ego will try to do everything possible to keep this from happening, so be prepared. Remember, the ego wants you to have pain. It doesn't want you poking around, trying to find the light. At the same time, though, the sensitive self is determined to be heard!

We are going to penetrate right through the ego's veil by asking the right questions. The first one is, "What is making me have this undesired feeling? What is causing me to be upset?" The answer is closer than you think.

By going straight to the source to ask, we will get an answer. Ask the Real You, the part of you that is connected to God, what is causing the pain. Ask and ye shall receive, remember? Be patient and keep asking. Ask until there is an answer.

The answer may just pop into your head. Pay close attention; it may come in a feeling or in a memory, a realization, or it may prompt an experience. Rest assured, if you keep asking, the answer will come.

Consistency and sincerity is what the child inside you is looking for, and all the answers to emotional discomfort are waiting within to be exposed. When you feel like you know what it is, then it is time to...

Experience

Going through this process may cause confusion or possibly even discomfort, but not to worry; just let it happen. If there is emotional upset, let it happen. Either way, avoid judgment, worry, or getting into analysis paralysis. At this point we want to take a deep breath and experience the feeling of the emotion. Let it flow and keep asking the question, "What is making me have this feeling?"

The natural desire is to find a time when this pain was experienced before, so we can trace it back to its source. What is the trigger, the hook, the reflection (memory) that comes alive and brings this suppressed pain to the surface?

Sometimes just a word can be the trigger. For example, let's say someone close to you called you worthless as a child. This experience hurts at a very deep psychological level and is locked away; the source of impacted emotional pain is seeking relief.

The minute someone pushes your worthless button again, it triggers an explosive, possibly even violent or painful reaction. It also could be the opposite, the feelings of shame, embarrassment, or disgust, which internalizes itself. The key here is to understand the wounded child; the sensitive self, deep inside, wants relief.

Picture a helpless young child hiding and crying in shame for being called worthless by a parent. The pain is so unbearable the young child, not knowing how to deal with it, locks it away. Deep in this inner vault the feeling sits waiting, hurting, and fermenting, for an opportunity to be healed and released. It seeks an outlet; a button to be pushed and "bang!" outcome the consequences. This kind of pain wrecks lives—not just for the person experiencing the pain, but also for those who are close to this person. This is why it is necessary to be persistent in seeking the source, the trigger of your pain.

Consider this metaphor: We are all walking around with a chest full of buttons. Each one of these buttons represents an emotion. Many of them are love emotion buttons. Some are pain emotion buttons. These buttons are just waiting to be pushed. Who pushes your buttons? What situation pushes your buttons? These buttons are what fire off your triggers. Behind the buttons is the answer to finding relief from your suffering and pain. Take the time to ask yourself what words are on your buttons. What words remind you of past experiences? What words do you have anchored to a scene or an opinion about yourself that is unpleasant? It takes courage to get to this point of reaching emotional *Release and Embrace.* This is the time when writing in a journal works great, and I highly recommend it to my clients that I help through this process. Also this is a time when talking to a trusted friend, counselor, or minister can be helpful. Because once we start to discover the button, then it is time to...

Express

Next we seek to express the emotions and qualities that we tend to interpret only as negative and undesirable. And there are wonderful things about yourself that you haven't even discovered yet.

All of us have parts of ourselves we just refuse to admit are ours; we fight to avoid anything that would bring us near them, when in reality we are blind to the fact that the problem is within. Joey was a client of mine who was stuck in a rut. Every area of his life was a mess. He struggled in business, he couldn't make a relationship last, and he hated his appearance. I noticed that Joey labeled several other people he considered close to him as losers. I asked him to tell me about these people. It was interesting to find out that every person he mentioned appeared to be relatively successful and not a loser at all.

It became apparent to me that Joey was projecting his own pain on to these other people when in truth, he felt like the loser. When I shared this with him, he got upset. I pushed his loser button, and bingo, we were making progress.

In order to undo a projection, you must move the unconscious, sensitive–self feeling causing the pain into the broader spectrum of the conscious mind where it has ego identification. Then it can be disposed of because the truth is out. The revelation here is the recognition that you are not a victim of your environment, you are doing this to yourself, and it is time to take responsibility for it.

As we discussed earlier, sometimes we have to do the uncomfortable until it becomes comfortable to get the results we seek. So what you are being asked to do is what Joey did. He accepted that his feelings of being a loser, which he hated, were eating at him so badly that he projected them onto others to get relief. Joey sat with his head in his hands crying his heart out when he became aware of the truth and expressed his feelings.

What good did this do for Joey? It made him stop holding back his own feelings and disgust with himself so he could move forward. Without expressing these feelings, he could find no peace.

The next part of expressing is to not only become aware but to reverse the direction of the projection. So now you are giving your sensitive self the floor and moving it into conscious-ness. If you want to see the sensitive self's view of the world, just amplify the emotion you have discovered. For example, Joey's realization was that his sensitive self saw him as a loser. I had him tell me in detail why he was such a loser. It got to the point that he was laughing hysterically at himself. When he took ownership of this opposite of his projection, he was ready to change.

It is very effective to go at emotions the way Joey did and express them after accepting them. This experience is not to be taken lightly. In fact, it is more effective if it is experienced fully. If you let someone get you jealous, try to experience more jealousy; if you get depressed, try to make yourself more depressed. If you feel angry, try to go to the next level of anger. When you do this exercise and throw yourself into it, you are throwing the sensitive self and the ego together. And we know which one has the authentic power and which one runs on lies.

When you can understand that you can make yourself more depressed, more jealous, and angrier, it will dawn on you that you can also make yourself feel less of these emotions! In other words, paying attention to the symptom delivers you right to it. This is a profound concept!

For the process to work, it takes commitment to feel and go deep into the emotion. A lighthearted attempt will not work. You literally have to go at those negative emotions and traits you hate in others and feel them, express, experience, and be them. Then you can release them, feel better, and heal. Next, you will be ready for the best part...

Evolve

The things you love or loathe in others are qualities of your own sensitive self. You wouldn't have these emotions and feelings if they weren't a part of who you are and who you are striving to be at the soul level. It makes sense if you think about it. Otherwise, why would these same feelings keep showing up and repeating themselves?

If you admire a trait in another person and you are attracted to them, it is because a part of your makeup knows it can be like them. The Real You knows no limitations. It's your own ego rule book and conditioning that steals your dreams.

The bottom line is this: To be happy, you have to understand and rescue your sensitive self, that hurting, wounded part of who you are. Until you can expose, experience, and express this part of yourself, you can never experience inner peace and evolve in your adult life.

Experiencing and evolving to emotional healing is a process—it can happen relatively quickly, but it is not going to happen overnight. Since we live in an instant gratification society, we want results now. If we don't get them quickly enough we are tempted to say, "The hell with it." The problem with this attitude is the ego wins and sends you right back into the emptiness and misery of a life not being lived on purpose. This sends us running for types of relief that are associated with unhealthy thinking, habits, and relationships.

Be Like the Stonecutter

Although there are many immediate payoffs to learning and applying the Valeo Method to your life, persistent effort provides the biggest payoff. You will soon reach a point where using all the steps are effortless and just a part of the way you think and live. This is the point at which you can realize that a transformation has happened seemingly overnight, but in reality, it is like the story of the stonecutter.

The stonecutter strikes sometimes hundreds of times in the same point with no apparent result. Then all of a sudden the stone cracks just where he needs it to. Even though it seemed like nothing was happening, on the inside each tap had an effect on the stone. It wasn't one tap that suddenly broke the stone; it was the combined, consistent effort over time. This is what happens with the Four E's and the entire Valeo Method. It is a process; it creates an internal shift of awareness and allows you to develop an inner strength and gain momentum in controlling your life and your future. It is designed to be gentle and somewhat unconscious while creating ongoing, noticeable, outward change. Otherwise, the change is too dramatic and drastic. This type of change we don't want because it usually doesn't last.

Here is some more good news—when the shift happens, it tends to be lasting. If there is a tendency to slip back, the skills you learned here provide a quick plan to correct and adjust your course. Once the body and mind reach this shift, it allows you to experience a whole new world without going anywhere. You just feel like a new internal person in the same external physical body. This makes it uncomfortable to experience the old thoughts and feelings. Like a wound that is healed, it doesn't reappear. A new wound might come along, but the old one won't reopen. Additionally, since you are now acutely sensitive to conditions that could create a fresh, new wound, you avoid them not just consciously, but unconsciously. Your authentic self becomes like a force field extending away from you. It repels negative and potentially injurious people, events, and circumstances from crossing your path. Your aura, or your body's force field, diverts them away, as well, and they don't recognize what is happening and neither do you; it just happens because of this work you have done. In essence, you have already begun to realize and evolve into the Authentic Self, the Real You, inside.

When Michelangelo was asked how he was able to sculpt the beautiful statue of David, his answer fits well here. He said, "I just removed the parts that weren't David, and there he was." There is something beautiful in all of us that deserves to be *exposed, experienced, and expressed* so we can *evolve* and become whole.

The Power of Pain

When you use the four "E's" you are going head-on at your negative emotional charge. It may seem difficult, but you need to look at the pain and discomfort associated with it as your friend. The pain is there for a Divine purpose, to draw your attention to what needs help and healing. The Scripture tells us, "*When trouble comes your way, consider it an opportunity for great joy. For you know that when your faith is tested, your endurance has a chance to grow. So let it grow for when your endurance is fully developed you will be perfect and complete, needing nothing.*"

If you don't face your pain, it never goes away, it just festers and gets worse. If you react to pain instead of responding to it, you are just chasing it away and it will come right back. The tendency is to turn away or run from it or get someone else to attend to it. The problem with someone else attending to your pain is they can't feel it or experience it; only you can. All spiritual study points out to us that God is within us. To believe this and experience it, we must put our attention inside, on the pain itself, where God can help us deal with it. Remember, the sender behind the messengers we receive is the eternal protector, the healer of our souls. When you pay attention to this truth, amazing things begin to happen.

So this is a challenge to stand your ground and not back down from the pain of the negative emotional charge. Saint Paul tells us, "*Mark out a straight path for your feet so that those who are weak and lame will not fall but become strong.*" This means we should always set an example with our walk. This allows us to influence people, which we even do indirectly, as they observe us.

Instead of reaching for a mask to cover up and hide from the challenges we face when making changes, we need to ask ourselves (and it bears repeating), "What is great about this? What am I supposed to learn from this? How can I use this experience to empower me?"

You are challenged here to review the summery at the end of the Embrace section. Remember, these are the skills you are learning, and repetition is the mother of skill. Review them often and make sure you are comfortable with them before moving to the next step, *Activate and Attract.*

Purpose of completing the Embrace step: To embrace the part of me that is locked away and needs to be loved and to uncover my unique and special gifts it holds for me.

Progress and Strategies

1. We all have suppressed emotional issues and childhood wounding that need to be addressed in order to go to the next level and live the dream of the soul.

2. I must challenge the person I think I am in order to set free the person inside me that I am capable of being and meant to be.

3. My pain and suffering has a purpose, a message for me. It is there to teach me and guide me. It is part of my intended path.

4. My issues with my sensitive self, my shadow self, are coming out one way or the other, sooner are later. It can be pretty or ugly; it is up to me.

5. I must journey through my suffering, pain, and frustrations, because real living is found on the other side.

6. To free my pain and embrace my authentic self and discover my gifts, I must be willing to expose, express, and experience my hidden feelings and shadows.

7. I am not the story I created of who I am. There is much more waiting to evolve and experience.

8. The AFIG process will open the portal to my sensitive self and my essence; my connection to my Divine and authentic power.

Summary and Action Plan

1. I will practice the "Awareness of Breathing" exercise at least twice per day.

2. I will continue to practice Catch and Release with every negative thought and with every negative emotion like doubt, worry, or fear, anytime they pop up.

3. When stressful situations, worry, or upset arise, I will immediately go to the AFIG process and follow the four steps. Before my final evening prayer, I will use AFIG to flush my mind. (It only takes a few moments and it is my mental and emotional cleanse before retiring at night. It's like washing my face, only better.)

4. I will ask myself these questions to make sure I am taking full re sponsibility for my life no matter what is happening to me:

    A. Am I blaming anyone for my situations in life?

    B. What behaviors or reactive negative patterns am I using to prove or validate that I have been wronged or mis treated?

    C. If I continue to blame others, how does this kind of thinking affect my long-term peace and fulfillment?

    D. How long have I let this behavior hold me back from the dream of my soul, my purpose, and my calling?

    E. If I let these excuses continue and I don't change, what is it going to cost me in success, relationships, happi ness, health, and peace?

5. I will practice meeting with my sensitive self (inner child) at least once per week in a peaceful, private environment. I will not discuss this process with others until I feel confident and safe; otherwise, I may get distracted by those who don't understand.

6. I will ask myself: Am I holding anything back that is keeping me from forgiving myself? If the answer is yes, I must go back through Catch and Release and AFIG more often.

7. I will practice the Four E's process until I find my source of pain and distraction. I will identify my triggers and face them head-on to evolve to my wholeness and truth about who I am as a person and what I am meant to be, do, and have in my life!

8. After completing this section of the Valeo Method and feeling comfortable with it, I will ask myself these questions:

    A. What skills or abilities did I receive from having these experiences?

    B. What was the gift/lesson for me from these experiences?

9. I will write in my personal journal about my experience thus far with the Valeo Method, including every breakthrough and emotional reaction, painful or joyous. This is very helpful in tracking my progress and creating long-term change.

PART VI

~

ACTIVATE & ATTRACT

Great works are not performed by strengths but by perseverance.
Samuel Johnson

The first three steps allow you to experience a mental and emotional *Release*. These strategies allow us to empty the vessel of the soul of what it *does* not need so we can fill it up with what it does need. You are about to be prepared to welcome your dreams into a fresher, more prepared vessel to carry you on to a life full of joy, confidence, and purpose.

There is one thing about life: it doesn't wait for us—time marches on. Is there something inside of you that just keeps nagging at you and will not leave you alone? It is best to pay attention to it. Within that voice lies your individual calling—the dream of your soul. Have heard from it much lately? Don't worry if you haven't. It is still there; it never goes away as long as you are breathing. It doesn't matter how many mountains you have conquered, how much wealth you have accumulated, how many accolades you have received, or how many times you have fallen down. Most of us know deep down that there is something else we are meant to be, do, or have.

This part of the Valeo Method is about activating the creative powers of God's universe within each of us and tapping into their omnipotent power. We are going to activate this power through our gift of free will. We are going to use our gift to activate unseen forces that are part of our eternal imprint. We are each individually a microcosm of the macrocosm of creation. Most of us spend our lives not activating this Divine connection and allowing it to help because we don't understand some basic principles of creating good in our lives. The *Activate and Attract* step is going to equip us with what we need to attract brilliant results in our lives.

It is possible to look at this process through spiritual and scientific lenses simultaneously. We are going to learn how to do just that while igniting our hearts with the power to attract and manifest. Before we go into the how to strategies to activate and attract in your life, we have to address the issue of purpose. I find that most people don't have a clue what their true purpose is.

The greatest joy of life is living our purpose, God's individual plan for each of us. What this means is embracing the opportunity to grow into who we are meant to be. How close are you to living your intended plan? Finding your purpose is critical. Death is not a tragedy; dying without finding your purpose is a tragedy. If one part of your life is going well and another part is awful, you're not there. If your finances are great but your relationships are suffering, you are not there. If your finances are great and you are letting your health go and not taking care of your body, you are not there. If your life seems good in all areas except your spiritual life, which is empty and lacking God's presence, you're certainly not living on purpose. If any of these situations seem familiar, you are living a life

with only temporary success and fulfillment—that is a guarantee. Living on purpose means experiencing all you were meant
to do, be, and have while at the same time not forfeiting your
intimate relationship with God.

Having a purpose means finding meaning in what you do. If
you don't have meaning in what you do, you don't bring value
to what you do. Just think about it, how many people are truly
happy? How many people really exhibit meaning and value
in what they do, let alone passion? People who don't have
meaning in what they do lack purpose and vitality. Those who
are living their lives on purpose have peace of mind.

Purpose is the anchor that secures us to life. It anchors us
through disappointment and crisis. Purpose is your soul's way
of declaring, "I feel good, and this is who I am!" Purpose brings
things together during times of uncertainty and loss. Carl Jung
said, "After age thirty-five, every crisis is a crisis of meaning."
We all need to find our purpose to survive and thrive.

Rufi, the thirteenth-century Sufi poet, wrote, "You might
do a hundred other things, but if you don't do the one thing for
which you were sent it will be as you had done nothing." How
powerful and well-said is this warning to us to not let our lives
slip away without finding our purpose. It is sad that so many
people just skim the surface of life and miss their calling. They
miss their sacred destiny. Isn't that sad?

Let's Go Soul-Searching

There are constant clues all around us seeking to help us
find our purpose. In fact, every person's life is designed to allow
the perfect circumstances and experiences to manifest so they
can develop the knowledge and skills to discover, proclaim, and
fulfill their purpose. Does that sound impossible? Remember
who we are dealing with here and who created this whole reality we call life.

Our job is to wake up and pay attention to the clues God
is showing us. Only then are we going to discover our gifts and
escape the endless loop of melodrama that the ego creates.
Do you know what your gifts are? Are you using them? Are

you letting them go to waste? Is it time for some serious soul searching? Here is a clue: If you can quit what you are doing and be happy you have not found your purpose.

Some people find their purpose easily while others have to seek it out, and it really takes an effort for some people. It means controlling the controllables while at the same time not worrying about what you can't control.

You have to ask yourself, "What are the consequences of not pursuing my purpose?" Our small, poor decisions may seem harmless, but when we add them up a picture begins to emerge. Are you associating enough pain to letting life slip away without finding your calling? Are you covering up pain because you don't want to endure the pain of the reality of what you are missing out on?

Isn't it time to stop making our gifts and callings wait on us? The real joy of living is embracing the opportunity to grow and be the person we are meant to be. This means believing you are never too old, it is never too late, and especially, believing you can never give up.

A person might be rich or sitting on a pile of accomplishments, but what does it matter if their soul is aching and empty because she missed her calling? What about all the things in life we think are so important? The new job titles, the rewards, report cards, prom dates, sports trophies, and even the opinions of others? In reality, it isn't these things we seek but how they make us *feel* that matters to us. Many times we exhaust ourselves striving for perfection and what we are really doing is just trying to be better than or like someone else. Real living is striving to become the best you can be while ardently seeking your purpose.

Chapter 45
Do I Really Have a Purpose?

*Many people have a wrong idea of what constitutes true happiness.
It is not attained through self-gratification, but fidelity to a worthy purpose.*

Helen Keller

Many times people get discouraged and give up on finding their purpose. They listen to their egos and other people, and it is easy to get discouraged. The often-used cliché, "Life is not a destination; it is a journey," reveals a powerful truth. A healthy soul is striving and seeking because that is the way it was designed—it is our natural, evolving nature. Just as our muscles atrophy without exercise, the soul can atrophy without attention.

One of my clients told me, "I would love to find my calling, but I don't know where to start." I told her to go outside anywhere and find a rock. She listened intently as I went on. Next I told her to take the rock and throw it up in the air. Then I told her to notice carefully where it lands, wherever that spot is, and start there. The point is, you have to get started. If you wait around for someone to come along and say, "Here it is, I found it, here is the place," you might miss out if you don't get started, so get moving right now. You have to be willing to get on a mission and do some serious soul-searching. When we are holding in our natural talents, we are resisting the natural flow of the universe. The best compliment you can pay God is to live the purpose he planted deep inside of you. You accomplish this by surrendering to it and letting it play through.

Erik Weihenmayer had ample reason to avoid pursuing his calling. At six months old, his doctor told his parents that he would be blind by his early teenage years. It actually happened at age thirteen. But instead of letting his future limit him, he searched his soul, found his purpose, and sought it with passion. His purpose was to overcome limitation and encourage others by example. He became a marathon runner, skydiver, skier, long-distance runner, scuba diver, and a member of the College Wrestling Hall of Fame. He climbed three of the highest mountains in the world, including Mt. Everest in 2001. He even dived off a forty-foot cliff just as his eyesight was beginning to go away!

The example Eric gives us is to pay attention, no matter what, to our circumstances and accept that they are there to help us discover our purpose. The only fear we should have is wasting all of our moments. Every moment, every thought in our lives has a purpose.

Your Purpose Might Surprise You

Sometimes when you seek your purpose too intensely, you can run right by it and miss it altogether! Many successful people find their purpose unexpectedly.

John Grisham, a Memphis attorney, never dreamed of being a famous writer and seeing his work turn into blockbuster movies. Writing was just a hobby. Neil Armstrong never dreamed of being an astronaut and walking on the moon; he was a Navy pilot. Sheryl Leech was a stay-at-home mom who, while stuck in traffic and trying to pacify her eighteen-month-old child, got the idea for a six-foot-tall dinosaur called "Barney," and we all know the results of that story.

In 1894, Dr. John Kellogg asked his brother Walt, a chemist, to create a grain-based supplement that he could offer to his patients. His brother mixed up a doughy concoction but was called out of his lab early. The next morning he discovered that he had left his stove on and the dough had boiled over, dried, and turned brittle. He had inadvertently invented corn flakes.

In 1905, Frank Epperson left a glass of his favorite soda outside on the back porch on a freezing cold night with a mixing stick in it. It froze, and he discovered a new dessert idea. Twenty years later he started sharing his treats, which he called Ep-sickles, which later became known worldwide as the Pop-sicle.

In 1902, William Carrier was working to design a device that could be used to remove humidity from the air inside printing plants. It didn't work, but it did cool the air. Orders start pouring in, but not for the dehumidifier; he had invented air-conditioning.

Your gift can be hidden too, waiting patiently to be unveiled. You may be closer than you think—all you might need is a little nudge, and your whole life can change overnight!

The key is believe with all your heart that you *do* have a purpose. It may be revealed like one of these examples one day, or maybe not. What matters is how are you going to find it? One thing is for sure—you can't wait on it, you have to seek it!

Are You Seriously Seeking?

Are you serious about seeking and finding your purpose? "Seek" is a verb that means to "search until you find; to not give up." It doesn't mean to look or glance, although that is what most people do. When have you set aside time and given the question of your purpose serious and focused thought? What follows are proven concepts and strategies to assist you in finding your purpose.

Ask yourself the following questions: What ideas or hobbies have you always wanted to try or explore? If you could get paid to do anything in the world, what would it be? What is the special gift or contribution that you alone offer? What unique trait or characteristic do you have that those who love and value you will miss the most when you're gone?

You have to look at your fruit. Most people don't know one citrus tree from another. You have to look at the fruit to know the purpose of the tree.

Here are the four things you can do to help find your purpose:

1. Listen to what the voice deep inside your heart is trying to tell you.

2. Listen to what your pain and suffering is trying to tell you.

3. Listen to what the patterns of your life are trying to tell you.

4. Listen to what is attracting and calling you; our desires are always informing us.

When have you listened to what the world is trying to say to you? Many people can tell you the television schedule for every night of the week, or their favorite sports team's schedule, but they haven't read a good book or had a peaceful moment of contemplation in weeks, months, or maybe even years. When is the last time you took a long walk to nowhere, watched a sunrise, cried with joy, held a puppy, kissed a baby, talked until dawn, called an old friend, or just sat in silence and cleared your mind? Life is too short to miss out on the good things, these precious moments, the juice of life. These are places where you can discover your purpose.

Emmanuel's Gift

A feature film was done about a Ghanaian man named Emmanuel Ofosu Yeboah. The film was titled "Emmanuel's Gift." The story is a testament to one man's courage, bravery, and determination and validates the fact that no matter who we are or what our circumstances, we all have a purpose.

Emmanuel was born with a deformed leg and as a result he had poor prospects for a good future. In his culture deformed babies were considered a curse on their families and they were usually abandoned in the street or left in the woods to die. Emmanuel's mother would not except this fate for her child. She named him "Emmanuel" which means "God is with us" and instilled in him a sense of value and purpose. Other children with disabilities begged in the streets to survive but Emmanuel knew he was meant to do more. He was determined to be self-sustaining instead of being rejected, humiliated, and without hope.

In order to prove he could overcome his disability and unable to afford a prosthetic leg, he rode a donated bicycle 379 documented miles around Ghana using one leg to pedal. His story gained national attention and inspired many who had lost hope. Emmanuel has since had an operation and gotten a prosthetic. Today he works tirelessly to create and ensure opportunities and a future for disabled Ghanaians.

Emmanuel says he knows his purpose is to help and encourage other disabled people and when he does he forgets about his own disabilities. His circumstances and challenges led him to his purpose.

In his book, *Man's Search for Meaning*, Author Victor Frankel writes, "We must never forget that we may also find meaning in life even when confronted with a hopeless situation, when facing a fate that cannot be changed. For what then matters is to bear witness to the unique human potential at its best, which is to transform a personal tragedy into triumph, to turn one's predicament into a human achievement."

If you love what you do it is impossible to fail.

While we are busy wasting time and thoughts, we miss the clues nature is trying to give us. God gave us intuition so He could use it to nudge us along to our destinies. He gave us free will so we could make choices to act on His promptings. How are you doing? How many of God's promptings have you missed?

What do you love to do when you have a free moment? What do you do that you can't get enough of? Is it art, sports, golf, chess, drawing, writing, gardening, playing a musical instrument, working on cars, designing things, exercise, or helping and encouraging others? The list is endless; what hits your hot button? The joys created by these things are clues to your purpose.

What did you love to do when you were a kid? Who are you jealous of? That, also, could be your purpose calling you and saying, "Hey you, look at this! This is what you're supposed to be doing!" What is something you could do all day long and never get tired of it? What do you do now whenever you have a free moment? When you follow your bliss, you will uncover your purpose. The lack of purpose in one's life can create unpleasant feelings and depression. If you ignore your purpose, it can begin to haunt you, it can make you sick.

A man was sentenced to twenty years in prison with hard labor. He was shackled to a large handle attached to a giant wheel on the wall. Every day he had to turn the wheel by cranking that handle until he was exhausted. He constantly pondered what his effort produced behind the wall. Could it be a grist mill making wheat or flower? Could he be creating power to give off energy that was being used to serve a good purpose?

At the end of his sentence, all he could think about do-ing was looking behind the wall to see what his efforts all those years had been producing. He was shocked and devastated to learn there was nothing on the other side of the wall. His efforts had been wasted as part of his punishment. The man's spirit was broken as he collapsed in tears to see his back-breaking effort had been for nothing. This pain to his spirit was worse than the twenty years of hard labor. We all need to seek our purpose; otherwise we rob our own spirit and cheat God out of the glory He receives when we live the purpose for which He originally created us. Even if we don't find our perfect purpose immediately, searching nourishes and soothes the soul.

Chapter 46
Dreams Ignite Purpose

In the world to come, I will not be asked, "Why were you not Moses?"
I shall be asked, "Why were you not Zusya?"

Rabbi Zusya

Purpose and dreams, peas and carrots, peanut butter and jelly—they all just go together. When we find our purpose we ignite our dreams. Dreams can also work for us in the opposite way—they can lead us to our purpose.

Dreams speak to our minds from the heart. Dreams say, "*Embrace* me, get out of analysis paralysis and run with me." A dream is a vision of a solution. If we look at the word "vision" in Hebrew, it means "glimpse of destiny." Dreams are also the base of a need. We could sum it up by saying a dream is a vision of a solution to a need in our lives and a portal to our destiny.

Dreams also give us life. People look and act differently when they have a dream. You can see it in their eyes and in their step. They feel alive because their spirit has been activated. A dreaming heart is a healthy and vibrant heart. Dreaming opens up the flow of nature in us because dreams are healthy.

Are you dreaming or asleep at the wheel of your life? As John Lennon said, "Life is what happens while you're busy making plans." We get so focused on the stuff of life, we neglect our dreams. Some people are so stuck in their thinking they remind me of the Peanuts comic strip character Charlie Brown, who said, "I'm still hoping yesterday will get better."

Discovering a dream to pursue is a blessing. Remember when you were a kid and peddling along on your bicycle when all of a sudden your chain came off? You were peddling like crazy, but going nowhere. That is the way life is without a dream; you are stuck wasting time and energy going nowhere. Then how did it feel when the chain caught hold again and you took off and sped away? Kind of a cool feeling, wasn't it? That is what it is like when you find your dream and pursue it. Life takes off!

Even if you haven't achieved a dream yet, it doesn't mean you don't have one. Also, dreams don't have to be simple or easy.

The following information in the *Activate and Attract* step will give you all the tools you need and a proven plan of action to live your purpose, realize your dreams, and tackle new ones.

Tap Into the Creation Process

Before God created the heavens and the earth, there was just God—omniscient, all-knowing, omnipotent, all powerful, omnipresent, everywhere. For some reason, God decided to create everything you and I know as our world and our universe. So that means everything, and I mean everything we see in front of our eyes was created by God out of nothing. In the Bible it says, *"By faith we understand that the worlds were framed by the word of God, so that the things which are seen were not made of things that are visible."* If we believe this concept, it means other things can also be created out of nothing, right? So, the question is how do we tap into the power of creation in our lives?

God gave every single one of us the ability to use this process. In fact, we can't keep from using it because it is the natural law of creation. It is backed up by science through physics, and most importantly, through Scripture. You can direct this process—slow it down, speed it up, use it with or without awareness, or obtain desirable or undesirable results—the only thing you can't do is stop it from working. It never stops working. Jesus said, *"My father is always working."* The question is simple: Are we in alignment with this energy dynamic or not? Being out of alignment with the benefit of this gift is living life the hard way. Each of us has been given the key to this life-advancing power. We can only use it properly when we understand it and realize its source.

God set a rhythm for life in motion. He began the never-ending creation process with the "first cause," which was God's thought. This was followed by a word and then followed by a result. This is the foundation for what we now know as *cause and effect.* Everything that is matter, or has matter (that matters) has a word buried in it that gives it physical reality. I don't want to get too deep into physics or Scripture on this subject; that is another book altogether. Let's just summarize it by saying that every breath of God combined with a word (sound) created all things, from the heavens and galaxies to earth to man and every creature alive and organism that exists. God's imprint is in all of creation. We see this Holy triune represented over and over all through creation. God operates in threes. We see it in Father, Son, and Holy Spirit; we see it in the mind, body, and soul; we see it in knowledge, experience, and being. This is the Divine expression process, the source of all knowledge, the source of all energy and matter. This process is eternally in motion; it never stops, it never rests, and it never gets tired.

Because of the creation process, it is extremely important that we pay attention to the thoughts we have and the words we use. We addressed this in detail in the section of the book on Transitional Language. This is also why it is important we use our language skills with integrity, because we have been entrusted with the power of creating our future reality with how we speak and how we direct our spoken words.

The Scripture tells us God created us in His likeness, in His image. Why did He do that? So He can use us to do great works! The Bible plainly says, *"God created each of us for his Glory."* Please let that sink in—you, my friend, are meant to be, do, and have something awesome. Are you ready for this? Guess who is the president of your fan club? God! He created each one of us so He could be like a proud Father, sitting in the stands at a little league game and watch us shine. It gives Him Glory! He created you so He could be proud of you, so doesn't it make sense that He would give you the tools to help you succeed with those gifts He gave you? In my seminars I kid around sometimes to make a point. I look at someone and say, "You have no talent." Everyone looks at me like I'm crazy. Then I say, "God has all the talent, and He just chooses to express certain special gifts through you."

All we have to do is get out of the way of the flow and let this natural process manifest through each of us. When some-one says, "You need to come to your senses," you may not realize it, but that means wake up and let what is trying to manifest naturally materialize through you. There's a difference between what we call acting naturally, or normally, which is living based on prior beliefs (rules) and acting supernaturally. We accomplish this by being sensitive to the power of all creation within every single one of us. We can learn the skills necessary to co-create a positive, fruitful, happy life instead of getting in the way of the great things that are seeking to manifest in our lives. Always remember: what seems outrageous, impossible, and supernatural is just another day at the office for God. Jesus said it this way, *"The things which are impossible for men, are possible with God."*

Creative Consciousness

There are some critical steps to activating, attracting, and manifesting good in our lives. These are processes and concepts that can come naturally to us, and they should. The challenge, as we have learned, is that we block the flow. There are endless sources of conscious awareness to which we can have access any time we need them. Saint Peter tells us that God is not a respecter of persons; that means He shows no favorites, so everyone, king or pauper, has the same access. Some ignore and waste this gift, while others recognize and nurture it. A lot of folks fall in between. Because there are no favorites, it means this process of nature works for us whether we believe it or not.

What you are learning in this step of the Valeo Method takes out the guesswork. Since life is not a dress rehearsal and we only get one shot at getting it right, doesn't it make sense to compress our time for optimum results? How does a sports team become a champion? They have a plan, they practice, they memorize plays, they follow the rules, they execute them, and then they are successful. The same principle works here.

Coming up are strategies to help you prepare to be a master co-creator and to become a master at helping others. The key is learning the steps and following them in order—then, you'll be ready for wonderful results as you head into the last step, *Manifest and Maintain.*

Chapter 47
Creative Visualization

Try out your ideas by visualizing them in action.

David Seabury

Creative visualization is about making conscious, desired choices in your life. It is about creating the vision of where you desire to see yourself in the future. It is about making a conscious choice to stay focused on what you dream of and having a habit that forces you to create positive momentum in your life. It is about living in an attitude of intention followed by expectancy.

We have discussed it, and now we are going to learn to apply some easy-to- remember tools to put your co-creating muscles to work.

God gave us the ability through our free will to make deliberate decisions. When we set deliberate cause and effect in motion, we activate a chain reaction of that unstoppable, universal energy. Once we have a thought it comes alive with our breath, and then the words we speak move our energy continuously until our thoughts manifest themselves. In other words, what we think about, we bring about.

The unaware and the unconscious spend their lives focused on the *effects* of this Divine process. They never realize that everything happening is the result of their previous thoughts. If the results are not pleasing to some of us, we play the victim or the "poor old me" game. We beat ourselves up with the "why me?" attitude.

Have you ever used one of those Fix-a-Flat cans when something gets stuck in your tire? It's designed to just get you to a service station. It is a temporary fix. Then you are supposed to remove the object and repair the tire. Have you ever just kept driving around for days or weeks before having it repaired? I know I have.

A stern father confronts his daughter's persistent boyfriend: "Young man, I would like to know if your intentions are honorable or dishonorable." The young man responded, "Oh, I have a choice?" Many times we can make different choices because we have better options, but since we don't know they exist, we do nothing and miss out. We are creating our world one way or another, aware or unaware, conscious or unconscious, every moment. Life is too precious to not pay attention to how our thoughts are creating our reality. Isn't it time to fix what is flat in your life permanently? To accomplish this, we need to understand something...

Thoughts Are Energy

Light is fast-moving energy. Sound is also energy, but it moves at a slower rate. If you magnify any type of matter, even a rock, enough times you will see the movement of the neurons and protons that hold it together. Everything in the universe, seen and unseen, is made up of moving molecules. Since everything is made up of constantly moving energy, if we attempt to slow down or block this natural process, negative consequences (pain, stress, and suffering, for example) are inevitable.

Thoughts create feelings; feelings cause us to have emotions; and our emotions represent the language of the soul, a powerful attraction power to which we have access. Because emotion represents energy in-motion, thoughts with emotion behind them are the energy magnets that attract our desired results. Understanding this concept is critical to the creation process. By thinking, then saying, then feeling, we activate the creation process. Once again, what we think about, we bring about.

Thoughts are the causal part of every reality behind every human experience. The thought is the beginning, just as it was when God began the universe with His first thought. That Divine law continues, whether we are aware of it or not. Understanding this concept of cause and effect is critical because it allows us to see that we need only be concerned with the causal point of anything, and then the results are automatic. There is an unseen thread beneath all thoughts that connect them to their ultimate manifestation. It may seem difficult to understand or accept this concept because we can't control the time line connecting the two. If we don't see results quickly enough, we give up. Have you ever had a thought or focused on something you desired, and then forgot about it totally, only to find it show up one day? It could even be years later, but it shows up! This is because you launched the thought energy, and that energy never ends. The thought did what you wanted it to do; you just gave up on it. Think of it this way—the journey is the cause, and the effect is always the result.

The only way this process is stopped, and this happens a lot, is when we launch a contradictory, negative, or opposing thought. It could be a doubt or a comment like, "That will never happen to me, it would be too good to be true." When you have thoughts like this you launch a heat-seeking missile to destroy the desired result that was already en route to you! When we launch our thoughts it is critical that we believe we will receive them—and not only that, we must expect to receive the result we want! How do we do this?

Living an Expectant Life

The exciting thing about using the creation process is that it is based on universal law; it has to work. Gravity is a universal law, it can't not work, and it is constant and never-ending. The

Law of Cause and Effect and the Law of Attraction are also universal laws. This means in the right circumstances these laws work perfectly, following Divine design. When we get in alignment with these laws we can use them to direct our course. When we set ourselves up correctly we activate and attract the power of these laws. This causes wonderful things to start happening in and around us. Some examples would be thoughts that pop into your head to do something that pays off big, or you might notice how good timing affects certain situations, such as when people unexpectedly show up to give assistance, encouragement, or provide resources—exactly when you need them. All kinds of seemingly uncanny coincidences show up more and more. This is an exciting place to arrive in your life's journey, and if you haven't been there yet it is time for things to change.

This process works for everyone; all it takes is desire, teachability, and willingness to step up and get in line with what is already there, waiting to connect with you!

Here is a thought to ponder: You are living in this moment as an answer to a question you asked in the past. So, the old saying, "Be careful what you ask for" has a lot of truth to it. We need to plan and control our thoughts; then, we are prepared to respond and not react to what shows up in our lives. We won't get blindsided with as many unexpected distractions on the way to our destiny. Here are some techniques called Future Framing and Dream Casting, which will help you develop your attraction power.

Chapter 48
Future Framing My Dreams

Vision is foresight with insight based on hindsight.

Dr. Myles Munroe

Future framing is a strategy we use in the Valeo Method that is modeled after the concept of reframing, which is used in traditional therapy. Reframing, simply explained, is taking a situation that causes an upset and reframing it into a different mental picture, thus allowing a person to perceive and interpret it in a different, more positive way. This allows us to create a different perception, and it frames events, experiences, and our dreams in a more positive way. This changing of our frame of mind, as we discussed in the Release step, can change our perspective, mood, outlook, and mental state immediately.

Future framing changes the way we look at things regarding the future. Pull your thoughts and visions for a desirable future together in a frame to create a frame of mind, or frame of reference of our future expectations. We are using our active imagination to actually create a picture in the future of what we desire, and we will plant ourselves into the feelings, reality, and actions (movements) going on in the scene. The clearer we see the future desires and the more focused we are, the faster we attract the manifesting energies. Remember, clarity is power. Most of us have so many random thoughts that move through us so quickly, it's hard to capture them in a frame, let alone isolate the ones we desire the most and manifest them. Be encouraged; you can do it, it just takes a little practice. It can also be really fun and exciting to put together.

First, visualize what you desire in a picture frame in your mind. Then add as many details as you possibly can. Next, step into the picture and make sure you are a living, moving part of the dream you created in the Future Frame. The movement of what you are picturing is very important, so make it like a movie. We do not want this to be a still frame picture! Adding details moves the picture closer to reality and activates feelings, which in turn fire off emotions and look out—here comes what you are seeking!

Associating with and adding emotions to the picture actually allows us to move into the Future Frame much faster; then, we attract what we want faster because our emotions are triggered and it feels real. Then, we can experience what it will be like to own what we desire.

Create a Personal Dream Cast

Now let's take Future Framing to another level and use Dream Casting to project a detailed scene into our frame. Future Framing just gets you started; Dream Casting is about actively setting goals. It is about having a strategy and knowing how to be detailed and specific regarding what you are building and putting in your Future Frame. It is time to do some serious dreaming and tap into your creative juices and get them flowing.

Now we will interject even more attraction power into our dreams. Creating the life you want is an ongoing and evolving process. You are a walking, talking, dream-manifesting machine, although sometimes you don't use the creation gifts you have been given. After you learn the skills of the Valeo Method, you will know you have the tools you need to create so you can teach others to do the same—you can pay it forward. This is where we get to use our creative muscles, so it is very important that we do this exercise.

A Dream Cast is simply a picture of how you see yourself at a certain point in the future, in detail and in writing. Just like a movie director creates a storyboard of how he sees a movie unfolding, you will create a scene that we will fit in your Future Frame and become your new, desired story instead of the story the ego would have you experience.

On a sheet of paper make a list of at least ten things you would love to do, be, and have in your life. Think of all areas, such as spiritual, family, career, love, achievements, education, charity, contribution, and wealth. The key here is to let your imagination go. Don't let the ego participate and interfere and bring fear and doubt in your mind—dream like a kid. The ego hates this process because it is out of control. This will not work unless you let go of your self-imposed limitations, so dream big!

Now, pick out a day in the future when you want to see these dreams come true. Three, five or ten years—it doesn't matter. The goal here is to learn to apply the process.

Next, place all these dreams in your Future Frame and sit back with a big smile and revel in the picture. Feel it, touch it, smell it, and experience the joy. The most important part is getting the emotions to activate.

There is something powerful about writing these dreams down and picturing them. Now write a few pages and describe these dreams like you are watching it in a movie, in real time, while it is happening. Make your Dream Cast come alive in your writing. Tell the story in detail so that anyone who might read it would see and feel exactly what you are Dream Casting. This takes some thought, so make it fun, and make it real—this is your dream, for goodness' sakes! Use massive detail. Have fun and get your spouse, significant other, or your kids involved. This is your life and your future. What else is more important?

Your "heart's desire" is the voice of God calling to you.

Does Writing it Down Help?

In 1953, Yale University asked its graduating seniors a question as part of a study. They wanted to know how many had written goals. How many would you think? Almost everyone I ask thinks the answer is more than it actually is. They discovered that only 3 percent of that class of seniors had actually written down their goals. In a follow-up study twenty years later they discovered something even more interesting: The 3 percent who had written goals in 1953 appeared healthier, happier, more emotionally balanced and grounded. But those results are all subjective. What is accurately measurable is financial well being and wealth. The 3 percent who had written down their goals were worth more financially then the remaining 97 percent combined! When I heard this story I never looked at setting goals and writing them down as an option ever again. It is a must, a good habit we have to have. Remember earlier when we talked about modeling success? What category do you fall in? That leaves us with a big clue: Writing down our dreams and goals are important and can make a huge difference in what we actually accomplish,

Not only do most people never write down their goals, most have forgotten how to dream. We get so beaten down with the grind of life and so caught up in just surviving instead of thriving, we miss out on a lot of the good stuff life has to offer. Life can be like a millstone; it can either grind us down or polish us up, depending on how we live it.

As you go through this process you will get excited and you'll probably start telling people about the changes and confidence you are experiencing. Just be cautious. Remember, the world is full of discouraged, negative people. These energy suckers and dream stealers are lurking around every corner waiting to get at dreamers. They could be at your work, among your friends, and even living in your own house. They want to take your dreams away. They don't understand what you're learning through the Valeo Method about yourself and your potential. Remember, many people are living with pain, and misery loves company. These people are tormented by their emotional wounding, their failures, and the incompletion in their lives. They are living with battered emotional bodies, and as a result their lives are full of disappointment, lack, and lost hope. The last thing their egos want to hear is your newfound hope, encouragement, and confidence. Ironically, what these people need is exactly what you are discovering.

<u>Garth's Story</u>

In the summer of 1985, an unknown man named Garth Brooks left Oklahoma bound for Nashville in his beat-up Honda Accord. He thought opportunities were on every corner there. He was overwhelmed with rejection and within twenty-three hours he was headed back home. He returned to his job in a sporting goods store. He played weekend gigs at local bars and wondered about his future. Two years passed before he got the courage to head back to Nashville and pursue a singing career. He found a job managing a boat shop and cleaned a local church once a week. Success evaded him again, and he went back home. He wanted to not just entertain with his songs; he also wanted to ignite hearts. He hung on and fought for opportunity. Record companies turned him down, one after another. He started to think he wasn't going to make it and would wind up in poverty. His wife Sandy told him she wasn't coming back again if he didn't make it this time.

Garth found a job as a songwriter, making three hundred dollars a month. Then he found an agent to represent him. The agent was able to get him auditions with seven of the biggest record companies in Nashville. He just knew he was on his way. Result? He received seven more rejections.

Discouraged and ready to give up and go home again, a voice inside told him, "One more time at the Bluebird Café, and give it all you've got." The Bluebird was a local bar famous for turning up talent. A record producer in the audience heard him that night, and Garth discovered his biggest gift was not writing or singing as much as connecting with the audience. He went on to sell more records than Elvis, win fifty major music awards, and make the Country Music Hall of Fame. He was credited with making country music cool.

An interesting note to this story is that Garth gave one thousand dollars of his first ten-thousand-dollar check to a minister in Nashville who was being evicted, along with his family, from his home at Christmastime.

Garth had plenty of opportunities to give up, and he did give up many times, but only temporarily. Remember, as you learn the steps ahead, know that you are always closer to your dreams than you think!

Focus on your Dream Cast and your Future Frame. Now it is time to learn how to turn your Dream Cast into your reality. Let's put together more easy-to-follow steps that will guide you along the way to your dreams.

Chapter 49
WOWIE ("I Am")

To say "I love you," one must first be able to say the "I."

Ayn Rand

This is a fun part of the Valeo Method. This is where you learn to turn wishes which would normally wind up going nowhere into reality. Now you will have a system, a step-by-step, easy-to-remember process for taking charge of your dreams and how to breathe life into them while teaching others to do the same.

We will use the mnemonic WOWIE "I Am" as an aid in remembering each step in the order that provides the best results. These are the steps:

1. W – Wish

2. O – Objectify

3. W – Want

4. I – Intention to Test

5. E- Emotion

6. "I AM"

The first W is for "wish." A wish is a desire without energy or action. It is a fantasy, a whim, a consideration towards a desire. Wishing is fun, especially as kids, because we don't have all those limiting beliefs. Since wishing requires no energy whatsoever, it is easy. We just wish and wish and wish. We learned how as kids but we know in our hearts as we get older that we probably aren't going to experience the reality of the wishes, and our thoughts of them just waste away. Wishing alone rarely brings you to your dreams. Sometimes a wish is a clue that a dream is calling you. For that very reason, wishing plays a significant role in the creative process. A wish could be a seed. Making dreams come true is rarely an accident. People do win the lottery, but let's not count on it. The steps in WOWIE I AM create a road map to help us develop consistent skills to produce a desired result in attracting and manifesting anything good we desire. The alternative is waiting around on luck to come through for us. The real meaning of luck is Labor Under Correct Knowledge.

So, overall, let's count wishing as good. Wishing is healthy if we take it to the next step. Adults get stale with their wishing and dreaming, and they give up. Here is the question: Are you just wishing for things to get better and stopping right there? Here is how to determine if a wish is meant to be a reality.

Objectify

This step is called Objectify. It means to get clarity on the objectives of your dreams. Then we can place this objective in the Future Frame so then we can visualize it and activate the Law of Attraction toward it. We have already spent time in the previous steps opening up the channels to the flow in our minds so we can be objective about our true desires. Now let's take advantage of that prior work and understanding.

Ask yourself, "What is the most important object of my desire?" That doesn't mean it has to be a physical thing; in fact, it probably won't be. It could be to create a foundation, find a soul mate, serve others, start your own business, be a parent, or travel the world. It could be learning a new language, or computer program, learning marketing skills, being a real estate investor, internet marketer, or designing things like clothes or home interiors. It could be learning to play a musical instrument or learning to paint or sculpt. It could be you that you want to be involved in taking the message of hope, peace, and salvation to others and help them find their way to the Lord.

The point is, you have to find something to put in the picture of your future. Keep searching and asking yourself more questions until you find that idea that gives you that warm and fuzzy feeling inside. Are you ready for some encouraging good news? What you are searching for is searching for you, too! Jesus said, *"Keep on asking and you will receive what you ask for. Keep on seeking and you will find."*

Wanting

The second W represents wanting, something most of us are quite familiar with. Wishing and finding your object of desire is important because it gets the mind going; it primes the pump for this next step. Now we graduate the objective to a want and we speed up the co-creating process. Wanting begins to stir emotions that activate the feelings about what it is that you want. This will be important later in the process.

There are some things to consider about wanting. Is what you want for the greater good of all concerned? Is what you want taking away from someone else, from the environment, or causing upset or unrest? You can't want something that will take away, deprive, or hurt someone else because it will go against the natural laws and flow of the universe.

At the same time you have to feel worthy of receiving what you want. The ego can step in and start reviving old limiting beliefs, causing feelings of inadequacy or negative internal dialogues. You can never let down your guard. Old habits die hard; just remember, they are no match for the power behind a determined soul.

The ego is standing by, ready to distract us and squash any new ideas that show up in our lives because these are the very things that threaten the ego's existence. So what is the ego going to do? Get ready for a barrage of excuses, reasons, and fears related to what you desire to see happen. The ego can even attract other "doubting Thomases" into your environment.

Get ready for the ego to cause you to have thoughts like, "You never did this before, what if you fail, you are going to be disappointed, embarrassed, blah, blah, blah!" All these thoughts are just a bunch of garbage talk from the ego. It's only true if you buy into it. Henry Ford said it best: "If you believe you can or you believe you can't, you are right."

Don't Focus on What You Don't Want

When people are not sure what they want, they tend to make negative statements. In fact, in my seminars people come up to me most of the time to tell me what they don't want instead of what they want. I have to probe them to get them to tell me what they *do* want in their lives. For example, I've heard, "I don't want to be upset any more. I don't want to lose everything. I don't want to have financial problems. I don't want my relationship to fall apart with my spouse. I don't want to be a failure." The problem here is that we highlight these statements in our subconscious mind. Science considers the soul-mind we discuss in the Valeo Method as the subconscious mind, and the egoic mind as the conscious mind. Considering this interpretation, the subconscious mind collects and stores information with no reasoning power related to it—the information is just stored away for future reference. This part of our makeup was not created to recognize and separate negative (fear-based) thoughts and words with positive (love-based) thoughts and words. Rest assured, anything negative you think or say or any fears you have, no matter how they are softened up, do not come from your spirit; they come from the ego. "I don't want" thoughts are negative.

With this in mind, all the negative statements you hear yourself think and say are just the ego's cunning way of keeping you off track. If we say to ourselves, "I don't want to be sick," the subconscious mind picks up the "I don't want to" part and connects it with "be sick." The subconscious mind has no reasoning power, remember? It will never recognize the "don't"

in "I don't want." It drops the "I don't want" part and sees
the "lose everything, have problems, relationship falling apart"
sections. When it receives these messages it goes out seeking
energy reflections of them and attracts them and their consequences. It is like being in quicksand; the more you flop around
and fight it (in other words, the more you say you don't want
something), the further you sink down into it. This is natural
law; it is the way our minds work and how we create unconsciously. Then we wonder why things are so screwed up! This
should help illustrate how important awareness is.

God did not create "don't and shouldn't" thoughts. Here is
an exercise to prove this to yourself. Don't think about a pink
elephant. Whatever you do, don't think about a pink elephant. I
said, don't think about a pink elephant!!! I mean it, you better
not think about a pink elephant or else! What are you doing? I
bet you are thinking about a pink elephant. This is exactly what
happens when we focus on what we don't want—we give it
energy and attract it into our lives.

The challenge many people run into with activating the energies and attraction power to get what they want is they aren't
being specific enough about what they want. You must avoid
using descriptive words that are not specific. Here are some
examples: more, better, some, prefer, like, and extra. These
types of words are weak and not specific enough to *Activate
and Attract*. It is like fishing with stale, old bait.

When asked, "What do you really want more than anything?" most people say, "I want to lose some weight, get a
better job, do something different and important with my life,
find my soul mate, make more money." All these are noble
thoughts, but they are unlikely to ever materialize. Also, making
comparisons is not much better. "I want a house like his or a
career like hers, or a family like hers" are just too vague to really activate anything; they fall in the category of a wish.

In one of my seminars an energetic young man in the front
row responded to my question, "What do you want more than
anything in the world?" with, "I want more money." I reached
into my pocket, took out a one-dollar bill and gave it to him,
and then I said, "There you go, get out of here." I wasn't trying

to be mean; I just wanted to make a point that if that's all he wanted, he could leave, because he asked for more money and I gave it to him. He didn't specify how much money he wanted, he just knew he wanted more. When we put out the statement, "I want more money," the response from the Universal Law of Attraction goes something like, "Okay, how much do you want?"

If you tell your child you want him to make better grades, it might happen or it might not. How about if you say, "If you take all of your C's to B's or better on your next report card, I will reward you with a special camping weekend." Now it makes sense because there is something to shoot for—it is specific.

Intention: Going Beyond Wanting

Next up is the "I," which stands for intuition. Let's look at how we have taken a wish or desire, intensified the wish and created an object of desire that you Future Framed for clarity. Now it becomes a want which you are specific about, so now the intensity goes up another notch.

Although it is natural to want to do, be, and have things in your life, this is where most people lose energy and stop. Most wanting gets stuck in a groove like one of those old vinyl records where it just plays the same thing over and over. I want, I want, I want. Not only do we say it to ourselves, we tell it to others. Do you know someone who is always saying what he wants but never gets beyond it? Some people stay in this mode for years, even decades, with no results. It becomes a habit; they get stuck in their story of wanting, and it becomes part of who they are—it is part of their story, their identity. Be honest—have you done this? Are you doing it now?

Intention is powerful; intention is the why behind our focus. Intention is the why that must go behind a want in order to get it moving. Here is a quick exercise: Write down three things you really want. Now say to yourself out loud as you read your list: I want _____ (whatever it is). Notice how you feel about wanting something; notice your physiological response. Does it inspire or motivate you to want something? If you are like most people, the answer is probably no. Have you said things like, "I want to lose thirty pounds, I want a new car, I want a home on the water, I want a more intimate relationship with God?" Do you look forward to wanting something? Does wanting make you feel satisfied with your life?

Don't get me wrong; I am not slamming you for wanting things. Wanting is a necessary part of the creation process. But we just cannot stop there. Wanting primes the pump of the creative process. Wanting sets us up for tapping into real power, the power of intention.

Chuck Yeager did more than want to break the speed of sound in an airplane. If he had only wanted to accomplish this historic feat, he would never have mustered up the courage to attempt it. Other men had died from their attempts. There were always plenty of uncertainties about whether it could be accomplished or not. Yeager knew if he could push through the violent vibrations without losing courage, and control the plane on the other side of the speed of sound, he would experience relief and the joy of victory. Yeager went from wanting to accomplish his goal to intending to accomplish his goal, and that's when he achieved it.

Now let's continue with part two of our exercise. Let's take the things you previously stated as wants and change just one word. Let's change "I want" to "I intend," and see what happens. When you say, "I intend to lose thirty pounds," instead of, "I want to lose thirty pounds," you activate the power of intention. "I intend to own a new Mercedes" is a statement that comes to life. Try it, practice changing all your former "sincere wants" to "sincere intentions" and feel them come to life.

Does this sound too simple? Try it for yourself and with others. Have someone tell you what they want, and then have them change one word, "want," to "intend." Pay attention to their facial expressions and their physiology. I use this demonstration in my seminars and the responses from the attendees by just changing this one word are amazing. This goes back to the power of awareness and why we must use Transitional Language to replace our disempowering words to change the outcome of our lives.

Wish and want thoughts are filled with doubt. For example, if you think, "I want to own my own business," the ego might respond, "Great idea, Buddy, but you are broke and have no experience at running a business." The want just gets stalled out or canceled—it never had a chance.

Thoughts that are backed up with intentions are different. When we intend something, the authentic self, the Real You, comes to life to access resources within you and powers from God's universe to help you. Intentions spoken with conviction and belief set the power of nature in motion. The cause and effect dynamic is launched and the only way to stop it is to think an opposing thought and cancel it out. Otherwise, get ready to receive—you can't set the time line, but the order is being processed.

Intention Needs Faith

When we begin to understand the power of co-creation we are off to a big start. To give power to your intention we need to add faith. Faith comes from the heart, not the head. Faith fuels intention; it sets it on fire. If you master faith, you will master life. Saint Paul tells us, *"All glory to God, who is able through His mighty power at work within us, to accomplish infinitely more than we might ask or think."* This power is God's gift and we are entitled to use it; He wants us to use it. But as great as this power is and as much as we are entitled to it, without faith it doesn't work, and there are certainly no guarantees. It takes faith to access this power.

Most of us have wasted a lot of precious time in our lives just going through the motions. We let life beat us up and toss us around like a ship lost in a storm. We miss out on many things because of fear, doubt, and anxiety. All these are created by our ego, so we are responsible for them. They were not given to us by God. The price of lack of faith is a steep one, which could lead to a lonely existence without the abundance God promised. Jesus said it very clearly: *"I have come so that you can have life and live it more abundantly."*

God intends for us to plug into his power within each of us. It's time to destroy fear, doubt, and anxiety and intend to have and attract our dreams into reality. It's time to stake our claim of prosperity. It's time to co-create a life of joy and accomplishments wrapped in peace.

Expectation

The "E" in the WOWIE I AM represents a power-packed combo—expectation and emotion. When we expect to experience something, it means we experience the emotion before it happens. Now we can harness emotions and direct them to help us create our intentions. By controlling our emotions, we become conscious navigators of our thoughts instead of unconscious victims of them.

When we co-create unconsciously, we are being led by the ego and we are subject to the consequences. We are being influenced by our own locked-away negative and positive emotional charges within our sensitive self. The pain triggered from the sensitive self can influence, change, and even stop our progress and momentum towards our intentions. By being conscious of the process, we can train ourselves to live by expectation and anticipation of what we intend to happen. Expectation means we are in control of our casual and causal thoughts, words and deeds, and we are directing them.

Get on the Horse, Get in the Gate

This is another fun part of the *Activate and Attract* process. It is also where many people give up and miss out on an intention they were very close to realizing. Most of us have been beaten down by allowing ourselves to be the victim of an ego-directed ride of life. We spend more time waiting to see what shows up than making it happen. As a result, we welcome some pretty nasty characters and situations in our emotional house. Being a conscious navigator means checking the intentions of others at the door of our minds.

From this day forward, we will "intend" for what we want to arrive at the door of our lives. We can do this by making our intentions real. Why does someone buy a new Mercedes? It's the gas mileage, right? Of course not; they buy it because of the way it makes them feel. Otherwise, they could buy a Hyundai and still save money. It is the same way with clothes, furniture, even the cologne we wear. Seeking to experience the feeling of a thing or event is what motivates us. And what is feeling, but emotion?

Why do so many rich and famous people become so visibly depressed? They have the money to buy almost anything they want, and they do, because it makes them feel good about themselves when their fame doesn't fulfill them. This is the same reason people drink alcohol in access, take legal and illegal drugs, smoke cigarettes, and overeat—the bad habits are substitutes for the feelings they seek. They need and crave the emotional feelings so intensely they are willing to destroy themselves in their pursuit of them. Some even pay the ultimate price, their life.

Think about this scenario. You go to a horse race and sit in the stands, the bell sounds to open the gate; you lift your binoculars and watch the race. No matter how exciting the race is, you're not in the race; you're just watching.

Now let's look at this experience a little differently. Picture yourself getting on a horse and being led to the gate. How do you feel as the rider? The horse prances and snorts, full of energy. Now you enter the starting gate and notice the anticipation in your horse as you get ready. You are absorbed by the excitement and energy of the environment. Now the bell sounds and you are off! Feel the massive energy and air rushing around you. You hear the pounding of hooves and the deep breathing of the horses. Now look ahead, you're in the lead! Here comes the finish line, closer, closer. Yes! It is time to celebrate, you won the race!

How does this scenario feel compared to the first one? Even though you weren't physically in the race, you were there in your mind. When you played along with the second part of the exercise, you were able to experience totally different feelings by directing your thoughts. This is one of the secrets to creating attraction power. Remember, like attracts like—it is a natural part of the universe. E-motion attracts unseen forces into your life to assist you in realizing your intentions.

Studies have repeatedly shown that the body experiences the same physical responses when a person thinks about a subject while relaxed and with deep focus and concentration as they do when experiencing the real event. Now it's time to stop watching life go by and get in the race. Practice feeling the emotion and the feelings of your desired outcome before you get it, and you will cause it to move faster into your life!

When EPCOT Center opened in Orlando next to Disney World, Walt Disney had been deceased for years. At the ribbon-cutting ceremony a man commented as he was introducing Walt Disney's son, "It is too bad your father did not get to be here to see his dream realized." His son replied, "Oh, don't worry; my dad had already seen every detail of this park exactly as it is." Disney's son knew his father had visualized his dream and experienced it clearly in his mind long before it ever became a physical reality.

It is called "fake it till you make it." This means practicing creative visualization every day to the point at which you can feel what it is like even though you aren't even close to getting there yet. The more real we can make our intentions in our minds, the more helpful ideas, clues, and directions will show up to guide us.

To take control of the *Activate and Attract* process, ironically, we have to also be flexible and allow God to weave His intentions through our own. We have to follow the steps, trust the process, live with expectation, know that it works, and then just let God have it.

How does a farmer wait? He plants his crops and waits patiently and expectantly for the sun and rain to bring them up. He expects to see the fruits of his labors. He did the work to prepare to receive, so he expects to get results. We have to do the same with our dreams.

If we are clear on what we intend and we activate our intentions through the Laws of Cause and Effect and the Law of Attraction, we are on the way to receiving them.

What if I am Not Getting What I Intend?

There were times when I was determined to use creative visualization to attract something in my life and it didn't come. Sometimes I thought I had done everything right and it still didn't come. I began to doubt if visualization even worked and if maybe I had just been lucky before.

One example was going to prison. I prayed and affirmed and intended not to go. Yet I spent three years in a Federal prison camp. Here's what I learned: God created the co-creation process, so He knows best and always takes care of those who believe and have faith in Him. I believe He wants to give us everything. But I also learned that God doesn't work on our personal or earth-based time table, He works on His time. Since He created everything, He can set up that way. Sometimes God is protecting us, sometimes He is saving us from something worse we could have experienced, and sometimes He is nurturing us. Sometimes we are being prepared and getting ready for greater things. Many times we intend and pray for something and we don't get it because God has something far better in store for us. That is why it is always good to pray for what you want, but add an addendum to your prayer: "Or something better." God may have something better planned for you that you can't even imagine. Rest assured, His answer will always be for the greater good of all.

The Great "I AM"

When Moses asked God who He was God answered, *"I am the great I AM."* He did not say I am the great "I was" or "Going to be." This could be interpreted to mean that God is everything, God is in everything, and everything is God. God is the spark of life in all our souls. God is the energy that moves the molecules in all matter and allows them to exist. This life force is eternal; it won't go away, and it never ends. We can freeze or steam water and change its structure, but it never disappears. We can break glass, crush it, and put it in a furnace and turn it into liquid or even gas. It changes structure, but it never goes away. This is because of the creative force of nature controlled by the Creator. This is the part of us that keeps all of humanity and every living creature alive and every inanimate object in existence. This is a very big fact to comprehend, but it is important that we grasp it to activate the individual power to co-create in our lives.

In our time-bound thinking the concept of eternal is not easy to metabolize. We only have to go to Einstein's Theory of Relativity for proof that time as we know it is an illusion. We can look at it through scientific and spiritual lenses; they will both bear the same truth.

The great "I Am" is the power of the Creator threaded through and imprinted in every molecule that exists, seen and unseen. This observation gets a little complicated when we look at it from the standpoint that this moment, "the now," is all there really is, that is, until ... the next moment and another "now." We tap into the purest form of co-creating when we understand that we are creating every moment, aware or not, because the "I Am" is a part of us.

The Bible tells us these three things: God created us in His image; He gave us dominion over earth, and it even says that God is working within us, giving us the desires and power to do what pleases Him!

We have to create. Everyone is creating every day, constantly. Just look around—what is going on in your life right now? What do you see in front of you right this minute in all areas of your life? You're seeing your past thoughts created! This is about getting in control of what we are creating by tapping into "I Am." The more we are in alignment with the great "I Am," the more we are co-creating with God the life we are intended to live instead of just showing up for some mess that we create on our own. God (literally) only knows how that could turn out.

Using the words "I Am" are the two most activating and powerful words in the universe. Don't misunderstand what I am saying here. I am not telling you to pretend or claim to be

God. We are talking about recognizing the part of you that is connected to the Creator who, were it not for Him, you would not exist. As we re-member with our original source of life and come in alignment with the good of all, something terrific happens. We activate, or turn on, the switch and let the creative energies of the universe flow through us. We become the conduit, the vehicle, the expression point of good that is inherent in everyone, our "before-DNA" purpose. When we activate the "I Am," the extension of God in all of us, we also tap into our own creative powers of cause and effect. The master teacher said, *"Ask and ye shall receive."* This means we were created to manifest good things in our lives, and we have the power within us, a God-given gift, to co-create.

We can only activate the "I Am" in us through faith. We need to believe that God wants to bless each one of us and show us His grace. "Grace" means "unmerited favor;" in that we don't necessarily deserve what is available to us, whether it be love, peace, prosperity, provision, or abundance, but that is what is available to us. Pretty cool, don't you think? God wants to give you what you want (as long as it is for good); He wants to give you more than you think you deserve, and He is ready "Now." We just have to have faith; we have to believe in the power within each of us to manifest.

This is critical because we are constantly creating anyway. This is where so many people miss it. Please pay attention to this next statement: If you have a thought that is opposite of the thought you want to happen, and that thought has equal strength, you will neutralize it—cancel it out. This is the reason some people say the Law of Attraction doesn't work for them. They are literally cancelling out their request before they give it an opportunity to manifest.

We discussed getting on the horse and in the race. Now let's make it real. When we say "I Am," we will add the verbs, doing, being, or having to fill in the blank, of what we seek to manifest, and we will therefore automatically activate the Law of Cause and Effect, which in turn activates the Law of Attraction. We are igniting the force of creation and connecting it to our good dreams and intentions. We're going to use the words

"I Am" as an activating part of our language and intentions. We're going to affirm our intentions by using "I Am" statements. The definition of the word "affirm" is "to make firm." When we write statements in the affirmative, we are creating "I am" affirmations. We need to write down, memorize, and even post our affirmations so they become a firm part of our thinking. Post them on the bathroom mirror, the refrigerator door, the visor in the car, and laminate them and put them in your wallet or purse, or make them into bookmarks.

Here are some examples of affirmations. Get creative and make your own or use these and have some fun with it—what a concept!

I am attracting the man/woman of my dreams now.

I am the owner of a successful _____ business.

I am creating an income of _____ per month.

I am at my desired body weight of _____

I am free from the habit of _____.

I am attracting a perfect job/career/business opportunity.

I am peaceful and happy and connected with God.

I am living God's purpose in my life. I am saved!

When you get in the groove with your "I Ams," you take away resistance. This is how we set powerful and unstoppable energy in-motion. Unseen forces are activated to assist and direct you. Intention is activated. Strong "I am" statements overpower negative, doubtful thoughts.

The challenge with most of us is that we lack patience and get discouraged too easily. We go into the instant gratification mode that society teaches us, and we want everything now. Just think if you could put on special glasses that would allow you to see the energies moving and connecting the things you desire in a Divine way to manifest your dreams. You would never get discouraged. You would understand why some things take longer than others, and you'd be happy to wait. You would live by faith that everything works out the best for those who believe and live according to their purpose. You would not dare have a negative thought or lose faith because you would know it would slow down the acceleration of your dreams and the realization of your purpose. You would know when you were blocking the flow. You would understand that lack of faith behind your intentions will cause you to lose power. This is powerful thinking; it is about thinking with emotions that are grounded in good—and in God.

Remember, emotions are easily transferred from one person to another. The person with the strongest emotion wins. If their negative emotion is stronger than your positive emotions, watch out! You will receive theirs! Why put the unnecessary drain and strain on your positive emotions and energy? This is an important part of living consciously and being responsible instead of playing into negative situations.

There are times when we have to let people go out of our lives. Many of my clients can't bring themselves to let go of a relationship or a friend who is ripping their lives apart. They work hard to get ahead and then let other people slow them down and rob them of their dreams.

We need to continually remind ourselves of our true emotions and our true intentions. There is a blind spot between what we intend to create and what is really happening in our lives. This is where the continuity of life occurs. By responding positively to what shows up in your life each moment, and only allowing people in your inner circle who bring positive energy with them and avoiding those who drain your good energy, you can speed up the attraction of what you truly desire. You want to compress time and not waste it on the unnecessary distractions and detours in your life. You want to be in the flow.

Chapter 50
How to Get Anything You Want

No one can make you feel inferior without your consent.

Eleanor Roosevelt

The Valeo Method is designed to teach you new skills and equip you with new strategies. A strategy is like the pieces of a puzzle or the recipe to a cake. Strategies take the guesswork out and relieve the frustration of trial and error— plus, they save a lot of time. Proven strategies stack the odds in your favor of getting a good and desirable result. So far, we have been accumulating ingredients, clearing the way, and getting prepared to find and live all our passions. This next step is a process called If I PAR. Here we have another mnemonic that gives us the recipe and shows us the right order to put it in. It shows how much of each ingredient we need. If we want to make a strawberry shortcake but don't know how much sugar, flour, or how many strawberries we need, we could have a lousy cake. If it is not prepared in the right order, we get a lousy cake. Realizing our dreams and goals works the same way. IF I PAR shows you how to get the best results in the least amount of time by understanding how to turn on our attraction power to ensure we get the best results.

IF I PAR

If you're not a golfer, don't worry; this is not about golf. It is a metaphor and we are just borrowing the word "PAR," which is a standard of consistency and success in golf. Par is considered a good score. It is considered a good job, a meeting of a high standard of accomplishment of the score at the golf course. Every hole in the course is different, but par score is established for each hole. The idea is to score par or better at each hole, and you have conquered the course. Any golfer will tell you that scoring par every hole on an eighteen-hole course is not easy.

The IF I PAR mnemonic breaks down the steps and the order necessary to get laser-beam focused on a goal or dream and get it moving toward you fast as you move toward it. If we could par our lives in all areas, we would be living a joyous, fulfilling life.

These are the steps to the mnemonic IF I PAR:

> I – Intention Statement
> F– Focus and Attention
> I – Intensity
> P– Passion
> A– Action
> R– Repetition

The first letter, "I," represents an "Intention Statement" we are going to create. It will be something you intend to do, be, or have. There are three steps:

1. Create the statement. It can be an "I Am" statement, but you have to use the word "intend." An example could be: I am successful in my new business (be specific) and I intend to make \$_____ per month in month_____ of year_____. Write it down and affirm it repeatedly. Put the statement in places where you will be constantly reminded of it.

2. Picture with clarity what you are declaring in your inten-
    tion statement, vision cast your statement, Future Frame
    the picture you see in your mind for the result you intend
    (not wish). Now put yourself in the picture.

3. Feel the emotions: see it, touch it, smell it, experience it.
    Remember, motion creates emotion. Having trouble?
    Don't give up; it is good to fake it till we make it!

Make sure your intention statement is real and believable to you.
Remember, scientists have proven that the feeling of having what
we intend to have is no different that actually having it as far as our
nervous system goes. Don't try to figure out the "how" of achieving your goals at this point. When you get the "why," the how will
come. It's not going to work out well if your intention statement
is: "I am a successful owner of my own business, even though I've
never done it before." That is letting negative energy creep in. Your
intention statement has no power this way. Most of us are so conditioned in our thoughts of doubt from our environment it is easy to
have half-baked intentions. Be careful who you tell your intention
statements to because sometimes even well-meaning people and
your family will discourage you.

Franklin D. Roosevelt could have listened to his family and
closest friends when they urged him to retire and give up on being
president of the United States. They actually told him that people
would not vote for a handicapped politician. Good thing he didn't
listen!

Doctor Seuss could have listened to the twenty-three publish-
ers who rejected his book and not found the twenty-fourth who
published and helped him sell six million of his children's books.
Alex Haley wrote dozens of articles and couldn't get them published
before writing his blockbuster novel, *Roots*. This is why you should
be careful about who you tell your intentions to and make sure
those you *do* tell really do want you to succeed.

What You Focus On, You Get

The next letter is "F" and represents "Focus." What you focus on is what you get. Where attention goes, energy flows. If you focus on lack and how bad things are, you get more of the same. When we focus on winning, victory, overcoming, constant improvement, and abundance, it starts seeking us.

Here is an example to prove a point. Have you ever bought a car that you really liked and made you feel unique? Then after a few days of owning the car, you see the same make and model everywhere! The car was always there; you just weren't focusing on it. We all have what is called a reticular activating system (RAS). This system locks a particular idea, concept, or thing in place in our minds, and we see the image and a trigger goes off. We can use the RAS as a tool to help us stay focused on getting a clear picture of what we seek to attract by continually focusing on it. Then when things pop up in our view the RAS is like a homing beacon, drawing us toward our desired result. The RAS becomes an unconscious magnet for what we seek.

Create a Treasure Map

A Treasure Map is a continued expansion of Future Framing and Dream Casting. This can be a notebook or a poster or a photo album or a software program into or onto which you put visual images of your dreams and goals. This step is designed to help cultivate the "why" behind your intentions. When people make major purchases, they buy based on their emotions most of the time. Emotions cause us to act. However, we justify with logic (which many times does not make sense). Treasure maps help you bring into focus what you desire, and it also helps you get clarity and focus.

I've seen some amazing creations with the treasure maps exercise. In group sessions I have seen the participants glow with excitement and pride as they shared their treasure maps with others in the class. They would get passionate as their dreams came to life in their treasure maps. It was exciting to me and the other participants to see the creativity and creams of others as they played out in pictures and as they explained them in words from the heart.

This is why a treasure map is powerful. It may sound silly or you may feel too busy to do this, but it is important to make your dreams come alive before they materialize. That is the problem many of us have; we are afraid to dream like we did as kids. We were born to dream; we just forgot how.

Your treasure map should include all the areas of your life, including spiritual, family, business, things you want, travel, and fun. Use pictures from magazines and the Internet, personal drawings and inspiring quotes to fill up your map. Pull out the stops, don't be afraid to let go. You may want to do your whole treasure map as a digital video—whatever works for you and gets you excited and stirs emotion is what you should shoot for—even if you shoot for the moon and miss, you will still land among the stars. There are no limits except the limits you put on yourself!

The creativity I've seen with treasure maps is nothing short of amazing. There's so much creativity and talent bursting to get out of you, so get ready to surprise yourself! What creams are waiting to be awakened within you?

Intensity Breathes Life Into Dreams

The second "I" stands for "Intensity." Most people spend more time planning a vacation than they do planning their lives. They wonder why everyone else gets the breaks. So many times we miss the message life is sending us.

Actor Michael Landon was on his deathbed when he said, "Somebody should tell us, right at the start of our lives, that we are dying. Then we might live life to the limit every day. Do it, I say! Whatever you want to do, do it now! There are only so many tomorrows!"

After getting focused on what you desire to do, be, and have, you are living the next step to getting what you want. But you must have intensity. Big dreams require big intensity to realize them. We are not going to drift our way to the top of Success Mountain.

Being intense means also being congruent. Being congruent means being in alignment with your dreams and having enough intensity to make them happen. When what we are feeling in our hearts and the words coming out of our mouths are the same levels of intensity, we are congruent.

Many of our lives are littered with the debris of past failures and lackluster attempts to realize our dreams. Our half-baked and half-hearted commitments to our dreams leave us lacking the confidence we need for future success. This is because we are incongruent, our hearts are not in it, and we lack intensity.

Hernando Cortez was a Spanish conqueror in the 1700s. He sailed to an island in the Yucatan Peninsula to attempt to take a huge treasure from a native dynasty. For two hundred years others had attempted and always failed. Cortez recruited all the best soldiers he could find. He left with a fleet of ships. Upon reaching land, he ordered all the ships to be burned. He said if we are going home we are going home on their ships. That is some serious confidence in yourself and your team! Retreat just wasn't an option. As the story goes, they realized a spectacular victory. What a concept!

It takes faith to have intensity toward your dreams. Faith is born in the heart; from there it moves to the head. Faith from the head alone is blind faith, which lacks power.

It is time to get intense. It is time to feel the weight of your future on your shoulders. It is time to stop making butt prints in the sands of time and get serious about your life! Leaders, champions, and winners are imbedded with unflinching determination and iron will. You have the same attributes within you; are you using them?

Sometimes just a little extra effort and intensity is enough. What can you do with 211-degree water? You can make coffee, wash dishes, clean away dirt and mildew. But what happens when you add just one more degree and reach 212 degrees? Now the water boils, which creates steam. Steam can push a multi-ton locomotive over a mountain, move a massive ship across the sea, and fire a fighter jet off an aircraft carrier.

How much clock-time do Olympic athletes win Olympic Medals by? Is it by minutes or seconds? Neither, it is usually by literally one-one-hundredth of a second. How long do they train and prepare for a chance to win? Now that is intensity! Intensity creates power. Since so few people have intensity or use it effectively, it gives a huge advantage to those who recognize it and use it.

Let's say you are going to learn to play chess. If you play one game every day for one year, you could develop some skill. If you play three times a day for four months, you play the same amount of games. But studies show that if you use the second example, you would be a better player even if you started eight months later than another player! Once again, intensity and compressing time gives you leverage and an advantage. If you are committed you're going to do it anyway, so why wait?

Passion: The Energy of Real Living

Are you thriving in your thinking and your life, or just surviving? Are you getting ready to go, waiting to go, or are you already in motion? Are you seriously ready to go to the next level? You can't get there without the "P" in IF I PAR, which represents a magical thing called "Passion." Passion is the fuel of excellence. Passion is what we get when we love what we are doing and when what we are doing gives us what we want in return. Passion is an energy that comes from finding and living your deepest desires and purpose.

Aristotle said,
"When talents and needs of the world cross, therein lies the vocation."

Deep within each of us is a voice, charged with energy, the voice that since your first breath of life has sought to be heard.

The key to tapping into your passion is to keep asking and searching your thoughts and your soul until you find that spark, that feeling that excites you like nothing else. Some people have a skill and they think it is a unique talent or purpose, but skills don't always carry that spark of passion. This is why we have to search for the work, career, or contribution that brings passion together with skills and talent. This is when personal power comes alive.

Passion drives conviction deep into your soul, and conviction produces excellence. Passion attracts others to your cause and to the pursuit of your dreams. Passion allows you to overcome insurmountable odds; it makes you unstoppable in your pursuits. Passion activates and fuels unrelentingly drive.

Goethe said, *"A man sees in the world what he carries in his heart. If your heart is aflame, your world that day will be on fire."* You are meant to have passion in your life. You are not supposed to do something and be happy; you are supposed to be happy and then do something! Isn't it time to get more passion in your life? How many of us are missing our calling? It is time to put an end to just skating through life, thinking our circumstances are going to change. It is time to break the chains of mediocrity and get rid of stinking thinking. God is busy working behind the scenes in your life right now. He is softening hearts and widening your path. He's making the crooked places straight, and He will move mountains for those who have faith and believe. The Scripture tells us, *"You will mount up wings like eagles; you will run and you will not get tired, you will walk and not faint."*

People love passionate people. Aren't they just great to be around? Maybe it is because so few have passion and so many want it. Passion creates massive attraction power within you. Passion is magnetic and available to everyone who seeks it, and with faith, they will find it.

Action

The "A" in IF I PAR represents "Action." When you have a burning desire in your heart for something, ironically, that something wants you, too. That is how the Law of Attraction works.

You also know that just wanting something doesn't give you much more than a state of need. By following the steps thus far, we have initiated the thought, word, and deed process to create movement of your intention toward you. When you take a step toward your dream, it takes a step toward you. We have to take the first step because even if we have faith, we are told, faith without action is dead. That sounds like we are supposed to get moving!

This is why we call it co-creating; we aren't alone; God is with us, but we have to do our part. Can you learn to swim by reading a book? Of course you can't, but what does it take? You have to get in the water and splash around, you have to get wet. We have to do something even when we are not sure if it is going to work. Some of us are asleep at the wheel of our lives. Will Rogers said, "You have to climb on out on a limb sometimes; that is where the fruit is." You have to get out of your comfort zone.

That may mean watching less television (also known as the electronic income reducer) and read a self-help or inspirational book instead. It could mean listening to motivational audio recordings instead of reading a mystery novel or a tabloid magazine.

How about asking a friend or acquaintance to coach or advise you on a subject you are interested in that they are familiar with? The wise author in Proverbs wrote: *"Those who listen to instruction will prosper."* It could mean changing your routine and getting up a few minutes earlier to pray, or changing your diet, or starting a new exercise plan. It could be as simple as asking a friend to help you find something on the Internet or getting involved in an online forum related to your interest. The key is, get moving. It is good to be employed, it is great to be deployed and moving toward your bliss! It is time to turn hope into expectation and expectation into reality.

I wanted to make time for prayer and meditation in the morning for years. I had good intentions right up to the moment I needed to take action. I learned to use the steps of the Valeo Method right in front of you to take charge of my life, and I found the discipline to do it. I had a ton of excuses. I thought I needed to make more money and have more success and couldn't afford to take the time. Now I realize how much easier my life would have been if I had been in control instead of my egoic mind.

The space shuttle uses about 90 percent of its fuel to create the propulsion to break through the earth's atmosphere and get into orbit. Upon reaching outer space, it only requires the remaining 10 percent of fuel to maneuver and return home. Once it makes the breakthrough into space, things are much easier.

A normally aspirated airplane engine struggles dramatically to climb in altitude after about ten-thousand feet. Soon, it has to return to earth to get more fuel to keep moving towards its destination. It never reaches massive speed with little energy (effort) like the space shuttle does.

Our lives are similar to these two machines. Most of us spend our time climbing our way to success; we just keep grinding it out and never get to the point where it only takes a little effort to keep it all going. How about putting out massive action in the beginning so that later, when you arrive at your dreams, it will take much less effort to keep it going?

I love to write. My goal is to write at least one hour every day. Some days I write for eight hours, but I always strive for one hour minimum and I usually make it. The key is to create a habit, a conditioned, positive action. Over a period of time your efforts start to compound and they produce great results. Discipline in one area of life will spill over into other areas. Every day I get up at 5 a.m. and I know my priorities. First I have to have my prayer and meditation time; second, I have to deal with my exercise for the day. If I have travel plans that interrupt my routine, I make up for that time later. I don't just skip out. I might not do as much, but I never just blow off my commitments. I find a way to make up for the interruption one way or another. I have conditioned myself to do what used to be uncomfortable until now it is not only comfortable, it is my comfort zone. Remember: Good habits are just as hard to break as bad ones.

When you have a lack of motivation to take action and do the things you need to do to get what you want, it is time to play the pain/pleasure card. Get a clear picture in your mind of your intentions. Sink into the emotions you experience from realizing your intentions. Continue to ask yourself: "What is it going to cost me if I don't take action? How will I feel if in five years, looking back, I realize what not taking action has cost me? How about ten years?" Remember, people will do more to avoid pain than gain pleasure. Make this a permanent part of your thinking. Joan Baez said it nicely: *Action is the antidote to despair.*

Another way to enforce your commitment to taking action is to make a public commitment. When I made the commitment to lose eighty pounds and display a six-pack of abdominal muscles, I knew I needed lots of leverage. I made a big public commitment. I told all my friends, family, and everyone who would listen to me what I was going to do and the time line that I committed to. I know they admired my goal but I don't think many of them believed me. I created so much leverage that I knew I would feel like a real loser (no pun intended) if I didn't hit my goal. Also, when I made that commitment I was in my forties and I had never seen my abs before! Every time I felt like being lazy and not taking action, all I had to do was remember how many people I had told about this goal.

I also cut out a picture of a man with a midsection like I wanted. I cut off the head and legs so all I could see was the midsection look I wanted. I put that picture in the bathroom so I had to see it every morning when I started my day.

I worked hard and hit my goal. It took twenty months. It has been years now. I feel half my age and I haven't taken any medication in years. The steps of the Valeo Method you are learning now helped me find what I needed inside to get myself to do what I needed to do to achieve success and prepare me for this major life change.

Don't be afraid to make mistakes. I got off track many times. I just followed what you are learning in the Valeo Method, and I got right back on track and never gave up.

What Michael Landon felt in his final months about not having time to do what he intended to do before he died is similar to how many terminally ill patients feel. This is an awful pain that none of us want to experience. What are you doing with the time you have left? None of us has a lease on life. Is your life going to be a warning or an example? Taking action keeps us from dying wondering what could have been.

Repetition

If at first you don't succeed try, try again. What a powerful statement. Winston Churchill once spoke to a large group of dignitaries. His speech was highly anticipated. The audience was surprised when he stood up and said simply, "Don't ever, ever, ever, ever, ever give up," and then sat down.

I teach a sales training course called, "The Passion of Selling." In the course, my participants learn the power of persistence and repetition, the big payoff for not giving up. One study about sales shows that 48 percent of all salespeople only ask one time for the sale; 25 percent make two attempts to get the sale; and 12 percent make three to five attempts. Yet 88 percent of all sales are made when the buyer is asked more than five times. This is an example of the power of repetition in one area of life. Success is buried right past frustration, unfortunately just where most of us give up. As Aristotle is quoted as saying: *We are what we repeatedly do. Excellence then is not an act but a habit.*

Michelangelo failed more than two hundred times to produce a satisfactory sketch for the Sistine Chapel. Thomas Edison failed more than ten thousand times before he invented the incandescent light bulb. It took more than twenty-five thousand experiments to invent the D/C battery we use today. Winston Churchill said, "Success is going from failure to failure with enthusiasm."

Calvin Coolidge said, "Nothing in this world will take the place of persistence, talent will not: Nothing is more common than unsuccessful people with talent. Genius will not: Unrewarded genius is proverb. Education will not: The world is full of educated derelicts. Persistence and determination alone are omnipotent. The slogan 'Press On' has solved and always will solve the problems of the human race."

Shortcuts are dead ends in disguise. Usually things worth the effort are not easy, but they are well worth it.

Have you ever driven around town with your emergency brake on? How did you feel when you realized it? That is the way many of us live our lives. We are riding the brake. We hold back from giving our best because we don't keep trying. Since this thing called life is not a dress rehearsal and we only get one shot at it, isn't now a good time to get going?

An African proverb tells us that in Africa, every morning when a gazelle wakes up, it knows it has to run faster than the fastest lion or it will be killed. Every morning when a lion wakes up, it knows it has to run faster than the slowest gazelle or it will starve to death. The moral of the story is that it doesn't matter who you are when the sun comes up; you had better start running.

A professional speaking coach told me, "Rehearsal is the work; performance is the relaxation." I never forgot that advice. Too many times we are unprepared for what life has to offer, and we come up short. Repetition is how the pros become pros.

Progress and Strategies

1. I have special gifts and talents like no one else. I am here on earth to dream, to decide, to declare and do what God intended for me to do. I will never be totally fulfilled until I do.

2. My purpose may surprise me. My purpose is looking for me just like I am looking for it.

3. I can "reframe" my current situation into a new "Future Frame" and move toward my new destiny as it moves toward me.

4. My dreams are meant to come true. My dreams are my sacred destiny. I was given the ability to dream as a child. I reclaim that gift now.

5. A dreaming heart is a healthy heart, a dreaming heart is a vibrant heart!

6. Dreams chase away worry and fear.

7. My purpose is behind my passionate dreams.

8. My job is what I get paid to do; my purpose is what I was born to do.

Summary and Action Plan

1. Make a commitment to find your purpose and live it. Other people do it; why not you?

2. Dream your biggest dreams, write them down, Decide to take ownership in their reality, Declare your dreams are yours (make "I am" statements about your dreams), and Do what is necessary by following the Activate and Attract step.

3. Create an Ideal Scene. Dreamcast a beautiful, detailed, ideal scene of where you want to be. Include your family and close trusted (positive-minded) friends in the process.

4. Take some serious time to understand WOWIE IAM and get clear on the difference between wishing, wanting, and intention.

5. Work on your Intention Statements and Your "I Am's" and put them in writing. Post them where you will constantly be reminded of them (bathroom mirror, car visor, in your purse or wallet). Re view your intention statements and say them out loud every morn ing upon awakening and the last thing before going to sleep at night. Say them with authority and congruency.

6. Use the word "already" and give thanks for your results. Example: "I am grateful I am already at my desired weight of ____ and feel ing healthy and vibrant," or "I am grateful I am already earning over $_____ per month."

7. Focus on your intentions at every opportunity and Future Frame them in your thoughts. Practice getting clearer and creating more details in your mind of your Dream Casting. The more details and the clearer you are, the faster your intentions will manifest.

8. I will use IF I PAR to condition myself to the recipe strategy for staying on track for excellence in all areas of my life.

9. Practice closing your eyes and feeling the emotions you will experi ence when you arrive at your dreams. The more you can experi ence these feelings, the faster your dreams will arrive in reality.

10. Always be alert for dream stealers and energy suckers lurking around. Avoid the negative influences of other people. They don't want you to make them look bad when you do well!

11. Live with passion; it is the fuel of excellence.

PART VII

MANIFEST
AND MAINTAIN

*Many of us spend our lives looking for success when it is usually
so close we can just reach out and touch it.*

Russell H. Conwell

What if there were two little-known and understood secrets that if you knew about and understood, you would know
exactly what to do to take control of your life forever? What
if there was one foundational cause behind all the suffering,
worry, and addictions in life? Would this be a good thing to
know? What if this secret was ultimately the key determining
factor behind all personal defeat or victory? What if this secret
factor was controllable, manageable, and could be directed to
change the course of events in your life? What if there was
another secret that was a little-known key factor that triggers the manifestation of all your dreams, but at the same time
it was the number-one reason the Law of Attraction doesn't
work for most people? Would you be interested?

Does it sound impossible, or too simple that these two little-known things could be so significant in creating lasting change? The last step of the Valeo Method is the best, for it reveals these secrets and more. In fact, you may be surprised what you discover.

The real power of the Valeo Method is how we line up five critical steps of the DREAM formula. Remember, each step is powerful in its own right, but when they are packaged together in the right order and put on the foundation of this last step, look out, life is a beautiful and flowing process! Most of us are already good at some parts of this process; the challenge comes from the parts we neglect or misunderstand. Some folks are like I was; they may do a decent job of keeping control of the first four steps. But because I didn't have this last step figured out, I kept missing the grand prize life has to offer. I could never be happy or satisfied.

This last step shows us how to reach a real breakthrough in our lives. The breakthrough comes when we realize the first secret, and that secret is: We are all ultimately seeking one thing in life more than anything else, and that is unconditional love. We have to experience it in order to keep the flow going in our lives. The soul is constantly seeking unconditional love and acceptance from our external environment. Unconditional love soothes the soul. We have delusions that other things will give us bliss, but in truth, they only give temporary satisfaction, and the yearning deep in the soul continues for unconditional love.

As we have also learned in the Valeo Method, an aching soul empty of unconditional love can be the source of tremendous pain when it is amiss. Previously, we discussed the effect of unconditional love on humanity and the power it has on the collective consciousness of society. Now let's take this force, which is the thread that holds the entire world together, and explore how it holds our individual lives together, and the one key that releases it faster than anything.

Harnessing this power creates an energy that removes all excuses, destroys all fears, and unleashes locked-away potential. Failure is not an option against this kind of power. There is no such thing as fear controlling you ever again. Accessing this power gets results because your intuition will show you how to adjust your strategies to get what you want. The force you have tapped into knows no defeat and never gives up.

Opening the Expression Point

In order to understand the first secret of the *Manifest and Maintain* step, I have to emphasize again that each of us represents an expression point in consciousness. Within this opening is where the Divine powers of creation manifest. Just as a lamp is an expression point for electricity, each of us is an expression point for God. First we must understand that God does not give talent to any of us. God maintains His talent and uses us to express it. Adam and Eve believed they were creators by themselves. As a result, they decided they didn't need God, and they messed things up. We as human beings are the instruments for creation, not the creators. When we begin to think we are the creators alone, rest assured that the ego, our false self, is certainly in control.

When we accept and relinquish the fact that all things are manifested from the unseen and invisible realm, we open the flow in our lives. Let us always remind ourselves that we have no power on our own. Our knowledge is not sharper than a double-edged sword, but we have access to what is. Our knowledge does not perform miracles through unmerited favor, but we have instant access to the power that does. In addition, if we understand certain principles and precepts, we will surely witness miracles of creation, healing, and abundance in our lives.

The same principles and precepts that demonstrate a penny in your life will demonstrate millions of dollars in your life if you are in alignment with the right source and you are not blocking the flow of creation. The problem with most of us is that we are so close, closer than we can imagine so many times, but we are blocking the manifestation of good because we are not aware of this next secret of supply.

In order to manifest in our lives, we have to transcend the mind. There is a huge difference between the spiritual truth about supply and the human belief about supply. In the spiritual sense, supply is not income; it is outflow. The opposite is true in the human sense. Most people, me included, have spent a big part of their lives seeking supply outside of ourselves. But that is not where supply is; it only seems that way to the unaware. All the supply we could ever need for the rest of our lives is waiting for us right now. But it is not "out there"—it is "in here"—inside each and every one of us. If you want to experience abundance and overflow in your life, you must find a way to release it from within.

Everything in the universe is moving. If we magnify the smallest particle enough times under a microscope we will see particles moving around, and that which is not moving is space. Space allows everything to move. The way to create in our lives is to create the movement, the motion, within our space that we take up in creation. We do this by giving. When we give, we are priming the pump for good in our lives. We are inviting the natural flow of the universe to happen. When we start giving of ourselves we create a vacuum in our lives. The universe is forced by its very nature to seek to fill up the vacuum (space) we created by giving. When we put out good, more of the same and even better energy keeps rushing in to re-supply us. If we stop giving, our flow starts to dry up; if we figure out how to give more we are back in the flow. That is called overflow, and a supernatural harvest and abundance is waiting to come upon you because of your giving!

Let's see what Jesus, the Master Teacher, said about giving which is very powerful: *"Give and you will receive. Your gift will return to you in full-pressed down, shaken together to make room for more, running over, and poured into your lap."* This sets up the second secret to priming the pump and getting a gusher of success flowing into your life.

So the second secret of the *Manifest and Maintain* step is giving. Giving does not have to mean just giving money or material things only; you can give of your time and attention to worthy causes or to help people who have a sincere need. You can give your love to those you have left out in the past. You can give love and attention to those who are lonely and broken-hearted. You could give forgiveness to someone you are holding negative feelings toward. You could give up things you have been holding onto that could serve others but are doing nothing for you. You could be holding on too tightly to money, and it is blocking the flow into your life. Maybe you could give ideas, counsel, and encouragement to someone who is struggling. You could give up feelings of jealousy, anger, or hate. You could give up the desire be in control of something, some situation, or someone. The Scripture talks about the importance of tithing. In relation to this subject, it is the only place in the Bible where God actually challenges people to test him. He says if we give Him his tithes, here is what He will do: *"I will open the windows in heaven for you. I will pour out a blessing so great you won't be able to take it in. Try it! Put me to the test!"* In Hebrew, the word "window" translates into "portal," so what God appears to being saying is He will open up a portal, a connection, between a giver and Himself. How can you get any more powerful than that as a reward for giving?

Just remember that our supply comes from the life force that resides inside of us. Our consciousness of this truth is our key to unlimited supply. The less we believe, the less faith we have, the more the supply appears to dry up. The supply never really dries up; we just lose access to it. There is as much available today as there was when Moses, Apostle Paul, and Jesus walked the earth. God is always the same; He never changes.

You may be like the fruit tree in winter. Your life may appear to be dull, sad, and uneventful or even a failure. That fruit tree may look barren too, but deep down inside it things are happening. The sap is pushing its way up through the trunk out to the limbs, out to the tips of those limbs to produce a blossom and then fruit. Know that same life-giving force that creates the fruit is accessible to us and the way to prime the pump and turn a drip into a gusher is to give.

This is the true secret to manifesting: Give. Test it! Try it for yourself! It is your apprehension and your realization of truth that manifests lack or abundance, sickness or health, and worry or peace in your life. Start with giving a lot of smiles and love away today.

Now let's go back and look at the point in time when your individual life began, the point where the individual spark of life was initiated. The fact that each one of us was created unique and different in the mind of God before we even had DNA makes us pretty special, don't you think.? Congratulations! That does make you someone special and unique. You are an original!

You might say, "Well, if God has already laid out my life, what is the use in me doing anything?" This is where we have to really reach down and stretch sometimes to get it. Remember this, God spoke through the prophet Isaiah and said, *"My thoughts are not your thoughts and my ways are not your ways."* We do have a say in our future; otherwise, God would never have given us the gift of free will. God knows what we are going to do. He knows if we will stand strong or give up; He knows if we will have courage or be a victim; He knows if we will believe in Him and have faith or live a life of chance. Remember this; God does not operate on our time frame. He operates on God time in the eternal now. According to Saint Peter, a day is the same as a thousand years, and a thousand years is the same as a day to God. The story of your life is in God's DVD case. He has seen the movie of your life and mine—He knows every detail, especially the ending. He knows what is best. This is why when we pray sometimes, it seems like God is not there or He is not listening. It is kind of like the Garth Brooks song that says, "Sometimes God's greatest gifts are unanswered prayers."

God knows best. Back in the very late 1800s, there was a great concern in America. There was a shortage of horses, and horses were the main source of transportation; in addition, they were needed on farms. Many religious leaders rallied their followers together in prayer for an answer regarding how to solve this serious problem and to get an answer from God. God answered and He solved the problem. It wasn't more horses, though; it was a horseless carriage!

Having faith is the easier way to solve our problems, even though the circumstances may tell us differently.

Let's go back to the bundle of joy we talked about in the beginning of the book. When the original infusion of life began we were nothing but pure, unbridled, unconditional love initiated by the creative thoughts of God. From that point on, our individual spirits begin a lifelong journey into and through life and back to our source, pure, unconditional love. This deeply programmed love is always seeking an outlet from other humans through affection, appreciation, adoration and, as we get older, approval and acceptance.

The only source to receive unconditional love outside of Heaven is from the part of God that is inside other human beings. In other words, our souls need each other to receive love until we experience the purest love by returning to our original source at the end of our earth assignment. From the time we are born our individual spirits are programmed to reunite with the original source of love. From our first breath (which is our first human inspiration from God) the quest for love is on. Unconscious at first, this feeling could be described as a deep yearning in the spirit to experience an individual reconnecting with its original source.

To master this final step of the Valeo Method, it is important that we grasp this powerful secret of human nature. This life force is with us every waking moment, whether we realize it or not, and it is ultimately affecting every facet and phase of our lives. Our individual spirits' desire for unconditional love is insatiable and is always seeking the reflection of the love it holds. Each of us has one innate, burning desire that drives us and will never let go until it is satisfied. Here it is: Each of us has to give and receive pure, unconditional love. Most of us spend our lives blocking the way to our source of Divine power, which is the only way to quench this thirst. When we learn to get out of our own way we open up the spigot to the ultimate power source of unconditional love. Unfortunately for many people, this never happens because we don't know how to get out of our own way and let the power inside us out that is trying to manifest our intended good experiences in life.

Our lives become the backdrop for an unceasing battle between two forces. The ego, the antagonist, and the Real Self, the protagonist, stay in a classic spirit vs. ego or good vs. evil dynamic that we have already addressed extensively in the Release and Embrace steps of the Valeo Method. Emotions are the language of the soul, and they speak to us through our inner turmoil and conflicts or love thoughts and peace, depending on which forces dominate.

The good news is it doesn't have to be this way any longer. Now we have a choice. We have learned the truth about the ego and exposed its falsehoods and tricks. We have learned to release our toxic thoughts, words, and emotions that keep us shackled to the ego. We have learned the huge effect of negative self-talk and personal labeling. We have learned we have hidden gifts waiting to be exposed and embraced and that the ego keeps us blinded from them. We have learned that controlling the ego is the key to unblocking our gifts.

When we unblock our gifts we are reconnecting with the unconditional love that came with our initial bundle of joy. We move closer to the dream of the soul, our unique individual purpose assigned by God. God wants us to find Him and know Him. He is ready to show us favor right now. We are told in the Scripture, *"Delight in the Lord and He will give you the desires of the heart."* How do God's blessings come? Let's look at what Jesus said: *"Pressed down, shaken together to make room for more running over, and poured into your lap."* I don't know about you, but that is exactly the way I want them!

Line Up and Cash In

The *Activate and Attract* step set up strategies and tools to prepare us to get the most from this last step. Now we are ready to get in alignment with all the good that the universe is trying to get to us.

The biggest mistake I have made and many of the people I work with make is seeking success outside ourselves. We addressed earlier in the Valeo Method how we establish our ways.

Early in life, we seek to act in a way that will get us love and approval from our parents; in our teenage years, this is transformed into a desire for acceptance and to fit in with our peers. As we reach our adult experience, our desires transform into a need to get ahead. What does all this mean? We are constantly trying to change ourselves or others so we can receive the one thing our soul seeks the most, unconditional love. The challenge is we can never find true, unconditional love outside ourselves until we release it from *within*.

When we are releasing unconditional love and receiving it from others, then we have arrived; we are in the flow. This is the point where we can ask with certainty and know that our words are from the spirit, they have life. This means there is nothing we cannot ask for that we cannot receive, and there is nothing we cannot do, including moving mountains, as long as we keep our faith. This is where we find all the answers, all the wisdom, all the abundance and the unconditional love we seek.

What happens if we don't receive unconditional love from all our outside seeking efforts? We get pain, and lots of it. How do we deal with the pain? Some people get depressed, some develop mental illness, and sometimes there is so much pain that people don't even want to live anymore. Most people just live with their pain and never find a way to rise above it. The real challenge is when the crutch turns into an addiction to drugs, alcohol, food, sex, or something that only masks the pain. Then, because there is only temporary relief from the pain, more appears to be better, and those consequences are never good. Even therapy and counseling produce few results unless the cause is addressed, and what is the cause at the core but the lack of unconditional love? All the Prozac, Zoloft, Paxil, and Ambien in the world are not going to do anything but mask the pain. The only way to get better and move on is to dive into the pain, find out what the cause is, and what is blocking our ability to experience unconditional love.

The only way we get rid of the pain, as taught in the *Embrace* step, is to go right at it. Then we find out what is causing the pain and what is making it difficult to find, receive, and experience unconditional love. When we go at the pain we find out something extraordinary; that behind what we fear, there is nothing. It is like the Wizard of Oz; it is fake. We also find something we created to protect ourselves (our egoic minds) is keeping us from the very thing we want most—unconditional love.

It may be hard to accept or believe that this one thing is able to control your life. It is not one person or a few people; it is not money; it is not fear. It is this one key motivating factor that is affecting all of our lives. It is the lack of unconditional love.

When I first made this discovery I tried to talk myself out if it. I kept saying to myself, "Could this be real? Why hasn't anyone ever made me aware of this?" I had been seeking peace of mind, success, and spiritual bliss for years, and no one had ever made me see this! I had literally found the number-one key to all my suffering!

Could all the chaos, drama, and suffering in all our lives be rooted in this one simple thing? Could being appreciated, admired, respected, and needed make so much difference and have such an effect in all areas of life? The answer is a re-sounding yes! Our need to be special to others, to be special to everyone, to be needed, is paramount. People are literally dying to get unconditional love.

If we could get a handle on this one issue, I am going to make a bold prediction of what could happen. We could elimi-nate all drugs for stress, anxiety, and sleep disorders. We could drastically reduce drug use and abuse, and alcoholism would see a huge decline. Suicide would only occur on rare occasions. World and economic outlooks and overall confidence would increase. We would see an upward shift in the collective con-sciousness of all society. We would see more "glass half-full" instead of "glass half-empty" attitudes. We would see a rapid decline in poverty, and the amount of people volunteering to help and serve others would explode. All this would happen if we could just do one thing as the human race: satisfy our deep, individual longings for unconditional love.

In other words, each and every one of us is longing to be a bundle of joy again so we can feel the unconditional love that accompanied us into the world. It is our innate goodness; it is the DNA of our DNA! We are genetically designed as the human race to seek unconditional love from our original, Divine source of life. We can never get rid of this longing, which has been with us even before we were born, until we satisfy it. We began as a piece of the fabric of unconditional love, and we will die craving unconditional love. Our ultimate bliss will come when we are a bundle of joy again. But here is the good news—we don't have to die to get it. It doesn't necessarily come easily, and it will take some work and determination, but it is our destiny, and we can experience it.

Frustration With God

Everyone at some point in their life gets frustrated with God; they blame God, get mad at Him, and some even curse God during really tough times. We think things like, Why all this suffering? Sometimes we whine and say, "Why me, why not someone else?" or "How come she gets all the breaks and I have to suffer?" When we suffer, we have to get to a place where we accept what is happening as not just bad luck or punishment, but part of our intended path. All past events in our lives up to this point are part of the play of our lives. To live in regret of our past and wish it weren't the way it was is to literally wish ourselves out of existence. Each one of us is exactly where we are supposed to be at this moment in time. We placed ourselves here using our free will and our prior thoughts. Our healing comes from accepting all and choosing best.

Let's look at an analogy of a small child going to a doctor. The child needs an injection of medicine. The doctor prepares a big, scary needle and is about to administer the medicine. The child is horrified and fights the doctor (the enemy) and the mother (the traitor) while trying to escape. Once the shot has been administered, the child clings tightly to the parent and feels relief, safety, and comfort.

How does the child go from feeling the parent is against him, the enemy, to a source of trust and comfort in just a moment? This is the way God works with us; sometimes we fight against hard challenges and circumstances we face when in reality, it is all part of our journey. Sometimes we just don't want to take our medicine, so we don't receive the message, the lesson, we are supposed to get. Our Creator knows what is best for us; we just don't like to take our medicine! When we accept our circumstances, He is always ready to embrace us and carry us through our suffering. He loves us unconditionally. How do we learn to trust God and choose to turn to our original source of life instead of some temporary and artificial relief? First, we have to realize it is easier than we might think, and it is certainly easier than suffering.

Chapter 51
Living in God's Economy

I have come that they may have life, and that they may have it more abundantly.

Jesus Christ

The *Manifest and Maintain* step is about reaching and living in a place of unconditional love at our core. It's about feeling the promise, protection, peace, provision, and prosperity that only comes from the one place that is indeed our connection to the oneness of all. It's not just about reaching this place; it's about living in it, feeling it, and being it.

When we move into this way of life, something exciting happens. Now we get the benefit of living in "God's economy." When we live in God's economy, the rewards are big, and not just economically. When we live in God's economy, the state of the world and national economy does not keep us from prospering. We are still going to have our challenges. God is still going to prune us and discipline us. The difference is, the correction we receive directs us toward, not away, from the success we seek and our purpose in life. Also, when we ask for help and direction and believe we will receive it, we get it. Maybe not on our time line, or the way we expect it, but we get it.

In fact, in God's economy, we do not even have to advertise what we do. We let people know who we are by "being" instead of talking about it. Our presence speaks volumes about who we are. The oneness of all that we share attracts like-minded people to us. It attracts people, energies, and situations that cause our lives to work. The more we recognize the oneness factor of life, the more vibrant, alive, and conscious we become. We become more sensitive to the message life is sending us. We recognize opportunities and situations that are attracted to us by the favor of God because we are more in alignment with our purpose in the mosaic of eternity. Doing business gets easier; sometimes things show up that amaze us, and we are tempted to think it is luck, but we know better. People find themselves wanting to help us and they are not even sure why. Something about life just feels right. This is because we are awakening to the oneness connection that is intertwined through all of humanity, the imprint of God.

We seek courage and wisdom, and it wells up inside of us. We seek supply, and it shows up. We stop walking past the clues and nudges the universe is sending us. When we live in God's economy, it is always a good time to start something new. Thriving becomes easier than just surviving. Struggling is a thing of the past. God's economy knows no scarcity and no limits. Fear has no power and challenges are welcome. In God's economy there is always a way. Even though we still have our ups and downs, they don't feel as uncomfortable as the peaks and valleys we experienced before, and they don't last as long as they did before.

This chart illustrates a person at the different phases of connecting with the inner power of God's economy. Here you will see the difference between getting in alignment with the true, authentic power of a multisensory being instead of doing it the hard way, on your own, with the artificial power of a five-sensory being.

The illustration shows the ADVANTAGE OF SEEKING Spiritual Enlightenment (Multi-Sensory) and AUTHENTIC POWER. This simple graph shows a powerful example of the phases of development of a person who is seeking to align their spirit with their original source of life.

QUALITY OF LIFE CYCLES

Cycles of Average Five Sensory Person
(Slow Steady Decline)

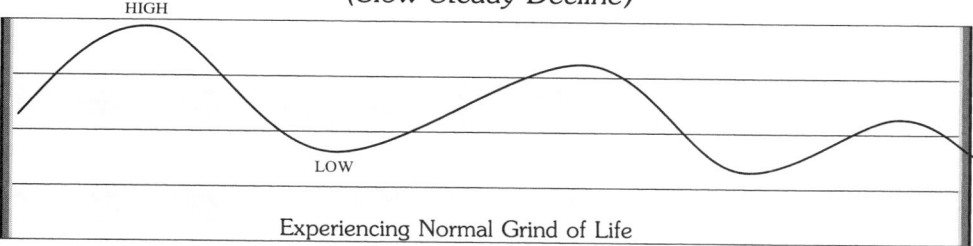

HIGH

LOW

Experiencing Normal Grind of Life

Cycles of Negative Five Sensory Person
(Faster Decline)

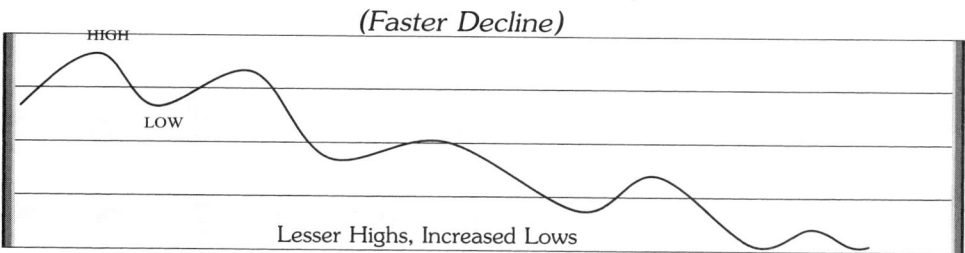

HIGH

LOW

Lesser Highs, Increased Lows

Cycles of Person Seeking Authentic Power
(Balancing)

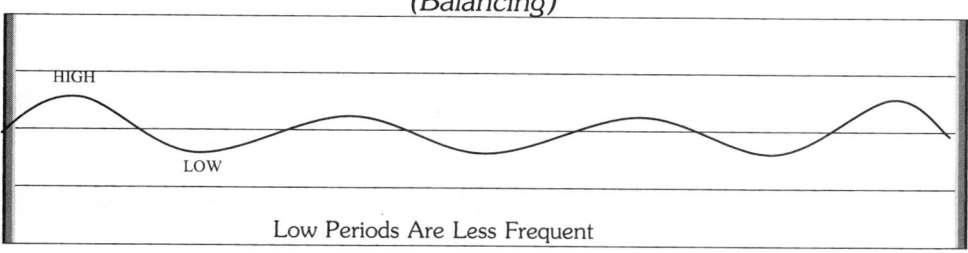

HIGH

LOW

Low Periods Are Less Frequent

Cycles of an Enlightened Mulit-Sensory Person
(Steady Increase in Joy and Success)

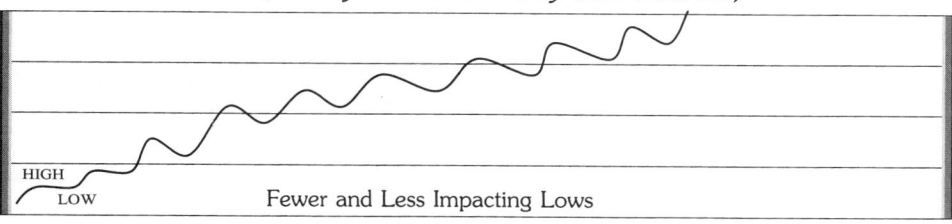

HIGH

LOW

Fewer and Less Impacting Lows

How's Your Cake?

Have you ever baked a cake or watched your mom do it? Sometimes when the cake is baking it looks like it is finished and ready for the icing and decorations. So you take it out, dress it up, and it looks delicious. But what happens some-times? We got in a hurry because it looked done; we put on the icing, decorated the cake and served it, only then we find the inside wasn't finished baking, even though it looked ready.

This is what happens to our lives without this last step of the Valeo Method. We are doing well and then we get full of pride and overconfident, thinking we are having success all by ourselves. When this happens not only is your cake not ready, you can have the recipe all wrong and the taste could be awful. There are rules to baking a cake that parallel life. There are strategies and a proven plan of action we have to follow. We need a recipe, then we need the ingredients, then we need the right amount of each ingredient, then we need to put them in the right order, then we can bake it at the specific temperature for the right time. If we don't follow all the steps and get them in order, no matter how pretty the cake looks, we could be living a lie and headed for disappointment or even disaster, just like some people who appear to be happy and have it all, but in reality their lives are a mess.

Get the Why

In order to tap into infinite power and experience and manifest ongoing success in our lives, we have to have either a burning desire or a burning discontent. This exposes the emotional, not logical, reasons for seeking enlightenment and authentic power in all areas of your life. When we find the "why" — the burning desire or the burning discontent behind what we are seeking—the "how" will come to us easily. The key to the *Manifest and Maintain* step is building our lives on a solid understanding that the source of our life force is spirit and then always nourishing that relationship. Our success is tied to the satisfaction of the soul. The soul can only be satisfied when it is dominated by love-based emotion from our original source and not from fear-based emotions created by the ego, the false self. Let's look deeper into the "why" behind the last step of the Valeo Method.

God speaks to us through intuition and through our suffering—both ways create awareness and draw us closer to Him. Some people ask, "If God loves me so much, why does He let me suffer, is He punishing me?" These answers are clear and stand out in Scripture. God always has a reason; He is always on purpose, and He always wins. He is also always teaching us and showing us that we belong to Him and with Him, but still many times we just don't get the message. One example would be as the Psalmist writes: *"For you, O God tested us. You refined us like silver. But you brought us to a place of abundance."*

Nothing pleases God more than when we ask Him for what He wants to give us. Do you want more abundance? Do you need guidance? Are you seeking a relationship, a soul mate? Are you seeking peace of mind to get you through your trials and challenges? Are you seeking to contribute, or to know your life purpose? If you are seeking any of these things, are you willing to cooperate with God, the laws of nature, and the original intent for your life?

It disappoints me when I see all the self-help and encouragement books on the market today that give great ideas and strategies, yet the authors choose to leave out the importance of having a relationship with God as necessary to being successful in life and whole as a person. I admire and respect many of these authors, and I know they are believers. I can only assume they are afraid to offend people by mentioning God in a self-help book.

I am not going to hold back the truth. I am not going to sugarcoat it or tiptoe around the power of God above all else to help, to heal, to give answers, and to give a life of grace (unmerited favor) and abundance. I have seen amazing changes, breakthroughs, and miracles, and I can prove it. The bottom line is this: Even though I might not know you personally, I promise you I care about you. I care about you finding the dream of your soul, your calling, and living your dreams. So if any of this is uncomfortable for you or you are having trouble accepting it, I have to say this, whatever you do, don't close your mind or stop seeking. You are reading these words right now, right here, today, for a reason.

When Abraham Lincoln was a young man he lived in a remote, rural area. There weren't many general stores back then. Peddlers would come by occasionally with a horse and wagon, selling goods. One time a peddler was going out of business and desperate. He stopped at Lincoln's home and persuaded him to buy his last barrel of assorted goods for one dollar. Lincoln, although poor himself, felt sorry for the man and just bought the stuff for one dollar to help him out. He put the barrel in a shed behind his house and forgot about it. He thought all that was in the barrel was junk. Sometime later he decided to look inside. He found the bottom half was full of law books. Lincoln studied those books and became passionate about becoming a lawyer, which led him into politics. The rest, as they say, is history.

You see, everything *does* happen for a reason and a purpose, and it serves us. Whatever good times or struggles you have in your life are blessings; you might not be able to see them today, but just give them time and you will. There is some message for you in this book, or you would not be reading it at this very moment.

You are closer than you think to your breakthrough, your supernatural harvest. I challenge you—don't give up. How many ideas does it take to radically and powerfully change your life forever, remember? Just one, that is all. I will leave this point with one more thought. My experience with my clients in over two decades of doing this type of work has been that those who leave out this step of the Valeo Method are living life the hard way. Why do it the hard way ? The school of hard knocks is a rough way to go. Having a life without this important part is not like having a wheel without spokes, it is like having a wheel without the hub in the center that holds all the spokes together!

Chapter 52
Pride vs. Authentic Power

The authentic self is the soul made visible.

Sarah Ban Breathnach

Pride is an emotion the ego uses masterfully to keep us in our five-sensory mode. Pride makes us feel that all we need are our five-sensory abilities to achieve everything we need in life. Pride convinces us we have all the answers without seeking help from a higher power. There is a story in the Bible about a king named Uzziah. The story says he was a devoted man of God and because of this, he and his kingdom were blessed abundantly. But something happened; King Uzziah got full of pride and forgot where all his blessings were coming from. He started taking all the credit personally for his success while forgetting about God and giving Him no credit. In fact, the Scripture says, *"As long as the King sought guidance from the Lord, God gave him success. But when he became powerful, he also became proud, which led to his downfall."* That brings us to one of the top reasons for failure.

Will Worship

Human nature causes us to seek long-term peace, release, and emotions of joy in our hearts and minds. We always have to remember the only permanent source of peace of mind comes from unconditional love. I spent years thinking if I could just make a certain amount of money or achieve a certain sales goal or owned a certain type of home, I would be blissfully happy. I also felt confident in my own willpower, to get myself motivated to put myself on the line to get the job done. My belief was, "I could accomplish anything I made up my mind to be, to do, or to have." One simple problem: I had it all backwards. I felt if I "had" the things my accomplishments produced, I could "do" what I wanted to do, and then I would "be" what I wanted to be.

In the Valeo Method we call this "Will Worship," which is believing that we can accomplish anything we want by our own will and volition without any Divine influence in any way. This is operating as a five-sensory being. We are totally counting on our own knowledge, ability, determination, and effort to do, be, and have all we are seeking.

If we go back to the illustration of God as an ocean of pure omnipotence, omniscience, and omnipresence, we get a clearer picture. Remember the comparison earlier of the ocean as a representation of God and how we could take that cup and dip it into the ocean, and it would represent a cup of God as an individual? If we take that cup and sit alone on the bank, away from God, we would be losing access to our spirit and our connection to the Divine power of God. We would be on our own power. In this situation a person has to depend on their own natural seeing, feeling, hearing, and thinking to carry out their plans and to survive and thrive. Without the connection to the power source, authentic power is lost. To the unaware or ego-dominated mind, artificial power can at times seem more than enough. Then they wonder why life can be such a struggle. They are living the hard way!

The Law of Human Limitation

Are you counting on the Law of Attraction paying big dividends for you? Here is the challenge: Another law is always in effect that is working non-stop against the Law of Attraction, and it can wreak havoc with the unaware. It is called the Law of Human Limitation. There's only so much you can accomplish as a human being or a human doing without the power of our original source. Your cup gets stagnant and sour, and the contents evaporate into an empty, unfulfilling life.

This principle can not only be measured in material success and wealth. It also can be measured, more importantly, by the ability to feel and experience the emotion associated with unconditional love. Without the connection to God, we are only able to experience the amount of love we have from our own little cup, not from our creator.

When the cup is disconnected on the bank of material life, it is fertile ground for fear-based emotion to grow because it has lost its connection to the power of the unconditional love of our original source.

God created every one of us with strong emotional and biological drives, and with a purpose. We are built to master those drives and live our purpose. So what does God offer us if we operate as a multisensory being and build our lives with a connection to spirit while we seek our original intent? How about over six thousand promises in the Bible, which include protection, provision, prosperity, abundance, and even eternal life on the New Earth? Another thing the Bible tells us is that God cannot lie: *"God has given both His promise and His oath. These two things are unchangeable because it is impossible for Him to lie."*

When we try to will what we want without having a spiritual foundation under our life, sooner or later we will be headed for rough waters. This is because some things just cannot be willed. Why is that, you might say, what about cause and effect? There is one thing we must never forget, and this is the element of God we always have to contend with and accept: If you're trying to will your life a certain way and it is against God's will for you and the dream of your soul, and if it is detrimental to your future, God is not going to bless your efforts. We have to remind ourselves we can't see the big picture like God can. Remember, He knows all things, He sees every life from beginning to end. God is not like a genie in a bottle. He doesn't come running every time we call, especially when we haven't been seeking Him.

Suffering is part of all of our journeys. Suffering allows us to learn from our shortfalls and mistakes. Then we have desire and emotion behind our search for a life of fulfilled dreams and happiness. Tests are put in front of us so we can experience trials and struggles; trials allow us to learn and turn to God and know Him. Then when we overcome our trials, it produces faith and confidence in us, which creates the testimony of our strength through the growing spiritual foundation in our lives. Suffering and trials are always rewarded with faith in God. We don't create faith on our own; we receive it.

Chapter 53
Why Trust God?

Faith is to believe what you cannot see;
the reward of this faith is to see what you believe.

Saint Augustine

Why should I trust God so much? It is not easy when we haven't been depending on Him as much as we did in the past. Is He really that much in control? I used to think, "If there are seven billion people on earth, how can He keep up with all of our thoughts? That has to be impossible." These thoughts caused me to start seeking answers. I wanted to know just how big and powerful God really is.

Here are some of the things I discovered after extensively studying the Bible, *A Course in Miracles* (a self study spiritual psychotherapy course in three books based on finding inner peace through the practice of forgiveness), and hundreds of other books on the subjects of spiritual enlightenment. These are things worth noting about God and His plans and purpose behind each and every life.

First, let's look at it this way. God created everything, period; this is His cosmic play. He chose each one of us to be a participant—that is, of course, unless a person chooses to assume there is no such thing as God and we all just kind of randomly happened along with the rest of creation. This makes about as much sense as a dictionary being the result of an explosion in a print factory.

Not believing in God is taking the easy way out; it is the lazy way. It is like just sitting in that cup and letting life dry up. If this is a person's choice, I pray for them. I say that sincerely and not sarcastically. I spent time in the doubting God modality. I learned something from being uncertain about who and what I am. It is like going against the flow of nature, swimming upstream. It may work for salmon, but I can tell you right now, for humans it is a rough way to live.

Let's look at some interesting facts about God's majesty and power. Let's look at some wonders of God. The Bible tells us God picks up the whole world like a grain of sand. After God created the earth, He created the sun, which is 1.3 million times the size of earth. The earth is at a 23 degree angle to the sun. If the angle were just 2 degrees off, earth would be covered in a polar ice cap. They would be no life on earth.

We are told by astronomers our galaxy is one of 140 billion in the universe. If our universe was the size of a pea, compare that to the fact that 140 billion peas would fill up a baseball stadium. We are told God created all the universes.

As a way to let you get an understanding of God's compassion for each one of us, we are given some clues. We are told God knows the number of hairs on each of our heads. We are told He has all our names written in the palm of His hand. We are told He saves every tear we have cried and keeps them in a bottle. As insignificant as a field sparrow is, He attends the funeral of every single one that dies.

We are never going to figure God out. His thoughts are definitely not our thoughts and His ways are not our ways. But if we can just get to know how compassionate He is, it will help us accept "what is" and understand it is okay if we *don't* understand. When we get frustrated with God, we can't understand why He is letting us suffer. But we must just trust His plan and keep asking Him to reveal it to us. Trying to figure God out is like picking up one piece of a million-piece jigsaw puzzle and thinking, "Why can't I figure this out?" Consider what Abraham Lincoln said: *I have been driven many times to my knees by the overwhelming realization that I had nowhere else to go.*

The Hard Way

Earlier in the Valeo Method, we discussed the difference between learning from the school of hard knocks and modeling successful people. There is a huge advantage to modeling success to get quicker, faster and better results and to compress time.

I explained my personal experiments with doing it the hard way and how modeling the success of others helped me. Now let's look at another strategy to avoid living life the hard way.

One of the subjects I have studied extensively is epistemology, the study of the origin of knowledge. Where did knowledge come from? What is the source? My studies convinced me that all knowledge comes from God. A graphic on the next page shows an example of all knowledge (held by God) broken into three categories: that which we don't know; that which we don't know that we don't know; and that which we do know. An example would be that we know we don't know how to do brain surgery or drive a submarine. In other words, we know we don't know certain things. Then there is all the other knowledge that we don't know we don't know, which takes up most knowledge.

What if we could tap into that **87** percent that we don't know we don't know? Could that be empowering? Could that give us an advantage? How about confidence? Peace of mind? That's what manifesting is all about!

I tried to live my dreams the hard way. I was operating totally on my own with artificial power, yet I was determined to reach my goals. Since I was disconnected from my authentic power, I had lots of stress and struggles, and my ego was always slowing me down, tripping me up and creating self-doubt. I was always pushing myself and never satisfied. Worries, fears, and doubt were always popping up, and I had to overcome them one by one.

I was always searching, striving, and thinking, "If only I could reach a particular level of accomplishment, I would be happy in life and everything would be perfect." (I'll bet you can guess what happened.) I was achieving some impressive results as a five-sensory being. Don't get me wrong; there is no doubt a person can achieve great things on their own, but that's the trap many of us fall into—it gives us a false sense of confidence and security. Sometimes the illusionary target of happiness can be like an oasis in the desert—when we finally reach it, it is either not real or it moves farther away.

The Easy Way

There is an old saying, "nothing worth having is easy to get." That may be true; but one thing is for certain—there is an easier way to get what we want when we compare authentic power to artificial power. When we compare a person functioning as a five-sensory being to a multi-sensory being, there is a huge difference.

When we understand how to tap into the **87** percent of knowledge that we don't know we don't know, there are no limits to what we can be, do, and have. Most people spend their entire lives seeking answers outside of themselves—facing out, when in reality they need to be looking inside, because that is where the real answers are.

Being multisensory means being aware of and accessing our authentic power that we receive through intuition, our sixth sense. It means claiming and declaring access to our all-knowing capabilities that so often go unrecognized and untapped. Tapping this power puts us in the know, in the flow, and on the way to an easier and more empowering life. Things that used to seem impossible now become conquerable challenges. We go from the belief system, "There is no way" to "If I'm committed, there is always a way."

THE TRUTH ABOUT KNOWLEDGE

What we know
we don't know

What we
do know

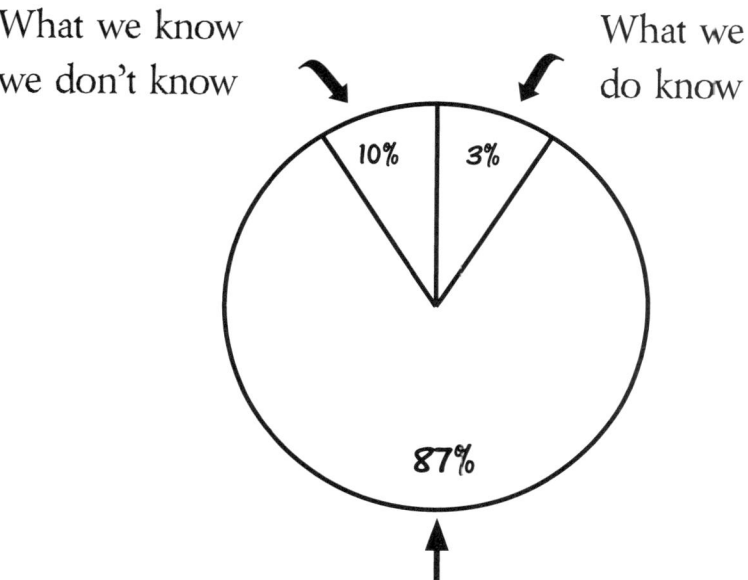

10%

3%

87%

What we don't know we don't know

The Valeo Method takes us through the steps to prepare us to receive authentic power. We went through the *Discovery* process to help us understand why we sabotage ourselves, and we discovered how we create our own suffering by allowing the ego to dominate our lives. We learned the power of going from unconscious thinking to conscious thinking and how to recognize the ego's never-ending tricks.

We learned to release the shackles of the self and remove the roadblocks to achievement that are put up by the ego. We learned how to get in the flow and how to recognize and embrace our own special gifts handed down by our Creator. We learned how to recognize our purpose and to build our lives on purpose.

Then we lined up the powers of the universe and equipped ourselves with the tools and skills to compress time and produce great, rewarding results in the least amount of time.

Now we are ready to go. Before we had these steps in place it was like trying to jump-start a car with rusty jumper cables. You get some juice, but not the full charge. Now it is time to turn on all five steps of the Valeo Method and manifest the life we were born to live. The good news is, now we are going to do it the easy way compared to the way most of us have been going at it up to this point. It is time to live the dream of the soul.

Perfect Timing - Perfect Plan

When we come to understand God's will in our lives, we learn to trust that He knows best. When He changes our course, we know there is a reason and that all things work out best for those who trust and have faith. I found different references to time in the Bible that helped me find patience. Here are some examples: "in the proper time," "at the appropriate time," and " in due time." There is a perfect time for everything to happen.

A man was shipwrecked, alone, and stranded on a deserted island. He realized he might be there a while, so he decided to build some shelter. For two days he worked and labored to build a makeshift lean-to which would protect him from the elements. Exhausted and starving, his next task was to search for food. When he returned from a fruitless day of searching, he couldn't believe his eyes when he looked up at his shelter he had worked so hard to build. It was engulfed in flames. He hit his knees and cried to God, "How could you allow this to happen to me? I am not a bad person. Where are you? Have you forgotten about me?" The man fell asleep on the beach only to be awakened the next morning by the shouts of a rescue team with the Coast Guard approaching to save him. "How did you find me?" he asked. The officer in charge replied, "We saw your fire."

You see, God specializes in tough situations, and His timing is perfect. If we could see our lives in front of us the way God can, we would see that every little detail that happens is part of a grand plan, and we wouldn't worry or be discouraged with challenges that show up in our lives. But because we can't see what God sees, the best we can do is tap into our authentic power and open up the channel to receive intuition. Because intuition is how God speaks to us.

You may be tempted to ask yourself again, "What about my free will God gave me? Why would he give me free will if he already knows what is going to happen with my life?" We do have the power to choose and direct our lives. Sometimes the ego has such control over a person they never tap into their intuition. They never reach a connection with the dream of their souls. This is why it is important we learn how to gain wisdom and build our courage so we can be in charge, one step ahead of our toxic thoughts and beliefs that are being propagated by the ego. It is worth bringing up again here: your ego is not your friend!

Let's look at it this way: What if we did not have free will? Let's say God created us so that we had to follow His plan exactly, giving us no free will. Let's assume every time we got off track we received a painful electric shock. The bigger the offense, the bigger the shock we would receive. We would be living according to suppression and direction, not by choice. Then we would all be screaming, "We want to be able to choose!"

Humanity is designed in such a way that we can play the main character in our individual stories of life. Plus, we get to do something very inspiring; we get to co-create our reality with the Creator of the universe. This is a wonderful gift, and we can use it for good and the dreams we feel drawn toward. We can also just show up, let things happen, and not really try to create good and live our calling. Unfortunately, that would be abusing a precious opportunity and ignoring our sacred gift, the dream of our individual souls. If we choose to ignore our calling, based on my experience in working with a large amount of people in diverse situations, this choice is an absolute promise of an unfulfilled and empty life, full of disappointments and uncertainties.

We are told that wisdom was created before humanity. This sends a powerful message to us that we need to be smart, and that His power begins with the power of speech, the power of the spoken word. We have already addressed the strategies to improve life with Transitional Language.
We have harnessed the power of the spoken word.

Where is an underlying, unseen thread that connects all our thoughts and words to the eventual deed or result. This thread is there to protect our power of choice. This is the reason we have to pay attention to the words we speak. When we speak, we launch a never-ending energy into eternity.

To most, the Law of Cause and Effect makes sense conceptually, but most don't believe or understand how they can use it to create a reality. Why? Because they lack the patience to see the results and simply give up. According to the Law of Attraction, every thought we have and every word we speak carries with it a power, an energy that is constantly seeking a reflection of itself. Have you ever really focused on something, had a sincere desire to have it or experience it, maybe you even prayed diligently about it, but then for some reason you lost interest and gave up? Then a while later, after you had long forgotten about it, all of sudden what you were previously seeking just showed up and surprised you? This is the way this natural process works. You had the thought, you spoke the intention, the unseen energies were launched, and it was just a matter of time until the result manifested. Cause was seeking effect, and at the perfect time you saw the result. How quickly we see a result is based on three factors: our faith that the desired result is going to happen; our persistent focus on the desired result; and God's will.

One other thing can happen and this is where most of us blow it and cancel out the manifestation of amazing things right before our eyes. When we have thoughts of doubt, disbelief, or fear and they are strong enough, we launch these energies and they cancel out the cause and effect process with negative, opposing energy. Our doubts neutralize our positive, good-seeking thoughts and stop them from manifesting. Ouch! Talk about avoiding negative thoughts—how is that for a good reason?

I know it is hard to stay upbeat all the time. We all have our down cycles when it takes more effort to stay on top and in control. This is why in the Manifest and Maintain step, we focus on working on and developing these skills. When we are beaten down and bludgeoned by life's circumstances and our fear-based thoughts, we have to keep reminding ourselves: "I am living today the results of my own prior thoughts. I am living in a situation that is a result of my prior intentions created by my conscious or unconscious self. My words are driving cause and effect, which is manifesting in front of my eyes. I can change what I am manifesting and therefore my experience. It really is that simple."

I encourage you to practice being acutely sensitive to your surroundings and what you are thinking in every moment, especially when you are speaking. I don't want to appear like I am preaching to you, but why is a curse word called a "curse?" Words are powerful and can cut like a sword. Our words can have an empowering or devastating effect on the course of our lives and those around us and close to us.

The spoken word is the most elevated facet of the soul. Remember: A word is planted in everything to give it reality (to make it "matter"); a word created the life of every living thing, plant, and animal, as God, and then Adam (instructed by God) named everything. The spoken word began creation. It arouses unseen forces beyond our imagination. The spoken word arouses the deep, spiritual roots of who we were before we were born; the spoken word creates life.

When we have a spiritual foundation underneath our thought-word-energy, we are bound to attract good into our lives unless we sabotage ourselves by concealing our good thoughts and words with negative or opposing thoughts and words. We may never know why some things we seek don't turn out the way we desire or intend, but many times, sooner or later, we do understand. How many times has something been a big disappointment, and later you realized it was the best thing that could have happened and in fact it probably was a blessing? When we can experience an event or situation that turns out not exactly like we had hoped and still accept it as being the best for us in the long run, we have arrived. When we can say, "What is great about this?" or "What is the lesson for me here?" or "How can I turn a lemon into lemonade here?" and really mean it, we are living at a higher level of personal growth and awareness. We are taking control of our thoughts and emotions and getting control of our destiny.

Sometimes when we ardently seek the dreams of our souls we wind up in a totally different career or life mission than we previously were pursuing. This is when we realize what was missing in our lives and why things weren't right. How many people spend years in careers or businesses that are not fulfilling, rewarding, or challenging to them before they find the courage to change and find happiness? How long does it take until they stop fighting the "flow" and get "in the flow" and discover the dream of their souls.

If things aren't working out the way you planned, God can be protecting you from death, disaster, suffering, or some other type of hardship or failure. When we are always seeking to be in alignment with God's will for us, no matter what happens, we are always covered.

If we are following our innermost passions and we have good intentions toward all, we are on course to arrive at our purpose in life. If our intentions are wrong, unhealthy, or hurting others, it is just a matter of time till they blow up on us.

When we lose wealth we lose a little, when we lose our health we lose something of a greater consequence, but when we lose peace of mind, that is the highest cost. The most quoted verse in the Bible is Psalms 46:10, *"Be still and know that I am God."* In times of trouble, God is one simple prayer away, ready to give us comfort. He is always ready to give us hope, encouragement, and peace if we believe Him and have faith. This is important to recognize because in stillness and silence, we have our strongest connection to authentic power.

Chapter 54
A New Level of Thinking

The highest revelation is that God is in every man.

Ralph Waldo Emerson

Einstein said, "The significant problems we face cannot be solved at the same level of thinking we created them." Einstein's wisdom lets us know we have to move to a different and higher level of thinking for things to change. If we don't like where we are today, we are not going to a higher level with the same thinking that got us where we are. If your life is not working for you the way you think it should, you have to change your thinking, and do it fast. All the answers lie within as we access universal knowledge through our oneness connection to God's universe. We make that connection when we welcome God into our hearts and acknowledge that He is in control. We must be willing to accept one simple thing and *Embrace* it: We may not know what tomorrow holds, but we know who holds tomorrow.

This kind of thinking helps us choose our state of mind before something happens instead of just waiting to see what happens and then choosing our state of mind. This way we can rest assured that in the end, good things are our destiny. Then we can manifest our experience in life with a guiding light instead of being caught in the fog.

Finding Unconditional Love

The *Manifest and Maintain* step is simple. It really means when we find the unconditional love we have been seeking since birth, we will be fulfilled and happy. God is the source of the unconditional love, first and foremost, and then we get it from other people who are dominated by their love-based emotions. When we find our oneness connection, we will be able to realize and live the dream of the soul.

If we don't seek this connection and relationship with our innermost self, we are fighting nature. Sooner or later the pain and suffering will get to the point where we cannot take it anymore. Then we either suppress it, which we already know can cause major problems, or we project it out onto others. Or, we can go right at it and face it the way we learned in the *Embrace* step and get rid of it for good. One thing is for certain: fighting the nature within us that is seeking to evolve and manifest in our lives is a losing proposition. Sadly, this is what most people do over and over, and they have to live with the consequences in all areas of their lives.

The soul is like a photoelectric cell; it needs the sun (light) to be energized. Lack of exposure to the sun (light) depletes its energy and its power to function properly. If our bodies are deprived of essential vitamins and nutrients, we become weak; our immune systems are compromised and we are susceptible to disease.

There is a story about a poor farmer back at the turn of the century whose wife was expecting their eighth child. A midwife was called in from a nearby town and she barely arrived in time for the birth. The father sent the other kids out of the house and asked how he could help. The midwife instructed him to hold the kerosene lamp so she could see to deliver the baby. As the baby started to come out, she said, "Come closer, quickly, bring the light closer, just a little closer please," and the baby was soon born. In just a few moments, the mother began screaming in pain. The midwife yelled to the father, "Bring that light closer again, even closer please; here comes another—you have twins!" The father, somewhat overwhelmed, wondered how he would raise two more children, and stepped back with the light. Almost immediately, the mother started screaming again. Once again the midwife yelled to the father, "Quick, bring the light, here comes another one, you have triplets!!" The father bolted out the door and took off running with the lamp. The midwife yelled, "Come back here! I need that light!" The father yelled back over his shoulder while running away at full speed, "No way! I think the light is drawing them!"

Have you ever found yourself afraid of what the light might bring? The soul needs the light from its original source. If the soul loses its connection to the oneness of all, expect to experience feelings associated with fear-based emotions. This is what happens when we can't put our finger on it, but something in our gut tells us something isn't right. This is the point where a temptation to turn to alcohol, drugs, food, or other bad habits can take over if we are not aware of what is happening and prepared to take control. All we need to do is nourish our souls like we need to nourish our bodies. We do this by keeping contact with our source of authentic power and not taking the temporary solution.

We do this by practicing the steps we have learned in the Valeo Method and by stopping the ego and our limiting past patterns, beliefs, and emotions dead in their tracks. We call them out and say, "Come on, I am ready for you; I know all about you, and you are not welcome here anymore. The past does not equal the future." Then we say to ourselves, "I am a fully developed and aware multi-sensory being. I know who I am and what I can do, and I know my source of life. I choose to take control of my thoughts and access my authentic power at this moment and overcome my former destructive beliefs, thoughts, habits, and actions. I decree and declare as of today that I am a new person in control of my destiny, now and forever."

We increase our own authentic power by teaching others around us to learn and use the tools and strategies we have learned with the Valeo Method. This in turn creates a sharpening of skills, because the best way to learn is to teach. In the final section of the book, we will address ways to grow even more by helping others.

Locking Into God's Tractor Beam: Authentic Power

Recent studies show that even the spiritual leaders of the largest religious organizations are spending less time in meditation and prayer than they feel like they need to. Why? Because they are human just like everyone else, and life is demanding. There never seems to be enough time. It is not a lack of time but a lack of priority that interferes with meditation and prayer in our lives. If people whose entire life is devoted to spiritual leadership are falling short in meditation and prayer; is it surprising the average person is falling short too?

What is the overall result? Our world, our nation, our community, and our environment is suffering as a collective consciousness of society that is vulnerable. We need strengthening of our group soul, just like we need strengthening and authentic power as individuals.

It is easy to make excuses for not making time to meditate and pray and seek a connection with our innermost self. Many of us slip into this trap. It is easy to just keep putting it off. Then there are the regrets, the lost time and opportunities that can never be made up. We celebrate New Year's Eve as a welcoming of the new year and new beginnings. What we are really doing is celebrating to take our minds off our shortcomings from the past year, where we failed to prepare, plan, and follow through on our previous years' resolutions and goals.

The charge to each of us in the *Manifest and Maintain* step is to stop wasting time and missing out on how good life can be. If we want to change things in our lives because we are unhappy or feel there has to be more to life than the portion we are enjoying, we have to be willing to change. Change means stretching, doing something different, and long enough so it doesn't feel uncomfortable any more.

You have many different levels of spiritual awareness. How is your situation? Are you satisfied with the effort you are making? Are those efforts causing you to feel good about yourself? Do you think your effort is enough? Only a few people answer yes to that question. My experience tells me we all can do better, and most people sincerely desire to do more; they just need a place to start.

There so many different techniques and strategies for meditation and prayer. There are least 2,500 books on the market today for meditation alone. In my search for understanding and clarity, I read hundreds of books on mediation and prayer related subjects, from a variety of authors with varying spiritual backgrounds. I respect all people who meditate and pray because all these folks are responding to their innate longing to connect with the Divine, their inner spirit that is calling to them. There are many different ways to accomplish a connection with your inner spirit. I am making some suggestions here, which I encourage you to try, but keep on seeking and find what works best for you. We all are programmed from before inception with this longing. The goal is to get there, whatever it takes, whatever works best for you. All my study and research on this subject has brought me to this simple conclusion. God wants us to seek Him, period. There are many rivers and tributaries that run to the ocean; in addition, there are many ways to find our way to God. Unfortunately, many of us have to experience major suffering and pain before we turn to Him. We are told in the Scripture that anyone who wants to come to Him must believe that God exists and that He rewards those who sincerely seek Him. We are told if we seek Him we will find Him, and if we move toward Him, He will come toward us.

What are more rewards for building your life on a solid spiritual foundation? I noticed things started to happen to me as I started seeking God and working to build a stronger spiritual foundation under my personal and business life. First, I noticed that I had more of a sense of peace. I recognized I was not alone. Before I thought God was so busy and there were so many other people to tend to that, at best, He only paid attention to me when I prayed. The more I put together and used the first four steps of the Valeo Method, the more I realized how critically important it is to have this final part of the method in place. The first four steps can create amazing and radical changes in a person's life, but without being grounded by this last step, it is much harder to keep going. When a person works on this part of the method it creates an environment for more intuitive realizations. As your sensitivity to your spirit and the Real You increases, your awareness goes up. In addition, naturally good people, good situations, and supernatural opportunities to grow in all areas of life start to show up on a frequent basis. They were always there; we just weren't prepared to notice them and receive them as part of our journey, so we missed out.

Before my discoveries and revelations in the power of this part of the Valeo Method, I had always operated as a five-sensory being running on artificial power. I had the attitude: "If it is going to be, it is up to me." When people would say, "I need to pray about a decision," I would think, can't they make up their mind on their own? I just didn't get it. But as I sought a more intimate relationship with God, the other parts of the Valeo Method became more and more effective in creating positive results in my life. I still had challenges; don't get me wrong—they just didn't affect me the way they did before. The Valeo Method was not actually a reality until the last step, *Manifest and Maintain*, was complete and in place.

Crab fishermen will tell you that when you catch crabs and put them in a bucket, you don't have to put a cover over them. When a crab tries to crawl out of the bucket, another crab will just pull it back down. The same thing happens to a lot of folks when they see an opportunity for help and positive change in their lives. They want to put a spiritual foundation under their lives, but sometimes people pull them down as they reach for their true place. That is what happened to me for a long time in my life.

Catch and Release and AFIG Again

Let's quickly review the Catch and Release and the AFIG process. Before we work on what we want to manifest, we have to have a clear and focused mind. If we are to get the full benefit and really up the power of the process, we have to be ready. It is like having the fastest car in the race but the fuel tank is contaminated with water.

Getting connected to the authentic power through an intimate relationship with your innermost being is not difficult, although it does require discipline and consistency. Now, let's address common challenges people run into and how to overcome them. Building a solid and intimate relationship with God is personal, so the experience is different from person to person. The end result is the same; opening up an ongoing connection and living with Divine power, authentic power, and allowing it to influence, direct, and empower our lives.

Chapter 55

Meditate and Open Up the Flow

Meditation is the tongue of the soul and the language of the spirit.

Jeremy Taylor

Meditation is an act of contemplation where you intentionally focus the mind on an idea. Meditation and prayer are considered communion, or communicating with a higher power. Meditation helps us prepare our minds and hearts to welcome God in. It is like a farmer getting a field ready to plant by plowing it first. When we meditate, we are plowing our minds, making them fertile, clearing away the debris, getting ourselves ready to receive the rain, which is called grace, or in other words, unmerited favor.

When we have faith and are sincerely seeking, the source of all light and life from the heavens is always ready to shine upon us. We are getting ready for good instruction, encouragement, and authentic power to be planted and grow within us. Meditation is a way to accept and receive "what is"—the real truth. We are welcoming the natural flow of creation through our being. We are preparing for an intimacy with nature, creation, and Divine power.

One of the biggest challenges we all experience with meditation is being able to quiet a noisy mind. Those 60,000 thoughts mentioned earlier that we experience every day wear us out. The hustle-bustle pace and mentality of the average person keeps our minds racing around on an endless loop, getting us nowhere. This is the very reason something that should be simple and easy like meditation, seems overwhelming to the average person. Their egos are dominating their every thought and running their lives. We say things like, "How can I stop thinking long enough to meditate? I have so much on my mind."

It takes desire, practice, and patience to meditate. Patience is the key. *A Course in Miracles* says: "Only infinite patience produces immediate results." Learning to meditate is simply remembering a natural act; we were built to meditate. Our bodies and minds need meditation to recharge, rejuvenate, and connect us to our authentic power.

Learning to meditate is learning to perform a healthy, natural, and life-enhancing act. Our bodies and minds need meditation to evolve just like we need fresh air, water, and food for nourishment. When we meditate, we are becoming conscious of our innate intelligence and eternal spiritual self. Meditation takes us past our ego and our "frame of mind" we discussed in the Release step that traps us. Wise King Solomon said, *"A quiet spirit can overcome even great mistakes."*

Meditation and Intuition

Meditation activates our inner directional guidance system; in other words, our intuition gives us the ability to live as a multi-sensory being. Without this connection, we are operating as a five-sensory being and intuition means little to us. As we open up and connect with the spirit/soul, we invite in and can expect oneness experiences on a regular basis. We can ask for them as guidance, and by being conscious to the process, they will respond. If we are too busy and occupied by our egos we can miss out on the message life is sending us, and that means we miss out on goodness, success, and joy in our lives. Oneness experiences are exciting because they confirm we are connected with the spirit and that God is with us. Our faith grows quickly as a result. Saint Paul tells us, *"For there is one body and one spirit, just as you have been called to one glorious hope for the future."* Meditations make us more conscious of truth. Then we are better able to accept that everything happens on purpose in our lives by perfect design.

Have you ever started to say something to a person and they took the words right out of your mouth? Have you ever thought of an idea and you told someone about it and they said, "I was thinking that same thing!" We usually take these moments for granted. We miss the message behind them because we are not connected deep enough to our source of life. All minds are mysteriously connected as part of the one infinite mind. This is how a person on one side of the planet can invent something and at same time, without realizing it, another person can invent that same thing or have the same idea on the other side of the planet.

Our personal prayer and meditation time is very private and personal. It's a good idea to use caution about even discussing your mediation practices with people who are not like-minded. Remember the NIOPs and the crabs in the bucket. Don't let anyone rob you of your destiny to experience the Real You and the inner truth about you, the unique message, the dream of your soul.

As a person learns to meditate and connect with a Divine source, the spirit of others recognizes the light emerging within you, and their spirit is subconsciously attracted to the light in you. They may not have a clue what is happening while spirit is being attracted to spirit. Miracles, surprises, and revelations await the sincere seekers of God through meditation. *A Course in Miracles* says: "Prayer is the conduit for miracles." Meditation and prayer change you in wonderful ways; they give you peace, bring you answers, and lead you to your purpose, the dream of the soul.

Getting Started Meditating

The process of reaching an inner, blissful state needs a spark to get it going. There are many models for meditation, yet foundationally they are all the same. Our focus here is on a simple, proven plan you can model and get results. At the same time, always be encouraged to explore new techniques that help or feel more comfortable. This is only the beginning.

The number-one challenge is getting a handle on our busy minds and our runaway thoughts. A person starts out trying to relax. They have good intentions, they breathe deeply and try to relax, but they get distracted. "Did I lock the door?" Exhale. "What day is today?" Breathe in. "I've got to get going, I have so much to do." Exhale.

As a result there is no effective meditation. Most people can't even quiet the mind for sixty seconds. So don't feel bad about it. This situation is called "drift," a departure from intention, a good-bye to the moment and the intention to meditate. It's all part of the process, and it is normal. The good news is, it can be dealt with and conquered.

Meditation Tips

Here are some key meditation strategies that will help to ensure good results:

- Wear comfortable, loose-fitting clothes (when possible) that help you relax, and make sure the temperature is not too warm or too cold.

- Find a place as quiet as possible. Reduce the noise in the environment.

- Turn off phones, televisions, and radios. This way the more you meditate, the less effect noise around you will have on your meditation.

- Sit or lie in a comfortable position. Sitting up is better because you are less likely to fall asleep. Some people enjoy meditating at night while lying down before going to sleep.

- Keep your head level when you sit up and look straight ahead. Picture a string attached to the ceiling, pulling you up.

- Relax your body, relax your jaw, and don't clinch your fists or your toes.

- Breathe in deeply, abdominal breaths through your nose to a count of four; breathe out slowly, releasing your breath slower than your inhale to a count of eight.

- Time yourself to meditate seven minutes minimum per session in the beginning.

    The task here is to begin developing your ability to quiet the mind and relax. Listen to your thoughts and ask yourself, "What is my next thought going to be?" This stalls the mind in the present moment, and that is the exact place we want to be. Pay attention to that moment and how it feels. It may be only a fleeting moment at first, but soon it will last longer and longer if you don't give up.

Conscious, Connected Breathing

The best way to begin meditating is to learn to pay attention to our breath. Most people use about 20 percent of their lung capacity. Just by paying attention to our breathing we can see quick meditation results. By limiting our breathing capacities, we are not only getting less oxygen, we are disconnecting from authentic power and moving away from present-moment awareness. The mind drifts from past to present to future, back and forth. Proper breathing brings us to the now, or the present moment. When we are fully present in the moment and breathing effortlessly, we are naturally drawn deeper into meditation.

We used breathing techniques to connect with the sensitive self in the Embrace step of the Valeo Method. We want to experience the aliveness of our inner spirit, not just the experience of relaxed breathing. Focused, connected breathing gets us ready to enter present-moment awareness. Some people new to meditation try to do what is known as "pushing the river"—they try too hard and don't allow themselves to get in the flow.

Think of meditation practice like chopping down a huge tree. Chop, chop, chop and nothing happens. Then, bit by bit, a crack appears in the tree and it is on the ground. It is not going back up either. Persistence pays off big in your meditation efforts, so be encouraged. You are closer than you think.

Let's practice paying attention to breath, which is the foundation of meditation and allows us to focus on something besides the noise in our minds. After reviewing the tips, find a comfortable place to start, a place you can relax that is quiet. After getting comfortable, sit and take seven deep, abdominal breaths. Inhale through the nose and exhale through the mouth. As you exhale through the mouth, imagine that you are releasing tension in the body. Let your exhalation carry your tension and worries away. After you have completed the seven deep breaths, assume a normal pattern of breathing. Bring your attention to where you feel your breath the most. You can focus on your nostrils, your chest, or mouth. Just find what feels right for you. Continue this exercise, striving to keep focused on your breathing and away from thought. Continue for seven minutes only, and then stop.

This is a simple beginning meditation. The goal is to make it a new habit to find and set aside at least seven minutes, two times a day, to meditate. Upon awakening and in the evening before retiring is a perfect place to start. The goal here is to continue this small but meaningful commitment for thirty days. During these seven minutes we are to focus on nothing except breathing, relaxing, and escaping from thought. Seven minutes twice a day is only ninety-eight minutes from a total of the week's 10,080 minutes. Doesn't seem like much when we look at it that way, right? You may already be way ahead of this strategy. Good for you, and God bless you! If you haven't set up time for your sacred self to discover the sacred wish of your spirit and soul, is "now" a good time to start? Meditation can be enlightening, therapeutic, and addictive, and it sets the stage for an awesome prayer life. Some people meditate for hours at a time and savor every moment. These people will tell you they thrive because of their meditation and prayer. It does not have to take months of practice to start noticing positive results. Many people start noticing an improvement in their peace of mind and self-talk, self-control and self-esteem right away.

Meditation and Time Perception

Meditation does something else for us. It takes us out of a time-bound mentality. The deeper the levels of meditation we are able to reach, the more we begin to see a change in our perception of time. This is how we know we are reaching a Divine connection. Most of us live our lives as slaves to time. If we don't pay attention while running from the ghosts of the past and confront the fears and illusions of the future, we miss out on an important part of life; the now moment. This is where we find our connection to source.

You might think, "That is easy for you to say, but my life is hectic, what moment? I'm busy every minute." Boy, can I relate to that kind of life. I used to be addicted to activity and action (there is a difference), although it is not all bad unless you get activity confused with action and you are wasting a lot of time and energy getting nowhere. If your life is running *you*, you are missing the present moment. You are passing right by the good stuff, the juice of life. In every now moment we are creating our future moments. Constantly remind yourself, "I created this. This is my handiwork. My prior thoughts delivered me to this place in my life. Whatever circumstances and situations I find myself in, I did it and I take responsibility. My prior state of mind and thinking manifested all this. The only way I can change is to create new thoughts with the right connection to my inner treasures and manifest what I deserve instead of this. I have the choice."

Usually, we forget our prior thoughts and moments. This is the problem; unconscious thinking and living. Remember the *Discovery* step of the Valeo Method, when we exposed how much living unconsciously and the lack of awareness had cost us? The Law of Cause and Effect and the Law of Attraction, just like the Law of Gravity, are constant. They work all time; they never forget; they never even pause—they never rest.

If you could control your now moments, does that mean you could control your future now moments and your future manifestations? Take some time to make sure this idea soaks in, because the answers is a big fat yes! We spend our lives having pity parties and asking, why me? when our prior now moment thoughts brought us where we are!

The more a person meditates the more the illusion of time disappears. In other words, meditating for thirty minutes can sometimes seem like only five minutes have passed by. This is a good indicator of deep meditation and connection to authentic power. When this happens, we have arrived at an empowering state of present-moment awareness, something no one will ever forget or want to live without again.

The Eye of the Storm

The word "meditation" comes from two Latin words, "medio," which means "center," and "sto," which means "to stand." Translated, this means "to stand in the center." The eye of the storm, even in a hurricane, is always calm. This is a metaphor for the storms, noise, and upset of life and how there is refuge at the center of our being. Unfortunately, the challenge most of us face is even though we do at times experience peace at our center, we get sucked back into the storms of life like we have no choice. Your problems won't survive in the eye of the storm because there is peace and calm at the center of your being just like the eye of the storm.

Instant Meditation

When you become a real pro at meditation, you'll be able to reach the same level quickly that you previously reached in a longer span of time. This is because you opened up a neurological association, a mental pathway, called an anchor or neuro-link. The neurotransmitters in the brain have recorded your progress in memory, making it easier to turn on the switches and return to meditation quickly. It is like taking a trip to a familiar place; every time we go back, it gets easier. Here are some tips:

- Take a deep breath and hold it for a count of three. One thousand one, one thousand two, one thousand three.

- As you hold your breath, hold back your thoughts.

- Repeat the following phrase to yourself: "While I release my breath, I will remember what it feels like physically and mentally to meditate." Breathe in and out slowly once again. Repeat to yourself again: "While I release my breath, I will remember what it feels like to physically and mentally meditate." Then say to yourself, while continuing to relax, "I am now experiencing meditation.

- Breathe deeply, slowly, and notice and focus on your breath; relax.

Creative Visualization and Meditation

After every seven-minute meditation, you have the perfect opportunity to fill your mind with creative thoughts. Visualize the dreams you put in your plans and goals. Think about the treasure map you created. See, feel, and experience the details of your dreams. Get in the picture and feel the emotions of living your dreams, of arriving at your dreams. Smile and thank God for the manifestation of all your dreams. Thank God for revealing your purpose. Use "I am" statements and be grateful for already having your dreams come true. Continue to relax with controlled breathing.

Here are some examples of "I am" statements:

- I am grateful for my prosperous and healthy life.

- I am grateful for my soul mate, with whom I share my life. (Even if you don't know who it will be yet.)

- I am grateful for Divine guidance in my life.

- I'm grateful for healing in my body.

- I'm grateful for reaching my desired body weight, blood pressure, dress size, body fat percentage, etc. (List anything you are seeking related to your health and physical body.)

Mentally picture yourself enjoying your dreams. Fill up your relaxed, empty mind with thoughts that will turn into words about your future which you can declare. Think of the words that will launch unseen forces and connect to you and draw the natural laws of the universe to manifest your dreams.

The ego is always prowling around like a hungry lion in your mind, looking to devour every good thought, hope, expectation, and dream you have. Don't let your guard down. The enemy can show up in clever ways to knock you off course with your hope and faith for the future. Be ready to call down the ego; to arrest it! Be ready to rebuke its illusions of lack and interference. Your egoic mind really has no power, unless an unaware mind grants it. It especially has no power over a right-thinking mind aligned with the power of God and His universe.

Chapter 56
Prayer's Role in Manifestation

Courage is fear that has said its prayers.

Dorothy Bernard

Because God gives us the ability to co-create good with Him as part of His creative process, we are able to produce wonderful results. I am a prime example of the challenge with this process. Sometimes we forget where our real power to create comes from. In other words, you think all you need is your own five-sensory, artificial powers to manifest results in your life. So what happens? Artificial power manifests artificial results!

In addition to the gift God gives us to co-create with Him, we also are the vessel He uses to display special gifts and talents. Saint Paul urged his spiritual son Timothy to wake up the gifts inside him. King Solomon wrote: *"Your gifts will make room for you."* Saint Paul reminded us of God's generosity when he said, *"God's gifts and his call will never be withdrawn."*

The challenge for most of us is just to calm down. We are so busy running around like a mouse in a maze that our gifts remain unopened. We miss out on the key, the secret, to our grand and unique gifts. The good news is, it is never too late to claim or reclaim our gifts because they are irrevocable. We just have to find the boldness and courage to claim them. In fact, they are always waiting on us, and even more, they are seeking us. Our gifts are a big key to living the dream of the soul and finding total happiness.

Making Your Prayer and Meditation Count

What is prayer anyway but a heartfelt conversation with God? When we pray, we are talking to God. How does He answer us? Through intuition and revelation, a dawning of truth or direction that comes upon us. Prayer is the bridge to intimate communication with God, and the rewards are a relationship with Him.

Any attempt at prayer is a good thing. Scripture tells us God knows our hearts, so meditating and praying to seek Him gets His attention. Not knowing how to pray discourages many people from experiencing intimacy with God. The key is to keep working on your meditation and to always keep praying. Jesus was quoted in the Bible as saying, *"When you pray."* He did not say if you pray.

The more face time with God, the sooner we see results. Having face time with God is like making deposits in your spiritual bank account. We can take a lesson from Jesus. He arose many hours before daylight to pray and prayed many hours every day, and when he needed to perform a miracle, it only took seconds. Prayer time is like plugging our spirit into the ultimate power source charger. Saint Paul told us, *"Pray without ceasing."* Your prayer never falls on deaf ears; the more you pray, the more your spirit will direct you on what to say and how to pray.

Prayer With Passion

Many people fall short when they are not present enough, or in the moment to be able to experience a state of prayer. Other times we aren't persistent enough, and sometimes we are not passionate enough. We all have found ourselves in situations where we just pray when we want something or we are in a crisis.

It takes a calm mind to make a spiritual connection. This is the reason you need to practice controlled breathing and mind-cleansing techniques every day. It takes repetition and practice, but the rewards are tremendous. The momentum of our daily thoughts is not going to stop on its own. Daily practice will give us what we are looking for, which is simply a reasonable amount of progress in a measurable amount of time.

We have all found ourselves rushing through prayers at one time or another with little thought or emotion. Jesus taught his disciples, *"Don't babble on and on as people of other religions do. They think their prayers are being answered merely by repeating their words again and again. Don't be like them for your Father knows exactly what you need even before you ask Him."* Jesus makes it clear; God wants our attention when we pray.

What if My Prayers Are Not Answered?

Many people wonder why nothing seems to happen when they pray. It is a good question, and here are some good answers.

If you are wondering why God is not answering your prayers, doesn't it make sense to ask Him? If you are sincerely seeking God, Scripture tells us that we will find Him. So why not just ask, "Lord, can you please show me and help me understand why my prayers are not being answered?"

The biggest challenge for us as new multi-sensory beings seeking an intimate relationship with our inner presence is our lack of patience. We think in human time while God operates on God time. Do you believe God will tell you why your prayers seem (notice I said seem) to not be answered? *"Ask me and I will tell you remarkable secrets you do not know about things to come."* Now, that sounds pretty simple. If we knew everything about our future the way God does, we would understand why prayers are not answered or they are delayed. We have to get ourselves to a place where we can believe, have faith, and trust.

God's answers and His timing related to your prayers is usually not what you expect. Sometimes what we are praying for is not the best solution, and God has something better in mind.

Maybe it is not the right time for your prayers to be answered. It doesn't mean God is not going to answer. Saint Peter addresses this specifically: *"The Lord isn't really being slow about his promise as some people think. No, he is being patient for your sake."* We don't know what God is up to in our lives. Accordingly to Scripture, He is always working. He is going behind the scenes, making our crooked places straight, getting things lined up and softening hearts so our prayers can be answered.

Surrender

There has to be a point in all our lives when we accept that our creation and existence as a human being was on purpose. That is, unless we choose to believe we are each the result of a random collision of energies, microcosms, and elements that just somehow showed up through happenstance.

We can look at who we are and where we are through spiritual lenses or scientific lenses. For many years, I have chosen to do both. I am the kind of guy who just keeps asking, why? As time goes on, the two perspectives of science and spiritual truth continue to align more and more as the reality of creation reveals itself through archeological, scientific, spiritual revelation, and discoveries. In my case, the more I studied the science behind nature, creation, and the human race, the more I became a believer in God, and the more I sought spiritual truth. If you aren't sure, or if you are confused, I truly understand, none of us want or need that kind of uncertainty in our lives. I urge you to keep seeking and you will find what you are looking for. Just remember that what you are seeking is seeking you, too.

Believing in a Divine power, an evolving, endless energy behind your existence, and coming to terms with some simple truths about your spirit is when true empowerment begins. This is the foundation of the *Manifest and Maintain* step of the Valeo Method.

When we can reach a level of trust and belief about who we are and the individual dream of our soul, our original intent, then we are ready to go to the next phase of enlightenment which is surrender; it is about trusting your source of life and breath, and trusting God to know what is best. Even when you don't understand what is going on with your life, it is knowing that what is best is always ahead for you as long as you believe in and trust God.

There is a famous story in the Bible about three young servants who served in the court of Babylonia under King Nebuchadnezzar. When the King asked these believers of God to bow down to his ninety-foot golden statue and ignore God, they refused. The King was infuriated and told them if they didn't comply he would have them thrown into a blazing furnace. He asked them, *"And then what god will rescue you?"* The three still refused to bow down and told the King that the God they served would rescue them. They told the angry King (who was not somebody to mess with), that even if their God didn't show up, they would not bow down (lose faith) to that statue. The King was so enraged he ordered the furnace turned up seven times hotter than usual. He then ordered the three to be bound and thrown into it. The flame was so hot it killed the soldiers who threw the three in.

The King jumped up in amazement as he saw four men, not three, walking around in the flames of the blazing furnace, unburned. He asked his men, "Didn't you throw only three men in the flames? Who is that fourth man?" The King was shocked as he shouted, "This fourth man looks like a god!" Immediately he ordered the men to come out of the flames, but only three came out and he saw that not a hair on their heads was burned; they didn't even smell like smoke! This experience convinced the King of the True God, and he ordered his whole kingdom to worship God from that day forward.

The key to this story is that even if God didn't show up, these men believed they would be safe in heaven with Him. This is a powerful testimony of faith. We have to trust God and know that even if He doesn't seem to show up (answer prayers) when we think He is supposed to, He is always there for those who seek and believe in Him.

Surrender also means having faith that your prayers are being heard. We are told by God in the Scripture, *"I will guide you along the best pathway for your life. I will advise you and watch over you."* How does that offer sound? Remember the first step of the Valeo Method, Discovery? We emphasized adopting the belief system that, "Everything happens for a reason and a purpose, and it serves me." When we can get to this point it is truly a huge step toward life mastery.

Have you ever had something uncomfortable or even over-whelming happen to you, something that appeared could never turn out well? Then you looked back one day and said, "Wow, if this bad situation or thing had not happened, I would never have reached this level, or learned this lesson, or met this person or overcome this limiting belief about myself!" We have all had these experiences. It goes back to what we focused on earlier about being a conscious liver of life, paying attention to what life is telling us. It is about being aware of what is going on around us. It is about being an acutely sensitive observer of the lessons we are meant to learn every day to grow and be the best person we can be. Warren Buffett put it this way: "No one can be a better you than you!'

Chapter 57

At Last...Faith!

*Faith is putting all your eggs in God's basket
and counting your blessings before they hatch.*

Ramona C. Carroll

Don't give up on God; He will never give up on you. There is something I love about God. He wants a close, intimate relationship with each of us. He says, *"Seek me with all your heart and you will find me, come toward me and I will come toward you,"* and then the best part He saves for last: *"For whoever finds me finds favor from the Lord."*

We all find great pleasure in many things in life—travel, sports, concerts, clothes, homes, cars, family time, and so forth. But the greatest joy and peace we will ever have is the inner peace of mind that comes from knowing we are fulfilling our calling, no matter what it is, and that we are pleasing our Maker. Then we know we have arrived, that life is good and getting better every day. Not sure what to pray for or how to pray? Pray for help. I turn to this Scripture when I need wisdom: *"If you need wisdom, ask your generous God, and He will give it to you. He will not rebuke you for asking. But be sure when you ask Him, your faith is in God alone."*

God gave us prayer as a gift and a tool to mine the golden nuggets of truth about ourselves and our individual roles in humanity. We should feel privileged and honored that we are given prayer—you can have an audience with the Sovereign of the universe, and that through your communication (communion) with Him, your role in life will be revealed.

God wants our love and devotion, the same thing He gives to us. This also means having faith. Faith means not being afraid to step out, to surrender. We have to be willing to trust Divine timing. What is the message in the Bible about trust? *"Anyone who trusts Him will never be disgraced."* We have to trust His awesome power, his infinite riches, wisdom, and knowledge.

If we surrender and depend on God to take care of all our needs and guide our steps, He will. This takes a commitment, and it may not be easy at first or at certain times. But as you go along it gets easier, and the favor comes more often. All of sudden something will start to happen in your life; I promise you, it will. Intuition, the ear of the soul, acts as a conduit from God to us and "in a moment," things change. Doors open that were closed tight, ideas come to you, people show up to help, confidence surges, and courage shows up right when you need it most. Peace of mind beyond understanding can be a part of your life. Now, when we are playing the game of life by God's plan instead of by our own plans or the plan of humanity, life makes more sense and it becomes a meaningful joy.

Ask-Ask-Ask Then Ask Some More

Another reason prayers don't get answered is because we don't ask enough. We just give up too easily. This goes back to belief and faith that our prayers are being heard and will be answered.

Jesus tells a story about a widow who had approached a judge to settle a dispute for her. The judge was unjust and did not believe in God. He turned the widow away and would not listen to her. She would not take no for an answer and persisted until the judge couldn't take her pleading anymore, so he gave her what she wanted.

This message repeats itself throughout the Bible: Be persistent, keep on asking. Jesus taught us to keep on seeking, and we will find. Keep on knocking, and the door will be opened to you.

I have seen amazing results from my seminars and in coaching clients who are persistent and consistent in their prayers. I have seen prayers answered with amazing detail to the request and in perfect timing and sequence, and even above and beyond the things prayed for.

Believe and Expect

In the beginning of the book I spoke about hope and how hope and expectation are really the same thing. Just remember that expectation is hope in action. We spent a large portion of the book (as we do in our seminars) focusing on the power of belief to create a life of joy or a life of misery. Belief is the foundation of all our thoughts and actions. We can pray intensely and we can have total forgiveness in our hearts. We can be specific and thank God in advance with all our hearts... and still not get prayers answered. Why does this happen? Because we don't believe enough in God's ability to hear our petitions and to answer us. Sadly, sometimes our impotent prayers of little faith are directed at our omnipotent God, and they are wasted and fruitless. Prayers without faith are like going into battle with stickpins instead of swords.

People give up on prayer and wonder why God is not answering them when in reality they have little or no faith that He will answer in the first place. They act like they are participating in some kind of prayer lottery where only the lucky winners get their prayers answered. What kind of god would that be? What happens to a sports team that doesn't have faith in winning? Does anyone ever go into battle or a sports event thinking, "Well, I might have a chance at this." What happens to a boxer who gets in the ring with doubt? What happens to a sick person who has no faith he will get well? If we want an overflow and abundant harvest in our lives, we have to expect one. Remember how the farmer waits after he plants? He knows his harvest will arrive! We have to be the same way—then stand back and watch what happens!

Jesus performed countless miracles on people who believed in Him. He would say, *"Your faith has healed you."* The *Discovery* step of the Valeo Method is designed to make us aware of how our limiting beliefs rob us of our quality of life. The Release step gives a proven plan to release the toxic emotions caused by our disempowering beliefs. When we release our limiting beliefs, we take away the ego's leverage, and then the ego can't get in the way of our right to answers to prayer.

The father of a son who was having violent seizures asked Jesus for help with his affliction, and he added, "If you can," to his request. Jesus replied, *"What do you mean, if I can? Anything is possible if a person believes."*

I have been blessed to see amazing miracles of change and total transformation in my work with individuals. I take none of the credit; all the glory goes to God, and I believe I am only a conduit for his unconditional love. I have learned amazing things while watching people go through and apply these principles to their lives. The unlimited source of blessings and favor available to us compared to the small amount most of us tap into and access is a gulf of space far too wide. With the Valeo Method, you can narrow that space and then eliminate it. In fact, we are already beginning to do just that through our team-building and pay-it-forward strategies. I hope you will want to learn more about your own life through the Valeo Method and then spread the good news that it stands on around the world.

Knowing all the answers to why things are the way they are in your life will not give you the peace you want. Knowing God and believing in Him will. God will always work something great in you; you just have to get out of His way with your lack of patience and belief. Allow God to do what He does so well—let Him manifest something magnificent in your life!

It's Not Your Battle

When you believe and turn your challenges and your dreams to God, it is no longer your battle. Now God is on the field of battle for you. King Jehoshaphat discovered his vulnerability and dependence on the Lord on a day of battle. He was grossly outnumbered and facing an overwhelming foe. He did the only thing he knew to do under the circumstances. He turned to the Lord and said, *"Our eyes are upon you,"* and the king was not disappointed in the outcome.

We have to keep asking, be specific, and never, ever lose faith. No matter how impossible things may look, never, ever give up. Success is buried right past frustration, and you are always, always closer than you think to victory! Remember, God's timing is perfect because He has already seen the end, and when you allow Him to coach your game of life, He will never send you in the wrong play!

What was the Lord's response to King Jehoshaphat? *"Do not be afraid nor dismayed because of this great multitude for the battle is not yours, but God's...you will not need to fight in the battle. Position yourselves, stand still, and see the salvation (deliverance from danger and difficulty) of the Lord who is with you...do not fear or be dismayed; tomorrow go out against them, for the Lord is with you."* When we live with the realization that the battle against lack and fear is not ours but the Lord's, we live with hope and promise.

So what happened? No director can do a Hollywood ending better than God. The Lord confused the minds of the King's enemy, and they started fighting among each other until the entire enemy was destroyed! God is ready to destroy all the enemies in your mind of doubt, failure, poverty, discouragement, sickness, and even death. Are you ready to do your part by having faith, believing and letting Him in?

Chapter 58
Pulling the DREAM Together

Cherish your visions and your dreams because they are the children of your soul; the blueprints of your ultimate achievements.

Napoleon Hill

I must say in closing the five steps that teaching and sharing the last step of the Valeo Method gives me the greatest joy of all. I know from experience that if you apply what you have learned and read here, you are on the verge of a breakthrough—you are opening up the spigot for overflow and supernatural harvest, and it is not far away in your life. The first four steps of the process work well on their own. However, as I mentioned earlier, the real power lies in putting this last step to work with the first four.

Now you can parlay what you have learned so far into exponential growth. You do that by harnessing the power of the Valeo Method and paying it forward to those around you, especially to your family and the other members of your team of life. Get ready to lock in a life filled with power, influence, and the ability to prevail over any problem as you use these five steps to live your dreams and build your "DREAM TEAM."

encourage you to take the challenge of implementing the *Manifest and Maintain* step as part of your daily routine and action plan now, today. Don't put it off one day or even one hour longer. Life is precious; every moment counts. Developing new habits usually takes less than thirty days. Make a one-month commitment of daily activities and budget your time to build on what you have learned from the Valeo Method. You and everyone around you will be glad you did!

Progress and Strategies

1. The first four steps of the Valeo Method only produce long-term results when you use this last step as a foundation.

2. My authentic power and the main key to my greatness is based on my understanding of the truth about unconditional love.

3. My own knowledge and five-sensory power will not lead me to my greatness.

4. My true source of supply is not from "income" but from "outflow."

5. When I release the power of unconditional love, I become a magnet for love and abundance.

6. Giving primes the pump for favor and grace in my life.

7. When we are not giving of ourselves, we are blocking the flow of blessings and intuitive guidance in our lives.

8. When I give, I create a vacuum in life, and God's design in the constantly moving universe is to fill that vacuum and create a flow of good in my life.

9. Meditation opens me up to access the power of spirit that gives me life to direct my way.

Summary and Action Plan

1. I will visualize myself as an expression point in the consciousness of God with a purpose He created to express uniquely through me.

2. I will pay attention to the power of unconditional love working in my life to satisfy any ache in my soul and the soul of others.

3. I will be conscious of slowing down by paying attention to the needs of others who show up in my life and their purpose and message in my journey at this time.

4. I will post my "I am" statements in places where I will be constantly reminded of them.

5. I will constantly remind myself to challenge my limiting thoughts and beliefs as they arise. I will ask myself: "Are these thoughts or beliefs based on fact or judgment?"

6. I will commit to, plan, and practice my mini-meditation sessions during my day and use "Instant Meditation" at every possible opportunity, especially when I feel stressed or worried.

7. I will have faith that my prayers are being heard by a loving and compassionate God and that the answers to all my challenges and the pathway to my success is already laid out and waiting within me to manifest.

Chapter 59

Building Your DREAM TEAM
(Together Everyone Achieves More)

Coming together is a beginning. Keeping together is progress.
Working together is success.

Henry Ford

Hardship and suffering changes a person. Unfortunately, it takes a lot more suffering than necessary for most of us to seek change. Sometimes changes caused by suffering make us better. Sometimes they save a life. Sometimes they cause us to give up. Some people have told me the experience of going to prison rescued them or saved their life. Their lifestyles had them on a collision course to disaster.

Why does it have to take a tragedy, a loss, prison, a major illness or accident, or even near death for many of us to wake up? And what about the people who let their circumstances make them bitter instead of better?

The quality of your life is the quality of your communication, both with others and yourself. Our lives boil down to a series of moments which you remember, but the time and space in between those moments seem to get lost. Most of us are just marking time and not moving on with our lives. We are not growing and creating a quality of life, full of memories and moments. When asked, "How are you doing?" have you ever responded, "I'm just surviving" or "Just hanging in there." What kind of attitude is that? No wonder so many people wake up in their twilight years and say, "Is this all there is?" God gives us free will, so we have a choice; we can set our own appointments to arrive in our desired future situations. So why not set some new appointments for better situations?

How can we change these cycles of loss, disappointment, and emptiness? Use the Valeo Method to create more "Team" in your life. Most people's lives are so boring and uneventful they can't even tell you three significant events that happened to them in the past five years. So, how do we create more team in our lives? First, let's get rid of the excuses. Leave the pity party. Who wants to hang around someone who is always backing up to dump their garbage on everyone? Use the (DREAM) Valeo Method to discover why your life isn't the way you want it. Use what you have learned to release your toxic thoughts, beliefs, and negative emotions. Embrace your sensitive self and the gifts your wounds are offering you. Activate the energies that attract the people, situations, and opportunities you seek into your reality now, through the power of your innate connection to God's universal Law of Attraction. Use prayer and meditation to get you closer to your Higher Self and access the authentic power of your God-consciousness to live on purpose.

Accept where you are as part of your journey and live to create special moments constantly in your life. Make special moments by giving your love and by giving of yourself. Remember that when you give you create a vacuum in the environment surrounding your life, the universe then seeks to fill that emptiness. What results is a natural flow of life; the more you give, the more you receive.

When you show love, you show God to the world. When you seek happiness only for yourself, it is hard to find. When you seek to give happiness to others and share it with them, then happiness will find you. When you give you are being like God; you are experiencing your own true God-nature through your authentic self. You might say, "How can I give? I'm broke, barely surviving, I'm in prison, I'm unemployed, bankrupt, handicapped!" No matter what your external circumstances are, you can always give unconditional love. This is your treasure to give.

Get creative, write a letter, send a card, make a phone call and tell someone you're thinking of them. Tell them you just wanted them to know how special they are to you. Let them know what a blessing they are in your life. Tell them something you admire or respect about them. Tell them how they made a difference in your life. Call a child (children thrive on encouragement), or an older person who feels forgotten, out of touch, or unappreciated.

I use this exercise with my classes and my coaching clients. I ask them to call someone they haven't talked to in a long time to just say hello. I tell them not to call for any particular reason except to say, "I miss you; I was thinking of you. I wanted you to know you always were an important part of my team." The results are amazing! You can only guess who gets the most out of it. This is a small and simple thing. Yet this simple gesture shows amazing love, and it creates a chain reaction of good feelings in both directions. I want you to try this exercise, but don't think about it too much because you might get in analysis paralysis and miss creating a moment—just do it.

Are you ready to build your team? Give a friend a copy of your favorite book (I have one suggestion). Take someone to lunch and surprise them by having another old friend meet you. Get home early and surprise your spouse with a flower, a card, or CD of his or her favorite artist. Better yet, surprise your spouse or significant other when he/she comes home by sprinkling rose petals from the door to the bedroom, put on some romantic music, draw a bath with fragrant oils, put chocolates on the pillow, and have two champagne glasses on the night stand. You don't need a reason—just do it! That, my friend, is called creating moments! Arrange for a surprise gift to be delivered to your child no matter what age. Just sign the card, "Just thinking of how special you are to me." Just do it for no reason. There are so many little, creative, fun things you can do for friends and family. Life boils down to a series of moments, so let's get busy creating them because this is what creates the quality of life. Be a "Moment Creator" for those around you and those you love. Think outside the box. Get outrageous and crazy, have fun, what a concept!

These are the things that make life have flavor and create what we remember. Stop living in a rut. It is worth repeating here, someone once said, "A rut is just a grave with the ends knocked out!" There is a line in the movie *The Shawshank Redemption* where an old man named Billy gets out of prison and says, I've got to get busy living or get busy dying." Which one are you doing?

God wants to bless you. Do you want blessings? Get busy using the gifts God gave you and bless others with them and watch what happens—let your joy shine through. Then get ready for doors to start opening. Miracles happen every day, every moment, all over the world. Aren't you ready for yours? God is ready, and He is more than able. Jesus said, *"To those who use well what is given, even more will be given, and they will have abundance."* So get busy giving so you can receive. Remember, you can never out give God, and you are never more like God than when you are giving.

As we seek spiritual enlightenment, we begin to understand the connectedness of all life with the oneness of mind and spirit. It becomes easier to see that we all need each other. To the new seeker of awareness, this concept might be a stretch in thinking and a little hard to understand and sometimes even hard to accept.

We do need each other, and we all need God. Together, everyone does achieve more. One thing life has taught me is that all people have a deep longing to be part of something, to be on a team. When two people who are like-minded and passionate about something good get together and get focused,

something amazing happens. They create synergy. This is a dynamic in which the energy and power of two becomes and feels more like three or more. Combine that with faith, and Jesus said, *"If two of you agree here on earth concerning anything you ask, my Father in heaven will give it to you."* What a great reason to surround ourselves with a faith-filled team!
California aspen trees grow in clusters. The reason is because they send new shoots up from the roots. In this grove of trees all of them are intricately connected together.

A giant California redwood can grow as high as **300** feet. You would expect a tree that grows that tall to have deep roots, right? Actually their roots are shallow because they need to capture lots of surface water. Their roots spread out like a maze in all directions intertwining with the other redwoods. By locking together this way the trees support each other in all the storms. Just like the aspen, they never stand alone.

What else is connected by a system of roots? People, and we are not meant to survive alone, we need to hold each other up. We get pounded by adversities and the storms of life we know are coming. We all need our team around us to support us!

Chapter 60

People Will do Anything to Be on a Team

Build for your team a feeling of oneness, of a dependence on one another and of strength to be derived by unity.

Vince Lombardi

People need team so much they will do anything to become a participant. Look what Olympic athletes go through just to qualify to compete. The sacrifice and discipline is incredible. They work daily for years just to get a chance to be on an Olympic team. How many get close but never make it? Then, after all that commitment and work, they win by only hundredths of a second.

People put their life on the line every day as part of our Armed Forces. When Hurricane Katrina hit New Orleans and the earthquake rocked Haiti, we witnessed an unprecedented outpouring of love and generosity from teams all over our country and the world. People gave and gave of their time, money, and resources. It was a beautiful example of the power and the spirit of teams coming together as the collective heart of God mobilized. Always remember the power of team in your life and that it is your nature to love being on a team.

We need more of this kind of love and team in the world. They say a person is institutionalized after a short term in prison, and it is true. But we are institutionalized as individuals and collectively. We are stuck in our thinking. We get lost and isolated in our little box of life, and then we wonder, "What difference can I make? Who cares anyway? I'm just one person. My life is screwed up for now. I'll wait till things are better and then I will contribute. Then I'll join the team."

Please know this, my friend—many people care, I care, for one, and of course, most importantly, God cares.

We are here in Earth School to learn and grow, and we need each other. The pressure of life not only separates us from our quality of life, it separates us from each other.

I may not know you but I need you. I need you on my team called Planet Earth and another team called Humanity to help me feel happy and fulfilled. Why? Because you are, according to the Word of God, a part of me. I don't care what color, race, creed, or religion you are; I don't care how good or bad your life has been. Neither one of us can escape it; we are connected. This collective consciousness is what influences the energies of our world. This creates a good reason to get on the winning team, right? The bottom line is that when we feel good, we do good things and have good thoughts, which in turn feed into everyone around us through the energies we share with all of creation. Everyone can make a difference; everyone can contribute to the good in their own way, to our world!

Team, Family, Friends

I woke up one day and realized something. I wasn't taking care of my team like I should have been. I was too caught up in conquering my goals and challenges and having things my way. I wasn't being mean to anyone I loved directly, but I was mistreating them with the lack of my love and attention. I was definitely missing the message life was sending me. I totally lost sight of the little things. Robert Brault says: "Enjoy the little things because someday you may look back and realize they were the big things." I realized I was guilty of letting my life run me, my ego control me, and I was missing out on one of the biggest gifts of life—having a team to enjoy. I was not only neglecting my family team. This is just how the ego works, and I knew better, but it got me anyway. The ego lulled me into giving up control of my life and the things that really mattered, and wow, was I missing out. I wasn't enjoying the people who passed through my life every day. Ask yourself if you have been guilty of letting this happen to you. Have you been so caught up in your agenda and the task at hand and in such a hurry that you didn't take the time to just stop for a second and look into the eyes of your spouse, significant other, and/or your child? Did you even take the time to say, "How was your day?" and really listen, or how about pausing for a moment, looking deep into their eyes and saying, "Hey, you, I love you!' Were you really that busy? Was it really that important? Today is the time to connect with the souls of those on our teams and let them know how we really feel deep down inside. The Valeo Method sets us up for that.

When we take care of our family team, our friendship team, our church team, our business team, and all others, they will take care of us. You might think, "Well, how about them working on my team? I'm not the only one dropping the ball! They need to help me build my team. I'm the one struggling here, I need some help!"

I have a reminder for you. All excuses are equal. Ouch! There comes that velvet hammer again. Sorry about that; it is all out of love, I promise. If you always do what you have always done, you always get what you have always gotten. The time is now to change what is not working and take control of supporting your team. I challenge you to take control of your team today and revel in the wonderful rewards that come with it.

Chapter 61

Share the Love –
Don't Dump on Your Team!

In order to have a winner, the team must have a feeling of unity;
every player must put the team first–ahead of personal glory.

Coach Bear Bryant

Build a team by being a blessing and not a burden to your loved ones and friends. Your family and friends don't deserve to suffer just because you are suffering, even though they love you and are willing to go through your pain with you. It is one thing to be a friend and lend a compassionate ear, but sometimes it gets out of hand. At some time or another, most everyone creates a pity party and invites all their closest family and friends. Is it really fair? Do you really want to hear it? Does it really accomplish anything? Let's bring good news and good energy to all those on our team and lift them up from now on and put up a big sign that says, "No more pity parties! No more poor old me!"

Your Team Needs You

When we give love and encouragement to our team, we are helping them but we are also helping ourselves. When a close team member calls you and says, "What's up?" and you respond, "Life sucks!" what just happened? You are dragging them down. How do you feel when you get an e-mail or letter that is negative or discouraging? If you keep doing this, your whole team loses positive energy. Then what happens? They will feed it right back to you and drag you down even further. It is a vicious cycle.

You might say, "You don't understand my situation; life is tough for me right now. I don't have much to be enthusiastic about. How can I encourage my team?" Remember the "focus" step in the IF I PAR process? Intention is the "why" behind your focus. Use the steps and change your focus. Ask yourself a better question: What are you happy about? What are you excited about? What are you proud of? What are you grateful for? Not sure? What *could* you be excited about, happy about, and grateful for? What you focus on is what you get. Your thoughts and words seek a reflection of themselves in the universe by natural law. What you think about, you bring about. Be the change you want to see. Before you get on the phone, write a letter, send an email, or visit a family member or friend, make up your mind to *change* your state of mind. Don't pollute anyone on your team. Remember, you need each other.

By slowing down and being sensitive to your energies and your awareness, you can lift your team up instead of dragging them down. Then, the positive energy you put out seeks more of the same and it feeds right back to you instead of the negative. Now, instead of people avoiding your presence, they will be subconsciously attracted to you. The team in you attracts the team in them.

If you positively affect five people a week with your attitude and empowering spirit and those people go on to inspire five people, that is twenty-five more. If those twenty-five people affect five more, that is 155 more people; if we stop right here, you get the idea. You have created a positive energy chain reaction.

Once when I was in line at a supermarket, the cashier was a pretty young lady but she had a bad attitude and a scowl on her face. I noticed how she was treating the folks in front of me (not very nicely). I decided to use my skills and have some fun. When it was my turn to check out I asked her with a totally serious face, "Miss, may I see your teeth, please?" Her whole demeanor changed; embarrassed, she giggled and asked me, "What did you say?" I repeated, "May I see your teeth, please? She smiled big and even laughed. I told her she had a beautiful smile and teeth and that I just wanted to see her smile. As I walked away from the counter, I looked back at the lady behind me who was smiling with the cashier as she explained what just happened.

Little things make a difference. That smile had a processional effect on others. It shows how easy it is to build a positive team wherever we go.

The bread you cast out on the water always comes back to you. If you don't cast it out, it is not coming back. It is up to you to build your team. The more you give, the more you get. When you drop a pebble in the water, does it just make a hole in the water and go ker-plunck? No, it makes ripples, right? That is what happens with our lives; our energies go out into other energies and ripple into our lives. This is why it is important to pay attention to what ripples we are close to.

Chapter 62
Team Spirit

*You need to be aware of what other people are doing, applaud their efforts,
acknowledge their successes, and encourage them in their pursuits.
When we all help one another everyone wins.*

Jim Stovall

People will do anything to be part of the team. Some join radical religious organizations, street gangs, terrorist groups. Kids in rough neighborhoods join gangs to feel safe, important, and respected. Teams aren't always good when they represent the wrong things.

People sometimes want to be part of the team so badly that when they get left out they do horrible things. Think of the Columbine High School massacre, the University of Virginia tragedy, what about the man who attacked the children at an Amish school, and the numerous disgruntled employees who have committed violent murders at their place of employment?

These people couldn't be on the team they wanted to be on, and it drove them to insane actions. These horrible events show how much a good, positive team is needed in all our lives and at all ages of life.

The Team in You

What is the best way to take care of the team in you? The best and most important thing you can ever do is learn to love yourself. Not from an egotistical standpoint, but from the gift of life God gave you. When you love, that essence of your being your true Higher Self, your spirit, comes alive. Appreciate your uniqueness. When we wake up our gifts, we are waking up the part of God's team inside each and every one of us and letting our light shine.

When we wake our spirit we smother our emotional garbage. We leave our past regrets and don't need to dwell on future worries. We recognize the juice of the present moment and how precious it is.

Some people live in a stupor; they miss out. They don't realize that we as individuals represent the unfolding, constantly revealing, active expression of God's will, and each and every one of us has a role in this magnificent cosmic play. All we have to do to live our bliss is step up and accept our role in life—the dream of our individual souls. When we do, we activate the expression of God as our opening in reality. When we accept our role, we are helping God build His team, and it doesn't get any better than that!

So I ask you, my friend, how badly do you want it? Do you kind of, maybe, think it would be cool to have a life full of joy and fulfillment? If that is how you feel, don't waste your time—stay in your story, your drama and trauma, and let your ego rule your life. But if that is not an option in your heart and you are determined to be, do, and have what you were meant to experience with every ounce of your being. I challenge you to make today the day you decree, declare, create, and prepare to experience a new vision, a new hope, and a new confidence.

Chapter 63

You Are the Movie Director

Commit your plans to the Lord and you will succeed.

Proverbs 16:3

Think of yourself as a movie director of your life. If you don't like the way that scenes are unfolding, you can change them. Is your life going to be a box-office crash or a block-buster? What makes a movie great is how it all comes together in the end. In fact, the more tumultuous it is along the way, the more we appreciate the movie when it has a happy ending. Is it time to work on your script? Is it time to rewrite the ending and create your Underdog Champion story? What was one of the most inspiring movies of all time? We talked about it earlier. A movie about a comeback, a story about a guy who is going nowhere, who took a long shot and became a world champion. An underdog named Rocky Balboa excited the hearts of millions when he prevailed over apparently over-whelming odds.

Why were all the *Rocky* movies so successful? Because everyone loves an underdog. They love comeback stories and stories of those who are in the midst of overcoming great obstacles and challenges. The underdog in *Rocky* brought out the underdog in each of us. It made us say, "Way to go!" and "Me too! I can relate to this guy." The movie showed us how setbacks and suffering can cause ordinary people to become extraordinary. It showed us that our most valuable possession comes from an unlikely source—the pain and suffering from our past. Our suffering gives us strength; it helps us find courage, and it ignites our hearts... if we allow it to.

Now is the time to stop the backward glances and start living in the now. It is time to grab the baton and move into the next scene of our lives with confidence and gratitude in advance of a beautiful unfolding story that gets better with every day!

It is time to direct the movie of your life into a masterpiece worthy of standing up and taking a bow at the end. It is time to stop making butt-prints in the sands of time and stake our claim. It is time to claim your gift of eternal life through faith in God's unconditional love.

As we close this part of our journey together, I want to leave you with a few thoughts. First, I pray that the investment of time and energy you have put into this book and these exercises has been rewarding to you. My goal was to over deliver in every way I possibly could with these writings. Every day as I wrote this book, I prayed to God that He would allow me to be the pen and He be the writer and that I would decrease and He increase, so that in some way I could serve you by serving Him.

I also pray that the Valeo Method will help you realize that when you are in alignment with God and you understand the concepts and principles taught here, profound life change is imminent for you. When you are living the dream of your soul, you don't even have to pray for opportunity because you will know that just as the rivers flow to the sea, it will come naturally. You will know that your life will be guided by God. In this same way, it is natural that God's grace flows to you. Your ability to receive may have been damned up by doubt, worry, and fear, or other negative emotions. Maybe you believed God was something separate from you and not aware of your needs. Now you can stand strong and tall and know you are person of favor; you are worthy; and your life is meant to be a masterpiece!

All I would like to ask is that you do me a huge favor and tell others about the Valeo Method and give them the gift of hope. Let them find their purpose and live their dreams. A gift is not a gift until you give it away, and you know what happens when you give. May God bless you and keep you. I wish you health, wealth, success, and most of all that you live the dream of your soul!

Be encouraged and live victoriously,

Benny Morris

Keynotes and Seminars

WITH DR. BENNY MORRIS

AUTHOR, PROFESSIONAL SPEAKER, AND LIFE COACH

Benny Morris is one of North America's most energizing, thought provoking, and dynamic speakers. Through his warmth, humor, and engaging presentation style he is able to inspire, motivate, and ignite the hearts of his audiences. His presentations address how to put life into our dreams, increase productivity, and overcome obstacles by understanding what limits us and holds us back. He shares with people how to use the principals of "The Valeo Method™" to put passion back in their lives and the work place.

His customized keynotes and in-house seminars are in constant demand by organizations who are seeking to energize and excite their employees, while helping them awaken their unlimited potential and work together better and excel as a team. Audiences are left invigorated, committed, and wanting more.

For a complete listing of Benny's programs & products please visit: www. DrEncourage.com

To book Dr. Benny Morris for your next conference or event, or to discuss hiring Benny as a corporate or individual Life Coach, please contact us at:

Toll Free: 1-888-926-0013

or

Email: DrEncourage@gmail.com

Don't let your journey end with the book!

Learn how to improve your skills with the Valeo Method and teach others these and many more transformational techniques to take charge of their destiny and live victoriously.

The best way to get what you want is to
help enough other people get what they want.

Zig Ziglar

For details on the "Live Victoriously Weekend Seminars" and the "Valeo Method Coaching Academy" go to:

www.ValeoMethod.com

For further information please contact us at:

Toll Free: 1-888-926-0013

or

Info@ValeoMethod.com

About the Author

Dr. Benny Morris is a noted self-help author, life performance trainer, platform speaker, and encouragement coach. His rise from adversity and his vast knowledge of human behavior and spiritual completeness qualifies him as a leading authority on personal development breakthroughs. He's the author of the groundbreaking book - The Valeo Method and the Founder of The Valeo Method Coaching Academy. His warmth, sincerity and dynamic presentation style at his Live Victoriously Weekend Seminars leaves audiences invigorated, encouraged and wanting more.